AFRICA

A Social Geography

AFRICA

A Social Geography

by

ANTHONY SILLERY

GERALD DUCKWORTH & CO. LTD.

3 HENRIETTA STREET, LONDON W.C.2

First published 1961

© ANTHONY SILLERY 1961

PRINTED IN GREAT BRITAIN
BY EBENEZER BAYLIS AND SON, LTD.
THE TRINITY PRESS, WORCESTER, AND LONDON

CONTENTS

123158

LIST OF PLATES

Between pages 68 and 69

MAPS

PREFACE

IT has been well said[1] that modern books about Africa fall into two categories: those written by journalists who are chiefly interested in the continent under the impact of nationalism and have very little idea of its nature and of its past, and those produced by specialist researchers. The former class has perhaps too much influence, the latter comes too late for practical application. This book is an attempt to compromise. Many years spent in various parts of Africa give me the right to claim some first-hand knowledge of the country and of its people, and I have also devoted a considerable part of the last decade to the study of African history. At the same time I have been at pains to keep abreast of modern developments, and have watched with interest and understanding, though not always uncritically, the growth of the movement towards self-government which has resulted in the establishment of independent African governments in many former colonies.

This book is designed to present a picture of Africa as it was towards the end of 1960. The political tempo is so rapid that I have preferred to concentrate on those things which, if not immutable, at least change more slowly than politics. These include geography, ethnology, culture, economics and racial relations. Some emphasis is laid on history, since it is impossible to understand the present except against the background of the past.

Even if I tend to neglect politics, my subject is still so varied and so wide that it is impossible in the available space to deal with any aspect of it except in the broadest outline. The book is therefore not meant for the specialist, nor as a reference book for those seeking statistics or other detailed information. It is meant simply to be read by the general reader to whom I hope it will give some idea of Africa and of the people who live in it.

One matter of orthography needs to be explained: When spelling Bantu tribal names it is usual nowadays to drop the prefix and use only the root; e.g. Ganda not Baganda, Chagga not Wachagga. I have followed no fixed rule, but have either kept or dropped the prefix according to which form I believe accords with common usage in each case.

[1] In a book review initialled H.I. in *Corona*, January 1961.

xi

Too much attention should not be paid to African statistics, especially population figures. At best these are only approximations, and probably wide ones at that. If it were possible by some magic means to discover exactly how many people live in the various parts of Africa, and how many cattle they possess, nothing would surprise me more than to find that my own figures, based on reputable reference books, were within 25 per cent of the truth. The same reservations apply, though perhaps in some cases with rather less force, to figures purporting to represent the areas of the various countries, and even to the geographical position of Africa itself: no two atlases agree on the exact co-ordinate of the continent's extremities.

Acknowledgements. One of the most encouraging things about writing a book of this kind is the ungrudging help one receives from other people. In the past two years I have ruthlessly pestered everybody who could be of use to me, and to all those in this country and in Africa who have so patiently answered my questions, read the draft, corrected mistakes and given me advice and information I now offer my most heartfelt thanks.

A.S.

Oxford
   March 1961

PART I
GENERAL

AFRICA
Important Physical Features

CHAPTER ONE

The Unknown Continent

THOUGH North Africa has been known to Europeans for thousands of years and the southern tip for centuries, it is only in the last hundred and fifty years or so that we have learnt what we now know about the rest of the continent. Up to the end of the eighteenth century a map of inland tropical Africa, if it was not 'a perfect and absolute blank', was largely guesswork:

> 'So geographers, in Afric maps
> With savage pictures fill their gaps;
> And o'er unhabitable downs
> Place elephants for want of towns'.[1]

The reason why Africa was for so long shut off from the rest of the world was no doubt largely that it is particularly well protected by Nature against penetration and settlement. In the north the Sahara Desert, though traversed by caravan routes in common use, was not adapted to regular large scale movement of peoples.[2] The African coastline affords few natural harbours, and much of it is backed by desert or semi-desert or by dense forest. The rivers are not easily navigable. Even the Nile is barred by cataracts which prevent easy access by boat to the upper reaches. The climate of the tropics was not good for Europeans and, before modern medicine, often fatal. Tsetse fly made animal transport impossible and in most parts travel was on foot with porters. The whole aspect was frankly unattractive and early European navigators like the Portuguese were well content to win footholds on the coast and sail on to the more accessible riches of the East Indies. Other Europeans who came later did little more than establish coastal trading stations. It was not until the late eighteenth century that Europeans set about seriously to explore the interior of Africa. By the end of the nineteenth century most of the blanks on the map had been filled in,

---

[1] Jonathan Swift, *On Poetry*.
[2] From the seventh century onwards Europeans could not in any case hope to penetrate from the north, since the whole of the Mediterranean coast was under Moslem control.

3

and the greater part of the continent had fallen under European
domination.

Configuration and Special Features

From its northern point, Ras ben Sakka, a little west of Cap
Blanc in latitude 37° 20' N, to its southern point at Cape Agulhas
in latitude 34° 50' S, the continent of Africa measures 5,000
miles. The width at its broadest point, from Cape Verde, 17° 33' W,
to Ras Hafun, 51° 25' E, is 4,600 miles. The area is about 11½
million square miles. The shape is in one sense fairly symmetrical:
on all sides the ground rises from a coastal plain to a plateau
which runs like a backbone down the whole length of the continent. This plateau has great diversity of relief. Generally speaking
the altitude ranges between three thousand and six thousand
feet and is higher in the south than in the north. But there are
in places great mountain masses which rise above the tableland,
such for instance as the Ethiopian massif with peaks above 15,000
feet, and some of the mountains of East Africa which are considerably higher. On the other hand there are basins or depressions
lying well below the general level, for example Lake Chad, the
Congo basin and that which lies in the great bend of the Niger
River.

Some time in the remote past a violent seismic disturbance
accompanied by great volcanic activity caused huge fractures in the
earth's surface. The result is a series of troughs, with sides more
or less clearly defined, which is called the Great Rift Valley.[1] This
is one of the most remarkable geographical phenomena in the world.
The Rift begins near the mouth of the Zambezi River and runs
northwards, including in its course the Shire River valley and Lake
Nyasa. North of Lake Nyasa it branches, forming the Eastern and
Western Rifts. The Eastern Rift goes on through Tanganyika and
Kenya, its progress marked by a chain of small lakes, Manyara,
Natron, Naivasha and others. It then runs through Ethiopia, cutting the Somali provinces off from the rest of the Ethiopian Empire.
The Red Sea is the link that connects the Rift in Africa with its continuation through Palestine. The Gulf of Akaba, the Jordan Valley
and the Dead Sea all lie in its bed, and it may be taken to come to
an end in Syria, its total length 4,000 miles. The Western Rift
branches off in a general north-westerly direction and contains the

_____
[1] Also called the Rift Valley, or just the Rift.

stupendous trough of Lake Tanganyika and Lakes Kivu, Edward and Albert. It ends not very far north of Lake Albert and is thus much shorter than the Eastern Rift. Lake Victoria, which lies between the horns of the two Rifts, is not thought to be of tectonic origin. (*Plate* 36)

In Kenya particularly the Rift presents a most majestic spectacle, and no one who stands on its edge, say at the point where the main road from Nairobi to Kisumu plunges down into the valley, can fail to marvel at the vast forces which so affected the configuration of the continent.

If now we look at a map of Africa our eye will probably first be drawn to four, and possibly five, great rivers. The Nile, which once nourished one of the great civilizations of the world, flows into the Mediterranean and is in fact the only African river of any size with an outlet in the north. It has a length of more than 4,000 miles and may be said to begin at the Kagera River, which flows into Lake Victoria. It is a river, as we shall see, with a great and romantic past, and it plays an important part today, for both the Sudan and Egypt are dependent on it, and it is so far the most developed of the rivers of Africa. The Niger too has played its part in history, particularly in recent history. After taking an enormous bend through West Africa for a distance of 2,600 miles it flows into the Atlantic Ocean in the Bight of Benin. The great Congo River also empties into the Atlantic. It is nearly 3,000 miles long and has innumerable tributaries and a drainage area of nearly $1\frac{1}{2}$ million square miles. The Congo is navigable in many parts and carries heavy traffic. The Zambezi rises in Angola but runs south-eastwards, at one point tumbling over a cliff to form the Victoria Falls, finally to flow into the Indian Ocean 2,000 miles from its source. The Orange River, further south, is included with some hesitation. It is shorter than the others, being only 1,300 miles in length; it does not, like the others, flow regularly but is often dry or reduced to a series of pools. But since it has played a part in the history of South Africa and remains of no small economic importance, it deserves to be mentioned. (*Plate* 3)

The great lakes of Africa are all except one in the eastern and central parts of the continent. The largest in area is Victoria, of approximately 26,000 square miles, as a freshwater lake second in the world only to Lake Superior. It is on the Equator and forms the chief reservoir of the Nile, which leaves the Lake by the Ripon Falls at Jinja. Lake Victoria is enclosed by Uganda on the north and

west, Tanganyika on the south and south-east and Kenya on the
north-east. It is a busy lake, with large populations on its shores
and many flourishing little ports. In many places it is also very
beautiful.

Africa does nothing by halves: after the second largest lake in the
world comes Lake Tanganyika, which is the longest, measuring as
it does 420 miles. It is also, except Lake Baikal, the deepest, sound-
ings of 4,708 feet having been taken. It lies in the Western Rift,
between Tanganyika and the Congo, and is quite narrow, being on
the average only 30 miles broad. Lake Nyasa, which lies between
the Nyasaland Protectorate and Portuguese East Africa, is 350 miles
long and has an average width of 30 miles. It is drained by the
Shire River into the Zambezi. Besides these three giants there are
other lakes, such as Albert, Edward and Kivu in the Western Rift,
Rudolf between Kenya and Ethiopia, Chad on the southern
edge of the Sahara, and many smaller ones in other parts of the
continent.   (*Plate* 35)

Africa boasts some splendid mountains, though they are not the
highest in the world. Still, Kilimanjaro, 19,340 feet, in Tanganyika,
the Ruwenzori range on the borders of Uganda and the Congo,
which has a peak of 16,763 feet, Mount Kenya itself, the Drakensberg between Basutoland and Natal and many lesser ranges, are
impressive enough.   (*Plates* 32–34)

CLIMATE

Only in very limited parts of Africa are temperate conditions
resembling those of Europe to be found. Most of the continent is
hot, and the heat is associated with great humidity in some regions
and great aridity in others. The most remarkable thing about
African climates is their symmetrical distribution in relation to the
Equator. Each kind of climate has its counterpart or approximate
counterpart in the other, in the same position relative to the
equatorial belt. The various climatic régimes are not, however,
sharply distinguished one from another but shade off gradually,
each merging imperceptibly into its neighbour.

Beginning at the Equator we find three variations of what may be
called the equatorial climate. The first two are both characterized by
high rainfall, great heat and a steamy humidity. But whereas in the
northern part of the Congo basin the rainfall is evenly distributed
throughout the year, the Guinea coast and its hinterland has an

annual dry spell, and even drought. In both these regions the predominant vegetation is thick tropical forest. The third variation is that ruling in the plateau lands of East Africa where the temperature is comparatively cool owing to the high altitude, and the rainfall moderate. The vegetation is a parklike savannah degenerating to thornbush.

On either side of the equatorial belt there is a broad zone which represents the transition between the hot, humid belt and the dry heat of the northern and southern deserts. In the north this transitional zone stretches across the continent from Senegal to Ethiopia, and in the south from Angola to Mozambique. This is the 'tropical' or 'Sudan-type' climate, still very hot, but with a well defined season of moderate rain. In the northern zone the oppressive heat is periodically relieved by a dry wind which though very dusty is conducive to health. In the south there is also a well marked contrast between the cool and the hot seasons.

Next come the two deserts, the Sahara in the north and the Kalahari in the south. Exceptionally, their arrangement is not quite symmetrical for whereas the Sahara with lesser deserts covers almost the whole of North Africa and in parts reaches to the sea, the desertic regions of South Africa are confined to the western and mid-western parts of the sub-continent. The deserts are very hot in summer with dry scorching winds. In winter the nights are cold, with occasional frosts and there are sometimes cold winds by day. Rainfall is scanty. Vegetation in the Sahara is exceedingly sparse but in the Kalahari light rains produce a cover of grass nourishing to cattle, and great quantities of wild melons.

Last of all we come to the subtropical climates of North and South Africa, without doubt the most agreeable and equable climates of the continent. The winters are mild and rainy, the summers warm. Both these zones once had good forests but wasteful felling has greatly reduced them, especially in the south. Thicket growth has replaced forest where this has disappeared.

On the South African high veld there is another type of subtropical climate characterized by hot summers, cold winters and an unreliable rainfall which is in any case concentrated in a very short period. The vegetation is mainly grass and there is no forest. On the other hand the east coast of South Africa, subject to yet a third sub-tropical régime, is warm, has a heavy rainfall (Natal has a rainy season of nine months) and luxuriant vegetation.

THE PEOPLE OF AFRICA

This great continent has perhaps about 225 million people, all as varied as the physical and climatic conditions in which they live. They do, however, fall generally into a number of groups, each group having certain physical, cultural and linguistic characteristics which distinguish it from the others. Provided therefore that we remember that the ethnic frontiers are blurred, and that the dominant features of one group are often to be observed in another, we may divide the population of Africa into Semites, true Negroes, Hamites, Nilotes and Nilo-Hamites, Bantu, Khoisan, and Negrillos.

Semites

The Semites are represented mainly by the Arabs, although not all who call themselves Arabs are of pure Arab stock. Indeed the term is sometimes applied to anybody who professes the religion of Islam, even though he may be quite negroid. It has thus very little ethnic significance but is useful in describing a large number of people of widely differing physical characteristics who are mostly Moslems and who speak Arabic. In Africa the Arabs of the north and east are those in whom the original strain is purest. The Arabs of the Sudan and those who are to be found as far west as Nigeria often carry much negro blood and are sometimes indistinguishable in appearance from the indigenous Negroes.

The Arabs of Africa are usually divided into three categories: the genuine nomads, the people of the camel, who are usually found in North Africa; somewhat less nomadic cattle owners; settled communities. How the Arabs came into Africa, and their impact on the people whom they found there, will be described later.

True Negroes

The black people of Africa are all popularly called Negroes, but for ethnical purposes we may distinguish a particular type whom we may call true Negroes for lack of a more specific name. These are the dominant people of West Africa from the mouth of the Senegal River, about 16° N, to the eastern boundary of Nigeria. Their main physical characteristics are a black skin, woolly hair and a tall stature. The head is fairly long in comparison to its breadth, the nose is broad and flat, the lips thick and everted, and the features are often prognathous. These people were formerly organized in powerful and wealthy kingdoms with an elaborate apparatus of officials, a priesthood in the service of a complicated and often cruel religion, a strong military organization and a notable body of artists and craftsmen associated with church, state and the secret and semi-secret societies that are a feature of West African life. Although the old kingdoms and hierarchies have either disappeared, or, where they have survived, lost much of their power, the true Negroes still live in well organized communities and have a high standard of material and technical achievement. They give an impression of exuberant and full-blooded vitality and are in many ways the most advanced and ambitious of the dark-skinned people of Africa. Their economy is an agricultural rather than a pastoral one.

Hamites

At some time in the very remote past Africa was invaded from Asia, possibly from southern Arabia, by a race we call Hamites. They were Caucasians and therefore belong to the same branch of mankind as Europeans. They also had strong affinities with the Semites. These Hamites came into Africa in a very long succession of waves. Some colonized the Nile Valley, others passed on into North Africa, while others gradually spread southwards into the heart of the continent. The last waves stopped, or were halted, in the Horn of Africa (the north-eastern tip, washed by the Red Sea on the one side and the Indian Ocean on the other) and now occupy the country known as Somaliland and thereabouts. These, together with the Hamites of North Africa, are those who have best preserved their physical characteristics down the ages to modern times.

We may conveniently divide the Hamites into two main groups or branches:

(1) the Eastern Hamites, who include the ancient and modern Egyptians (allowing for strong infusions of foreign blood in the latter), the Beja, the Nubians, the Somali, the Danakil, the Galla, and, with some reservations, most Ethiopians.[1]

(2) the Northern Hamites, who include the Berbers, the Tuareg, the Fulani of West Africa and an extinct people of the Canary Islands called the Guanche.

So widely distributed, and over much of the continent so mixed is the strain, that it is not easy to give a description of Hamitic physical characteristics. Among the Eastern Hamites the build is

[1] See, however, pp. 145, 148.

fairly tall and often spare, the nose straight and sometimes aquiline, the lips thick, but not everted, the beard thin, the hair often frizzy but sometimes straight or wavy, and the skin variable in colour from yellowish to black. Many Hamites, especially the Berbers, are of distinctly 'Nordic' appearance, having long heads, narrow noses, and even in some cases white skins, blue or green eyes and fair hair. These are to be found alongside other types, swarthier, with broader noses, some with long heads and some with rounder heads, some with negroid characteristics.

There has in the past been a tendency among anthropologists to ascribe any signs of superior culture among Africans to Hamitic influence. 'The civilizations of Africa,' wrote Professor Seligman, 'are the civilizations of the Hamites.'[1] The generalization is too sweeping. The advanced true Negro civilizations of West Africa are not Hamitic, and conversely there are a number of comparatively pure Hamites with no very impressive civilization. In our present state of knowledge we may accept the view that invading Hamites mixed with indigenous negroes to produce new strains; and that in some places they imposed themselves as a pastoral aristocracy on sedentary agricultural Negro populations. To go further would be to do injustice to people who have evolved spontaneous civilizations of their own.

Nilotes and Nilo-Hamites

In the southern Sudan and in East Africa there are several peoples of considerable importance presenting a mingling of Negro and Hamitic elements and generally regarded as falling into two divisions, Nilotes and Nilo-Hamites. The Shilluk and Dinka of the Nile Valley, tall, long-headed and dark-skinned, are typical Nilotes and the division is represented as far south as Lake Victoria by the Luo or Nilotic Kavirondo. Nilo-Hamites include the Masai (known to even the most casual visitor to Kenya), the Nandi, the Lumbwa, the Suk, the Turkana, the Karamojong, probably the Didinga and Topotha of the southern Sudan and the Iteso of Uganda. They are fairly tall, fairly long-headed, often narrow-faced, with fine features and a skin (notably in the case of the Masai) that is somewhat brown. Nilotes and Nilo-Hamites are predominantly but not exclusively pastoralists, and devote to their cattle an almost religious esteem. This veneration extends to objects associated with cattle, such as milk and grass and some tribes will not kill cattle except on

[1] Seligman, *Races of Africa*, p. 85.

ceremonial occasions.[1] It must here be stated that the distinction between Nilotes and Nilo-Hamites is mainly based on linguistic grounds about which opinion is not unanimous.

Bantu

This is really a linguistic term but is used ethnologically to describe a very large negro group whose languages have certain unmistakable common characteristics. Allowing for Nilotic and Nilo-Hamitic 'islands', the Bantu occupy the whole of the southern two-thirds of black Africa. Apart from the bond of language, they are diverse in appearance, and though all have certain common features, they differ considerably in their culture from tribe to tribe and from region to region. What link other than language, one asks, unites the aristocratic Bahima, true Nilo-Hamites in all but speech, the industrious and homely Sukuma, the handsome cattle-loving Kuria, the powerful, disciplined, warlike Zulu, the broken, partly islamized tribes of the coastal areas of East Africa, the intelligent, vocal, ambitious Chagga, the hardy, independent mountaineers of Basutoland? That certain very loose bonds do exist we shall see later. But spreading as they do over a great part of the continent (unlike the Nilo-Hamites and Nilotes whose habitat is comparatively circumscribed) the Bantu have been subject to a great variety of environmental influences that has caused a similar diversity in the characteristics of the various groups. Obviously, people living in arid plains will develop in a different manner to those living in swamps or mountains, while the presence of this insect or that, for instance the tsetse fly or the mosquito, will determine a whole way of life.

The Khoisan

These are the Bushmen and Hottentots of South Africa. The Bushmen are the oldest indigenous race of Africa and were formerly widely distributed over the continent. Harried in the past by Bantu and European enemies they are now confined to the Kalahari desert and its neighbourhood.

Bushmen are short in stature, with a yellow or yellowish-brown skin, 'peppercorn' hair, prominent cheekbones, narrow eyes and very flat noses. One of their notable characteristics is the prominence of the buttocks in men and pronounced steatopygy in women. Further north, the swamp Bushmen of the Okavango delta

[1] Seligman, *Races of Africa*, Chapter 7, *passim*.

are taller and darker. Bushmen live in an exceedingly primitive way and are almost completely unaffected by contact with higher civilization. They obtain their livelihood by hunting and gathering edible roots and plants, neither practising agriculture nor keeping cattle. In spite of this precarious way of life, they are an exceedingly merry people, much given to dancing and singing. Above all, the race has produced a notable form of art, the so-called rock paintings, scenes of people and animals and daily life executed on the rock walls of caves. The colour is extraordinarily vivid and the pictures themselves have high artistic merit, but the art has now died out completely and the paintings we see today must be very old, though exactly how old it is impossible to say. There are said to be over 50,000 Bushmen still in existence,[1] but the numbers are believed to be dwindling. The conditions that made their life possible, un-limited space and plentiful game, are vanishing. The Bushmen are becoming merged with other peoples by intermarriage and will doubtless disappear as a race in the not distant future. (*Plate* 7)

The Hottentots, whose habitat is now mainly South West Africa, are the result of the mixture of Bushmen with early Hamites. They are taller than Bushmen and differ from them in that they are a pastoral people, possessing cattle and sheep. Their culture is generally superior to that of the Bushmen but they do not appear to have made rock paintings.

The Negrillos

These are the Pygmies of the Congo forests. Their existence was known to the early Pharaohs of Egypt but little is as yet known now of their language and culture, although they are said to be excellent dancers, singers, mimics and actors. They live mainly by hunting and collecting and their way of life, primitive as it is, seems to be ingeniously adapted to their environment.

Non-African races

To complete the African scene we must make some reference to those races which although comparatively recent immigrants have now made Africa their home. The most important of these are Asians and Europeans.

The Asians consist mainly of Indians and Pakistanis and are to be found in Zanzibar, where they have been settled for a longer

[1] P. V. Tobias, 'On the survival of the Bushmen' (*Africa*, Vol. XXVI, No. 2, April 1956).

time than elsewhere, on the East African mainland, and in Natal. They fall into two principal communities, Moslems and Hindus. There are also Sikhs, predominantly artisans, and Goans from Portuguese India, many of whom are office workers.

There is a whole European nation in South Africa, large immigrant communities on the shores of the Mediterranean, and other smaller ones in Central Africa and in the eastern highlands. To these we must add the traders, missionaries and officials scattered all over the continent, powerful agents of the introduction of European civilization.

AFRICAN CULTURE

To the European explorers of the nineteenth century tropical Africa appeared to be savage and primitive, given over to tribal war and cruel superstition. With important exceptions the people lived in conditions of poverty and insecurity, lacking elementary amenities and struggling under difficulties for the essentials of life. The social and political organization seemed either excessively simple and backward, or, when more highly developed, barbaric and oppressive.

It is of course true that Africans were at that time comparatively uninfluenced by the outside world. Such contacts as they had had with higher civilizations in their more recent history had done them little good. What they had seen of Europeans or of Arabs, whether in the south, west or east, must have persuaded them that these were people to avoid. The only beneficial, or at least innocuous agents of European or Asian civilization were occasional Christian missionaries and the traders of many nations who usually kept to the coast. No doubt there was always some communication among the African people themselves, some interchange of ideas, some handing on of skills and practices from one community to another. Various crafts, the raising of certain domestic animals, the cultivation of certain plants, were at one time or another introduced from outside and in due course spread across Africa. But the breezes that blew from outside from the time of the Hamitic invasions, whenever that was, to the modern era, were very light and the culture that evolved over most of the continent, except of course in the Arab and European areas, was truly indigenous.

There are signs scattered about Africa that this culture was not an unsuccessful one. Zimbabwe in Southern Rhodesia with its

massive stone walls and towers, the most important of several such
sites in south central Africa, is now widely believed to be the work
of a native race, and not, as was formerly held, that of Semitic
immigrants. At Engaruka in Tanganyika there are the ruins of a
stone-built town large enough to have housed thirty or forty
thousand inhabitants. This too may be the product of a native
civilization. At Mapungubwe in the Northern Transvaal there is a
burial ground rich in golden ornaments and other metal objects
which seem to be of local inspiration and origin. There is no cer-
tainty in these matters and any conclusions must be tentative. We
shall probably never know for certain who built Engaruka and
Zimbabwe nor who was buried at Mapungubwe; nor shall we know
how and when and why their various cultures disappeared. But
these and other relics of the past do permit us to suggest that at
various times there may have existed south of the Sahara native
communities who had reached a state of civilization considerably
superior to that in which much of Africa was found by nineteenth-
century Europeans.[1]

To leave the past and to come to modern times, African culture
varies enormously in kind and in quality from tribe to tribe and
from place to place, and ranges from that of the simple, primitive
societies of say, the pagans of Northern Nigeria, to the highly
organized system of the Baganda. But it has enough aspects common to all regions and tribes to permit us to draw, in very broad
outline and with all possible reservations as to detail, a general
sketch of African culture as the first European travellers found it,
and as it still very widely is.

RELIGION

Most Africans believe in a Supreme Being, often associated with
the firmament. He is the creator of all things, but plays little part in
the life of the individual. Though there are some tribes who believe
in a personal God who answers prayers and grants favours, to most
Africans the Supreme Being is remote and impersonal and takes
little interest in His creation. From Him are derived numbers of
lesser gods, who may be graded in a descending scale and may be
associated with natural phenomena. By far the most important
aspect of African religion is a belief in mysterious and occult forces
that influence human life. These forces may reside in human beings,

[1] Early African indigenous culture is attracting increasing attention nowadays,
but research in this field is still in the early stages.

animals or things and can be used to strengthen life and assure its continuity in descendants by observance of the correct ritual. Associated in some way with the life forces are the spirits of departed ancestors. Africans believe that the spirits of the dead have power to bring good or evil fortune to their living descendants. The ancestors must therefore be honoured and propitiated, it may be through the head of the family or through the chief or through priests. This belief was the reason why in some tribes it was thought necessary, when a chief died, to kill his servants and the women of the palace, so that they might attend their master in the next world. This idea is not of course peculiar to Africa, but seems to belong to mankind's common stock, different items of which keep appearing all over the world among people widely separated in space and time. It was also the custom from time to time to kill people in order that they might act as messengers to carry the news of the chief's activities to his departed ancestors. Fortunately most ancestor cults were not so bloody as these, and usually took, and still take, the form of invocation and an offering of food and of some small domestic animal.

The African also believes passionately in sorcery, which is the misuse of the life forces to bring harm to other people. Sorcery is regarded with the utmost horror, and to defeat it African society has provided itself with a class of persons whose profession it is to detect the sorcerer and to undo his spells. These are the witch-doctors, whose beneficent activities are often confused by Europeans with those of the very sorcerers whom the witch-doctors seek to frustrate. Allied to witch-doctors are other doctors who provide remedies for less personal disasters. In this category are the 'rain-makers', a most inappropriate term which they themselves would be the last to claim. All they purport to do is to ascertain why rain does not fall. This may often be because someone in the community has offended the ancestors, and the doctor will advise how the offence may be purged. He may also perform certain rites in order that the offended spirits may be appeased. 'Rain-makers' are therefore diagnosticians and intermediaries and nothing more. Other practitioners specialize in preventing plagues of various kinds, e.g. grain-eating birds, others, more positively, in ensuring supplies of food,[1] and the chief himself often carries out the rites designed to

[1] One chief whom I knew on Lake Victoria was a noted fish-doctor. His greatest triumph was when two or three fish fell from the sky. The rational explanation was that they were caught up and carried by a waterspout.

remove all obstacles to a successful planting and an abundant harvest.

How The African Lives

It is impossible in one general chapter to describe the way in which all the people of Africa live, nor is it wholly necessary. We may disregard recent immigrants like Europeans who have brought with them the culture of their homeland and have merely modified and developed it in their new surroundings. Even the Arabs, who arrived many centuries ago, do not differ widely from Arabs of one sort or another anywhere else. We need therefore only concern ourselves with the Negroes between the Sahara and the Cape who have lived in the continent so long that they may now be called indigenous. They all have certain peculiarities of thought and behaviour that distinguish them from other races, and enough characteristics in common for us to be able to speak very generally of an African way of life.

The Community

The great mass of these people belong to communities called tribes that may be large or small. Tribes are distinguished among themselves by language and by cultural differences. In one respect however they are all similar: they all have a well marked social structure. This may range from some simple organization of a few family heads, with perhaps one elder whom the others regard as their senior, to the elaborate machinery of the nation state, with a king at its head and around him justices, ministers, and representatives in many towns and villages. It must however here be said that African despotisms have in the past been rare. Tyrants there have certainly been, but on the whole the African system has usually contained safeguards against the unbridled and capricious exercise of power by one person. The chief is surrounded by well defined groups of councillors whose advice he is bound to respect. Most chiefs, however powerful, find it advisable to listen to what their councillors say.

In addition to his secular powers, which are political, judicial and social, the chief has religious powers as well. Many regard him as the intermediary between the tribe and the more powerful ancestral spirits; and it falls to him to perform the rites incidental to seedtime and harvest and to the other important events of the year. In

some tribes the chief's person is the object of extraordinary veneration; in others he inspires no more than the respect due to a social
superior.

There are of course many Africans who do not live in a tribal
state at all. These are generally town-dwellers, people who have cut
themselves off from the traditional organization and are now subject
to some form of urban government. Yet so strong is the pull of the
old order that people of the same tribe will often tend to group
themselves together wherever they may be, even though their for-
bears may long ago have moved away from the tribal home.

We must expect the tribal system ultimately to give way to other
forms of political organization, based perhaps on European models.
Whatever the ostensible model it is safe to assume that these systems
will be strongly permeated by African sentiment, and that they will
be obviously moulded to suit the ideas and characteristics of the
race.

Common to all African societies is a strong sense of community,
of communal existence and action, of collective responsibility. The
African does not regard himself primarily as an individual before
God and before man, as does a European. He is firmly embedded
in his family, and if not totally detribalized, in his clan and in his
tribe. Alive or dead his kith and kin are around him, concerned with
all aspects of his life, sharing his successes and his failures, his good
and his evil fortune, living in him as he lives in them. If an African
commits an offence, his community is responsible with him. If he
prospers and reaches a position of wealth and power, the family and
the clan will expect to benefit. This sense of community has many
admirable sides. The African tribe is itself a complete welfare service. The old are cared for and the needy are fed. Widows and
orphans are 'inherited' by some male relative whose duty it is to
look after them. As long as there is any food no one will starve. In
addition to these material advantages the tribe gives a feeling of
'belonging' to something ancient and respectable, of communion in
some continuing spiritual order, of balance and stability. The idea
of strictly personal responsibility, introduced by European missionaries, traders, administrators, lawyers, has done much to destroy
the communal conscience which admittedly tended to blunt initiative and progress and to foster an excessive conservatism. Nevertheless there are some who regret the passing of something that
modern Europeans are none the better for having lost: a sense
of obligation to something wider than the individual.

Justice

African justice ignores the difference between civil and criminal law, and is based on the principle of redress and compensation. Thus if I injure a man in any way, whether by striking him, or by stealing from him, or by negligently letting my cattle eat his crops, or by failing to pay him a debt, his remedy is the same: I must make suitable payment in compensation for his injury or for his loss. Punishment in our sense is alien to traditional African practice except in witchcraft and perhaps in offences specifically against the chief. The distinction between crimes and torts has no part in African legal theory. This however, has changed under European doctrine and we now find the division between criminal and civil clearly marked in most African judicial systems.

Subsistence

The evidence of travellers shows that at the time of the European penetration of Africa in the last century the people's subsistence was simple and precarious. In the course of the ages the African had managed to adapt himself reasonably successfully to his environment; but he had never learned to dominate it. He got his living partly from agriculture, partly from cattle raising, sometimes exclusively from one or the other, occasionally adding to his larder and his wardrobe by hunting wild animals. Yet only in the last pursuit was he really successful. In a continent where rainfall is either excessive or scanty, where the soil is on the whole rather poor, where soil erosion and soil exhaustion are widespread, where pasture is seasonal, traditional agricultural and pastoral habits tended to accentuate the adverse effects of these factors rather than to mitigate them. Among comparatively few Africans was it the practice to irrigate or rotate their crops, conserve the soil or fertilize it (except by wasteful cutting and burning of forest), store winter feed for their stock, or cull their herds. When the soil or pasture was overworked in one place, the African simply moved away from the desert that he had made and went to make one elsewhere.[1]

The neglect of elementary animal husbandry is all the more surprising because cattle play a vital part in African life. They are not only, or even primarily, regarded as an economic asset. They are

[1] There are of course exceptions. To quote one known personally to the writer, the people of Ukara Island on Lake Victoria use their land in a very efficient and ingenious manner.

a social factor of first importance. They constitute an essential ingredient in the institution of marriage as dowry paid by the bridegroom to the bride's family. In Ruanda-Urundi the custody of another man's cattle establishes a sort of feudal relationship between the two men. In many tribes cattle are the object of a cult and are regarded with almost religious veneration.[1] Many Africans will not sell cattle except when forced by dire necessity to do so, and do not habitually slaughter them for food. The result of this attitude is increasing pressure on scanty grazing and water. This is a commonplace of African agronomy and need not be laboured here.

In the domestic arts, houses were built with what lay nearest to hand, mud and sticks and grass, a ready prey for the white ants but easily built and easily abandoned. Clothes, if worn at all, were of simple, homely materials, such as bark cloth and hides, and here it may be said that by means of crude but very thorough processes the African contrived to make clothes that were both elegant and durable. Machinery in the modern sense did not exist. In one way only had the African risen above his circumstances. There is in him a boisterous vitality that has enabled him down the ages to triumph as a race (though many individuals succumb) over bad and insufficient food, disease, numberless germs and parasites, and all the disadvantages of a bad climate. To these are now added diseases acquired by contact with aliens. Before the coming of European government this vitality was the African's only protection. Now, while admitting that civilization brings ills of its own, we may expect that with European medicine to help him, and with education, child welfare guidance, and better economic conditions generally, the African will proliferate exceedingly.

The Arts

It is perhaps not too much to say that the African is the most musical person on earth. This does not mean that he has yet produced a Beethoven or a Bach, as far as we know. But it does mean that his whole being, his whole life, is permeated with music. There can hardly be an African who is not familiar with, and incapable of adding to the folk music of his community. It is a gift that is fostered at a very early age, and children of the tenderest years are expected to take part in music making, in singing and in dancing. New songs, new music are constantly being made, for the African sings about everything and about everybody. This racial trait persists

[1] Especially among the Nilotes and Nilo-Hamites (pp. 10, 162).

far from the ancestral homeland, and the Calypso of the West
Indian is just another form of the same art which is practised in any
African village at any time of day or night. Europeans have unwisely
tried to teach music to these intensely musical people, but the
African genius has been equal to the test and the children whom one
may hear in the morning singing the Tanganyika national anthem
to the tune of Clementine[1] revert quite naturally to the ancient
musical themes of their race in their homes at night.

With music and singing goes dancing. Just as he always sings
about his business, so is the African under compulsion to translate
all his activities into rhythmic movement. An African dance is a
thing of power, full-blooded, sensual, witty, dramatic; the move-
ments are exuberant and often complicated; the rhythm of the
dancers and the drums subtle and faultless. The effect is tremen-
dously exciting—and quite inimitable. Modern European mani-
festations of the neo-African craze, from the early jazz of the
'twenties to the jive and rock and roll of today, are sad imitations of
the real thing.

In the plastic arts the true Negroes of West Africa are outstanding and the sculpture of Ife and Benin is famous. Some Bantu tribes
of the Congo have produced a wealth of wood-carving. In other
parts of Bantu Africa where the indigenous tradition is not so strong
artists and craftsmen are coming forward under foreign influence.
Recent years have witnessed the development in several parts of
Africa of a literature European in language and form but African
in inspiration. The ancient artistic tradition of Ethiopia expresses
itself in painting, fine writing and illumination, architecture and
music and is deeply transfused with Christianity. Ethiopian literature also finds its focus and inspiration in the Christian religion.

African Languages[2]

Apart from European languages introduced by recent immigrants, the languages of Africa can be divided into five families:
the Sudanic, the Bantu, the Hamitic, the Semitic and the Bushman.

The Sudanic family reaches in an irregular band across Africa
from Cape Verde to the confines of Ethiopia, with a number of out-
liers in the territories of other families, such as Kunama in the

---

[1] This is a memory of the past. Tanganyika has perhaps by now adopted a more
authentic national song.

[2] The reader who wishes to be more fully informed is advised to consult Werner:
The Language Families of Africa.

north of Ethiopia, Luo at the north-eastern end of Lake Victoria, and Mbugu in Tanganyika. This family comprises over two hundred languages, including most of the better known ones of West Africa, but not Hausa.

The Bantu family spreads over the whole of southern and central Africa, north-west as far as the Gulf of Cameroons and north-east to the Tana River. This enormous field is interrupted by enclaves of other languages to which we shall refer below, while there are also languages of a Bantu character, described as semi-Bantu, in the Sudanic area of West Africa. There may be as many as 250 Bantu languages and a great many dialects. Some of these languages differ from each other no more than, say, Italian from French but they all have unmistakable common characteristics and there is no true Bantu language that is not immediately recognizable as a member of the family.

The Ancient Egyptians spoke a Hamitic language. So did the Libyans and the Numidians and so do some of the people of North Africa today. Hamitic languages are now found in their purest form in north-east Africa, which is the home of several Hamitic peoples such as the Somali and the Galla. It should be mentioned that the Hamitic languages show some indications of a remote affinity with Semitic, as if in the very distant past they had been one branch which later became divided.

The most ancient African representative of the Semitic family is Ge'ez, the old liturgical language of Ethiopia. The most widely spoken is Arabic, which is the language of North Africa and of Egypt and has spread far south into the Sudan. Arabic has profoundly influenced the Hausa and Swahili languages of West and East Africa respectively, and is closely associated with the spread of Islam.

Finally, we come to the Bushman languages, spoken by the Bushmen of South Africa. These are politically unimportant, but, it appears, linguistically very interesting. One characteristic, a number of so-called 'clicks', sounds produced by the tongue, teeth and lips, has been much discussed. There are other tribes in Africa who use clicks: the Hottentots, the Zulu and the Xosa of South Africa, and the Sandawi of East Africa.[1] Comparatively little is known about the Bushman languages, and there may be little time left in which to study them. They seem to be giving way to the

---

[1] The Zulu and the Xosa may have acquired their 'clicks' from the Bushmen or the Hottentots.

languages of the surrounding populations, European and African, and will no doubt disappear altogether before very long.

It must not be thought, simply because African languages were until recently unwritten and spoken by comparatively untutored people, that they are barbarous, primitive, devoid of structure and grammatical rules. Even if they were, they would still deserve to be studied. 'The most barbarous language,' wrote Dr. Werner, 'is, in its degree, an instrument of human thought, and as such, worthy of a careful and reverent scrutiny.' Those who have studied African languages at all thoroughly (the writer speaks from a knowledge of several Bantu languages) knows that they are highly organized and flexible, in many respects well adapted to render precise meanings, and often exceedingly melodious. Furthermore they are the vehicles of a very rich folk-lore. To speak an African language well requires time and plenty of hard work but the task is by no means insuperable. For those who intend to live and to work in Africa the effort is well worth while. To the missionary and teacher, the farmer, trader and administrator, a command of language is a tool of the trade. Those to whom it is not a necessity will find that as a means of communicating easily with a pleasant, interesting, awakening people, it opens a window on a new world.

HISTORY OF AFRICA

Ancient Egypt

Some five miles west of Cairo in the desert of Egypt stand three great pyramids. Weathered and rough and stripped of their former marble casing but otherwise intact, they still stand, grey and massive, constituting, with the Sphinx, the best known symbols of Ancient Egypt.

Though palaeolithic tools and neolithic graves have been found in the Nile valley, the history of Egypt begins 'officially' with Mena, first king of the first dynasty, who is also the first king of Egypt about whom anything is known historically. The division of the Egyptian kings into numbered dynasties is due to the historian Manetho (c. 270 B.C.) who wrote a history of Egypt from the records then in existence. His manuscript was deposited in the great library of Alexandria and is presumed to have been destroyed when the Moslems burnt the library in A.D. 642. Some fragments, however, copied by other historians, remain.

The authorities vary as to the dates of the earlier dynasties, some placing the first as far back as 5000 B.C. and beyond, and others as late as 3000 B.C. Whatever the date it is quite certain that the first dynasty marks, not the beginning of a civilization, but the continuation of one that is already well developed and already old. Carvers and gold workers were wonderfully skilful, hieroglyphic writing (the beautiful writing of Ancient Egypt) was coming into common use, and there was an advanced religion, with a well organized priestly hierarchy.

The practice of building pyramids, for a purpose that is still not altogether clear, was begun by the kings of the third dynasty. Zoser built the 'step' pyramid of Saqqara and Snefru built one pyramid at Medum and another at Dahsur. The three great pyramids of Giza were built respectively by three fourth dynasty kings, Khufu, Khafra and Men-Kau-Re.

Most of our knowledge of Ancient Egypt is derived from inscriptions and works of art in the tombs of the kings and nobles, from buildings such as temples and pyramids, and from papyri or from monuments. Many of the tombs so far uncovered—very few compared to the thousands that must still lie buried in the sand—had been rifled before they were found by archaeologists. Tomb robbery is a very ancient craft in Egypt and began in the time of the Pharaohs themselves. Nevertheless we have enough to provide us with much reliable knowledge of the history, religion and culture of this humane and artistic people, far more, for instance, than we have about our own ancestors of a much less remote period, who were neither artistic nor, probably, humane. Unfortunately these are matters on which we cannot dwell in a book of this kind, and those who wish to learn more about these people, their writing and painting, their art and science, their religion from which so much sprang, should consult one or two authoritative works on Egyptology and should also, if possible, see the Egyptian collections in the great museums of Europe or in the Cairo museum. It will be sufficient here to note that the Nile Valley, four or five thousand years before our era, was the nursery of one of the most remarkable, and certainly one of the most enduring civilizations ever so far evolved by man.

Egyptian civilization was carried by traders and soldiers far up the Nile into continental Africa. The ruins of Meroë, about a hundred miles downstream from Khartoum, testify to a culture closely derived from Egypt. The Meroitic kingdom, which occupied the country enclosed in the bend of the Nile between the fourth and sixth cataracts, provided Egypt with its twenty-fifth or 'Ethiopian' dynasty and rose to a position of great power and influence. It fell from this position in the fourth century A.D. when Meroë was destroyed by the kingdom of Aksum in what is now northern Ethiopia.

The history of Ancient Egypt may be said to have come to an end with the annexation of the country by Alexander the Great in 332 B.C. if indeed we do not date it two centuries earlier, at the time of the Persian invasion. But even at the later date, the old religion had enough vitality left to cause Alexander, no doubt as an act of expediency, to travel to the Siwa Oasis and worship at the temple of Jupiter Ammon. Perhaps from our point of view the most important feature of the Ptolemaic period that followed was the inscription on stone steles of a decree that special honours be paid to Ptolemy V. One of these steles was the Rosetta Stone, found by a French engineer officer not far from the town of Rashid or Rosetta in 1799 and now in the British Museum. The Stone is inscribed in three characters, first the hieroglyphic, which was the old picture writing employed for nearly all state and ceremonial documents intended to be seen by the general public; second, the demotic, that is the conventional, abbreviated and modified form of hieratic (a cursive form of hieroglyphic which was in use in the Ptolemaic period); and third, Greek. The hieroglyphic text corresponds to the last twenty-eight lines of the Greek text, and since the Greek character was, of course, perfectly known, the Stone thus provided the key to the deciphering of the hieroglyphic.

As every schoolboy knows (at least every boy who has read Shakespeare), the line of the Ptolemies ended with Cleopatra, and Egypt became a Roman province. After many vicissitudes, a weakened and impoverished country was easily conquered in A.D. 639–640 by a Moslem army commanded by Amr ibn al Asi, a general of Omar, the second caliph. At this stage, the beginning of a new era, we leave Egypt for the time being and move westwards to North Africa.

Berbers and Carthaginians

The first people of North Africa of whom we have historical knowledge are a race of light-skinned Hamites whom the Arabs called Berbers,[1] who later provided Europeans with the name

---

[1] The etymology of the word is not settled. Some say it is derived from Arabic 'barbara', to talk noisily or confusedly, others favour derivation from a Greek and Latin word describing anyone who was not a Greek or a Roman.

Barbary for the whole of the North African coast. Phoenicians began to colonize the coast about the twelfth century B.C., first founding settlements at Leptis, Oea, later Tripoli, and Sabratha in Libya, and then moving westwards to found their most important North African city, Carthage near modern Tunis. By the sixth century B.C. Carthage was the prosperous centre of Carthaginian power, wielding supreme influence from Syrtica in the east to the Straits of Gibraltar in the west. The Carthaginians were essentially sailors and merchants and their occupation of the coast was probably neither intensive nor continuous. On the other hand they undertook immensely long voyages. Carthaginian vessels sailed north as far as Britain for the tin of the Cornish mines and a Carthaginian admiral, Hanno, was said to have sailed round the west coast of Africa to the Gulf of Guinea and possibly beyond to the Gaboon River. Her wealth and power founded on maritime commerce, Carthage was mistress of the Mediterranean.

Much of the history of Carthage is the story of her wars with the Greeks in Sicily and with the Romans. The Sicily wars continued intermittently and with varying fortunes from the beginning of the fifth century B.C. for about 200 years. The mighty struggle with Rome, the so-called Punic wars, began in 264 B.C. and covered a span of 118 years. These were the wars that threw up one of the great figures of world history, Hannibal, the Carthaginian general (247–183 B.C.), a man of extraordinary character and powers of organization, no doubt the most dangerous enemy that Rome in her great days ever encountered. The Punic wars came to an end in 146 B.C. with the fall of Carthage to Rome and the total destruction of the city. The supremacy of the Mediterranean passed to Rome.

The early history of eastern Libya or Cyrenaica is different from that of other parts of North Africa. As in the rest of the region the earliest inhabitants of whom we have any record were Berbers. They seem to have been more or less continuously at war with Egypt, and Ancient Egyptian reliefs commemorating the victories of the Pharaohs often show Libyans in the most unfortunate situations— being hit on the head with clubs, crushed under chariots, or being led into captivity. There is no firm record here of Carthaginian colonization. Cyrene was founded by Greeks, who then built four more cities, Berenice (Benghazi), Barca (il Merj), Apollonia, and Teucheira or Arsinoë (Tocra). At the beginning of the third century B.C. the country became known as the Pentapolis from the federation of the five cities. Cyrenaica formed part of the empire of

Alexander the Great and after his death in 323 B.C. came under the dominion of his successors in Egypt, the Ptolemies. The last Ptolemaic ruler, Apion, who died in 96 B.C., bequeathed the country to Rome, and it became a province of the Roman Empire. (*Plate* 70)

The Romans in North Africa

The Romans tried at first to restrict the occupation of their newly conquered territories to a comparatively small area round Carthage, which they called the Province of Africa. But they soon found that it is impossible to limit the responsibility of government at will, that one commitment inevitably leads to another, and that no sooner has one frontier been established than it becomes necessary to establish another wider one to protect the first. After several conflicts with rebellious tribes, Numidians, Garamantes and others, the Romans extended their rule over the whole coast from Cyrene to the Atlantic and southwards to the Fezzan.

The Roman domination of North Africa lasted for nearly six hundred years and was a period of great material prosperity, as many magnificent remains of towns and buildings testify. Agriculture and forestry were encouraged, public works developed, trading settlements grew into prosperous and beautiful cities, all under the protection of garrisons deep in the desert at places like Bu Ngem, Ghadames, and even Garama, the modern Germa, capital of the powerful and warlike Garamantes. It is also worth remembering that North Africa gave Rome a great emperor, Septimius Severus (A.D. 146–A.D. 211) who was born at Leptis. (*Plate* 69)

North Africa's connection with Christianity is an early one. From the many Jewish communities settled along the coast there was 'one Simon, a Cyrenian, coming out of the country', on whom was laid the Cross 'that he might bear it after Jesus', and in the account of the Pentecost in the Acts of the Apostles men from 'the parts of Libya about Cyrene' were among those who received the gift of tongues. Tertullian, creator of Christian Latin literature, and St. Cyprian, bishop and martyr, were both of Carthage in the Roman province, while St. Augustine of Hippo, one of the greatest fathers of the Latin Church, was born at Tagaste in Numidia.

Decline and Fall

With the decline of the Roman power North Africa fell on bad times. The troubles began in the fourth century with the rebellion of the Donatists, a schismatic sect representing in some sort the

masses against Church and State. In A.D. 428 the Vandals with
Genseric at their head poured into North Africa from Spain and
occupied Carthage. The Donatists made common cause with them.
Genseric had the sense to preserve the old administrative machinery
and was thus able to maintain law and order, but the country was
once more plunged into anarchy when he died in 477. A Byzantine
army under Belisarius liberated the country from the Vandals but
this victory brought no peace. The bridgehead of civilization in
Roman Africa had always been a narrow one. Inland were savage
tribes always ready to take up arms against the settled communities
on the coast. As long as the Pax Romana extended as far south as the
Fezzan, the inhabitants of the coastal towns could sleep sound in
their beds. But those times were over. Now the barbarians of the
interior watched the Byzantines and the Vandals at war and rose
against the victor. The revolt was suppressed with difficulty and the
Byzantines did what they could to reorganize the life of the province. Proper administration was re-established and Christianity,
after its long subordination to the Vandals and their Donatist allies,
was restored and extended to the inland tribes. But the spirit had
gone from the place, the rulers had little faith in their task and the
people were apathetic. When the Arabs invaded North Africa in 642
only the Berber tribes, with their passionate love of liberty, offered
much resistance.

The Arab Invasions

Until the seventh century the Arabs lived pretty well within the
boundaries of Arabia, some as town dwellers, some as nomads in the
desert. About 571 there was born among them a man named
Mohamed who, proclaiming himself to be the prophet of the one
God, founded Islam, 'submission' (to the will of God), one of the
great religions of the world. After the prophet's death in 632 the
Arabs, aflame with their new faith, burst out of their frontiers and
poured into Africa. They invaded Egypt in 639 and subdued the
country in 641. They met with little opposition. Egyptian Christianity was torn by dissensions, and its hold on the masses was
certainly not strong enough to inspire in them a spirit of resistance.
Similarly, when the Arabs resumed their westward march in 642
they easily overran Cyrenaica and Tripolitania. Here and there the
Christians went down fighting (the town of Tripoli withstood a siege
of six months before it was captured) but it was the Berbers who put
up the most obstinate resistance, actually succeeding at one stage in

driving the invaders back to Egypt. But this success was only temporary and early in the eighth century the Arabs drove across the
country from east to west and in 711, strongly reinforced by
Berbers, invaded Spain and Portugal and there developed a remarkable civilization which has exerted great influence on all aspects of
life in the Iberian peninsula. The Arab conquest of North Africa
was completed in the eleventh century by two tribes of marauding
nomads from Arabia, the Beni Hilal and Beni Soleim. The Beni
Soleim stayed in Cyrenaica but the Beni Hilal passed on to the
west, harrying and destroying wherever they went. The devastation
that they caused was such that the country has never fully recovered
from it.[1]

Although the Berbers managed to an astonishing degree to preserve their purity of race and in some places their language, the
greater number in the end adopted the Arab religion, dress and
speech and many Arab customs. Christianity virtually disappeared
although it had survived further east in Egypt, and in Ethiopia
which was never conquered. The effect of the invasions was to
stamp North Africa indelibly with the Arab mark, and to turn it into
the Maghreb or western part of the Arab world.

Morocco

The Arabs called Morocco Maghreb al Aqsa, which means the
Far West. It is a country of mountains and narrow plains with a
plentiful rainfall, very different from the country through which
they had passed on their long march from Arabia. Here they established the Idrisid dynasty, a branch of the family of the Prophet,
and contemporary with Haroun al Raschid, Caliph of Bagdad. Here
also they built the city of Fez, intellectual centre of the Maghreb.
In the eleventh century Morocco was invaded by the Almoravids
(*al murabitun*), Berbers and puritan Moslems, who built Marrakesh,
extended their rule as far as Algiers and overran Moslem Spain.
The Almoravids were succeeded by the Almohades who further
enlarged their dominions, making them stretch from the Tagus to
Tripoli. An empire so extended could not survive for long. In the
thirteenth century the Maghreb split into three parts. The governor
of the old Province of Africa proclaimed his independence and so
established the Hafsid dynasty; the Abd al Wahid dynasty took the

---

[1] 'The most serious consequence of the devastation was that enormous areas went
permanently out of cultivation and the desert crept in. Directly or through their
herds, these wild Arabs also destroyed most of the forests . . .' Bovill, *The Golden
Trade of the Moors*, p. 58.

central Maghreb round Algiers; and the Merinids succeeded the Almohades in Morocco. The present reigning dynasty in Morocco, that of the Filali, which originates from Tafilalet on the Saharan side of the Atlas Mountains, came to power in the seventeenth century.

The Reconquest of Spain

The Arab occupation of Spain lasted for about 500 years. Spanish Christianity, where it did not compound with the invaders, retreated to the north where the idea of an ultimate reconquest was fostered and kept alive. The occupation was punctuated by frequent outbreaks of fighting but was on the whole marked by tolerance and a spirit of 'co-existence' on both sides. Tolerance, however, later gave way to fanaticism. On the Moslem side this was due to the coming of the Almoravids, who had no sympathy with Christians, and on the Christian side to the arrival of monks and warriors from France who communicated to the idea of reconquest the spirit of a crusade. In the thirteenth century the Christians vigorously assaulted Moorish Spain and by the middle of the century the kingdom of Granada was the only Spanish state under Moslem control. It survived for 250 years before falling to the Spaniards in 1492 after a hard-fought war. During this time there was steady pressure on those Moslems who remained in Christian Spain either to abandon their faith, or go to Granada, or leave Spain altogether. Many chose the last alternative, and in 1610 the remaining Moriscos, Moslems who had become converted to Christianity, were expelled from Spain.

Trans-Saharan trade—the Empires of West Africa.[1]

Long before the dawn of Islam, the people of the North African littoral had traded southwards across the Sahara with the Negroes of West Africa, exchanging salt from the mines of Taghaza, Taodeni and Taotek for gold and slaves. This trade was carried by camel-caravan along recognized trade routes running from the cities of North Africa through the oases and the salt mines to the towns on the southern edge of the desert. There were three principal routes: a western one from Morocco to the great northern bend of the Niger and the country to the west of it, a central one from Tunisia to the country between the Niger and Lake Chad, and an eastern one from Tripoli and Egypt to Lake Chad. The trade they carried flourished

[1] Much of the material for this section comes from Bovill, *The Golden Trade of the Moors*, and Fage, *An Introduction to the History of West Africa*.

down the centuries until the arrival of European traders on the
west coast and anarchy in the western Sudan[1] combined to
turn the direction of trade south towards the sea and commerce
with the north declined.

From about the beginning of the Christian era, North Africans
began to migrate across the Sahara and to settle in numbers north
of the Niger and Senegal Rivers, establishing dominion over the
Negroes whom they found there and gradually merging with them.
These migrations were intensified by the Arab invasions of North
Africa from the eighth century onwards, but in due course the
Arabs themselves came south of the Sahara, and the mixed people
of the region, products of the fusion between Berber and Negro,
became converted to Islam.

The outcome of these invasions from North Africa was a succession of great territorial empires in the country north of the West
African forest. These empires were founded either by the fair-
skinned invaders themselves or by Negro or semi-Negro peoples
who had learnt the ways of successful warfare from their contact
with North Africans. The secrets of success were a social organization of a military character and the possession of horses and camels.
The Negro tribes were no match for people endowed with these
assets, and the conquerors extended their empires rapidly, only
stopping at the forest, where cavalry was not effective. The earliest
of the empires of which we have any substantial knowledge is
Ghana, which may have been founded, perhaps by Cyrenaican
Jews, about A.D. 200. Ghana was absorbed into the Sosso Empire of
Kaniaga at the beginning of the thirteenth century, and Kaniaga in
turn was swallowed by the great empire of Mali, which reached up
into the Sahara and stretched from Futa Jallon in the south-west
to Gao on the middle Niger. Mali's greatest days were during the
first part of the fourteenth century, after which came a steady
decline; and as the greatness of Mali waned, so did that of the
Songhai kingdom of Gao gradually develop. Towards the end of the
sixteenth century, however, the Moroccans, not content with the
trans-Saharan trade, sent an army against Gao in the hope of securing the gold of West Africa at its source. The Songhair empire,
weakened by wars and dynastic quarrels, was no match for the
invaders and soon collapsed. But the Moroccans had quite misunder-

---

[1] 'Sudan' is used in this context to describe the great savannah belt that stretches
across the continent south of the great northern deserts from Senegal to Ethiopia.
The term 'western Sudan' covers broadly the sub-Saharan interior of the West
African region described in Chapter Seven.

stood the true nature of the wealth of Gao. This depended, not on possession of the gold mines, which were far away in the south, but on trade with the people in whose country the mines were. The Moroccans were in no position to conquer the gold-producing areas or to ensure the peaceful conditions necessary for the pursuit of the trade. Their victory was therefore a hollow one but the army managed to maintain itself in the western Sudan for nearly a hundred years, living on tribute from the local chiefs, electing its own pashas, and keeping up its numbers by recruiting Negroes. As time went on the authority of the pashas waned, the efficiency of the army decayed, and by the end of the seventeenth century such political authority as there was in the western Sudan had passed to powerful native rulers.

Between the Black Volta and the great bend of the Niger River a comparatively small group of invaders from the neighbourhood of Lake Chad, possibly refugees from Berber invasions, founded a number of states called the Mossi-Dagomba States. These were more stable than most of the great sub-Saharan empires and when the Europeans arrived at the end of the nineteenth century were still ruled by direct descendants of the men who had founded them 500 years before. Further east, other states were established by Hamite-dominated Negroes who spoke a language called Hausa. These Hausa states were conquered by Fulani between 1804 and 1810 in a *jihad* (war of religion corresponding to a crusade) and so became the Fulani emirates which the Europeans encountered when they entered northern Nigeria in the latter part of the century.

Europeans in West Africa

The title of 'Navigator' bestowed on Prince Henry of Portugal (1394–1460) was scarcely deserved, since the Prince himself never in his life went further afield than Tangier. Yet his services to African discovery can hardly be exaggerated. He drew together skilled geographers, founded a school of navigation and an observatory, and promoted and equipped expeditions to places hitherto unknown. During his life and after his death the Portuguese made a series of brilliant voyages of exploration down the coast of Africa, which towards the end of the fifteenth century were to take them round the Cape of Good Hope and into the Indian Ocean.

Henry's enthusiasm for exploration sprang from several motives. He knew all about the gold trade between West and North Africa and wanted to tap the source by out-flanking the Sahara. Then, he hoped to find a way round Africa to establish contact with the fabulous monarch Prester John of Ethiopia. Such a contact would be doubly meritorious: in itself it would tend to the unity of Christendom, and at the same time it would outflank the Moslems, who stood astride the road to the east. Finally, Henry may have been moved by sheer zeal for knowledge. The voyages initiated by him were not isolated ventures, but formed part of a definite plan. All the results were collated and compared, and each expedition, armed with the accumulated experience of its predecessors, was part of a scientifically organized system of exploration. As the Portuguese pushed further south along the coast, so perhaps would their plans develop and expand, until, with the rounding of the Cape and with the Indian Ocean open before them, they had the trade of the Indies almost within their grasp.

Meanwhile on the west coast Portuguese settlements multiplied. They were usually small, consisting merely of trading stations or off-shore islands, though at some places substantial forts were built, as for instance at Elmina on the Gold Coast. Small as they were, the stations had great commercial influence, and Portuguese trade on the coast, especially on the Gold Coast, was of considerable importance, and it was moreover a trade in which the Portuguese at first had no rivals. This preponderance was of short duration. It was challenged quite early by the Castilians and towards the end of the sixteenth century several other European nations set out to break the Portuguese monopoly and to establish trading stations of their own. First the Dutch, then the English and the French, not to mention Brandenburgers, Swedes and Danes, all threw themselves into the contest with zest. Except for French attempts to develop the trade of the Senegal River, European traders did not go inland themselves, but contented themselves with establishing trading stations on the coast. The main function of these stations was to hold the slaves, who constituted the chief article of trade, between their delivery from up-country by native slavers and the time when a ship was ready to take them across the Atlantic.

The arrival of Europeans on the coast brought about a profound change in the condition of the hinterland. West African contacts with the outside world had hitherto been through North Africa. The empires created and ruled by the Berbers and others stopped short at the forest fringe, and though indeed the northerners visited the forest peoples, it was only to trade and to raid for slaves and not to settle. Now the direction of trade changed towards the coast, and as the forest tribesmen flung themselves heartily into the slave-raiding game they acquired firearms, became wealthy and strong and founded states comparable with those whose connections were with the north. Such, for instance, were Oyo, Ashanti, Dahomey and Benin. Like the northern states, these were formed by comparatively small groups of alien immigrants, and their organization was in many respects similar to that of Ghana, Mali and Gao. They also had considerable resemblances one to another, since they were formed from people with a common cultural tradition. And as they rose by the Slave Trade, so by the same accursed traffic they fell. Their frenzied participation in the Trade led them into ruinous wars, corrupted their rulers, promoted internal divisions, decimated the peasantry, and inhibited the development of any proper economic order.

In 1578 young King Sebastian of Portugal, obsessed with the idea of a crusade, dragged his reluctant people into a war with the Moors of Morocco. He met complete defeat at al Ksar al Kebir (Alcazar) where an army of 26,000 Portuguese was annihilated. The King himself was killed and with him the flower of Portuguese chivalry. The direct result was that in 1581 the Crown of Portugal passed to Spain and the Portuguese overseas empire collapsed. Though Portugal regained independence in 1640, she had already been supplanted by the Dutch as dominant power on the west coast. About the middle of the seventeenth century other European nations, particularly the British and the French, were attracted by West African trade. Following the Dutch example they created national trading companies with charters giving them the monopoly of their nation's trade on the coast. The Dutch lost ground to the British and the French between whom there presently ensued a bitter fight for world power. The consequence for West Africa of the Anglo-French wars of the eighteenth century was that Britain became the dominant power in West African trade.

It must be emphasized that this predominance was not accompanied by extensive territorial possessions. Competition between the nations was for trade, not for sovereignty. In 1764 the British made an unsuccessful attempt to constitute a crown colony, that of Senegambia, but in the main European colonization was an affair of forts and factories necessary for operating and defending trade, on land recognized as belonging to the natives. The companies regarded themselves as tenants of the local chiefs, without whose goodwill and assistance trade could not be carried on.

Arabs in East Africa

There is an early 'pilot' or guide to trade and navigation called
the *Periplus of the Erythraean sea*, compiled about A.D. 80 by a
Greek merchant seaman, which describes in detail the voyage down
the Red Sea and the African coast of the Indian Ocean. Many of
the geographical features mentioned in the *Periplus* may be easily
identified, but the interest of the guide lies rather in what the author
tells us of the politics and commerce of the day. We learn that the
people were apparently of negroid stock and ruled by chiefs. But it
also appears that these chiefs had long been under some kind of
Arab suzerainty and that there was already a well-established trade
carried by Arab and Indian ships between Africa, Arabia and India.

For several hundred years after the *Periplus* information about
East Africa is scanty, but there is enough evidence to show that
inter-continental traffic prospered and spread. Between the fifth
and sixteenth centuries the Arabs were masters of the Indian Ocean.
East African trade reached beyond Malaya to China and there was
a large Arab 'colony' in Canton. Nor was the trade by any means one
way. Indian ships called at East African towns, and although there
is no certain evidence of *direct* contact with China, Chinese books
often refer to East Africa and Chinese coins are found on the East
African coast.

In due course, probably in quite early times, the Arabs proceeded from trade to colonization. We do not know when the first
Arab settlements were founded or where, but the process was no
doubt a gradual one. By the early middle ages there was already a
string of Arab colonies from Mogadishu to Sofala, each one a city
state usually at odds with one or more of the others. At no time was
there anything like an Arab 'empire' of East Africa. The nearest
approach to unity was 'the overlordship exercised for varying
periods over a varying number of other towns by the one which
happened at the time to be the strongest or the most aggressive'.[1]
The unwarlike tribes of the coast submitted to the colonists
without much difficulty. Intermarriage quickly took place and
produced the Swahili, the mixed, indefinable people of the coast.
The Arabs attempted no systematic exploration or colonization of the hinterland. Their only interest in the tribes of the interior
was trade; and if in the course of their trading expeditions they
established permanent inland settlements, these too were not for

---

[1] R. Coupland, *East Africa and its Invaders*, p. 26.

administration, nor for the establishment of plantations, nor for the exploitation of natural resources, nor for anything else but trade. Unhappily the principal and most valuable article of trade was slaves, of whom great numbers were taken to Arabia and India and a few as far as China.

As the years went by the Arabs of East Africa attained a state of considerable prosperity, living in large towns, wearing fine clothes and surrounded by luxury. The great Arab traveller Ibn Battuta, visiting East Africa in the fourteenth century, was most impressed by their wealth and civilization, describing Kilwa as 'one of the most beautiful and best built towns', and Mogadishu, where he was well entertained by its hospitable and pious people, as an 'exceedingly large city'. This advanced, if predominantly material, civilization was almost destroyed by East Africa's next invaders, the Portuguese.

The Portuguese on the East Coast

The west coast of Africa, valuable as its trade proved to be, was only a stage in the Portuguese plan of expansion. In 1485 Diego Cão reached Cape Cross in latitude 21° 50′ S. In 1488 Bartholomeu Diaz, blown far to the south and turning back towards the north-east, found that the coastline was now running east. He had rounded Africa without knowing it. He got as far as Algoa Bay and sighted the Cape on the return journey. In little more than twenty years after this significant discovery the Portuguese had achieved the mastery of the east coast of Africa. The assault began after a reconnaissance by Vasco da Gama in 1497–99. First da Gama himself in 1502 compelled the Sultan of Kilwa to acknowledge the supremacy of the King of Portugal; in 1503 Ruy Lourenço Ravasco obtained the submission of Zanzibar. In 1505 a fleet of twenty ships under Almeida occupied Sofala and Kilwa and destroyed Mombasa; in 1506 another fleet of fourteen ships under Tristão da Cunha and Albuquerque persuaded Lamu to submit and destroyed Oja and Barawa, sparing Mogadishu only because the sailing season was drawing to an end and time was short. In 1507 Mozambique was built up into a permanent settlement, with church, fort, quarters for garrison and staff. By 1509, when a governor-general was appointed, occupation of the east coast was complete. Combined with footholds at the mouth of the Red Sea and in the Persian Gulf it assured the Portuguese command of the Indian Ocean.

The effect of the Portuguese conquests on the Arab colonies was disastrous. The Portuguese claimed and enforced a rigid monopoly of the sea trade of the Indian Ocean, the old Arab connection with India was cut, and even coastal shipping was made as difficult as possible. On land the Portuguese employed every effort to destroy Arab commercial relations with the inland tribes, but made no more impression themselves on the interior than the Arabs before them. The Portuguese conquests therefore, while destroying the wealth and power of the Arabs, had few positive results.

With the annexation of Portugal by Spain, and the collapse of her empire in the first half of the seventeenth century, the Portuguese lost their hold on the eastern trade. Their ejection from most of East Africa was soon to follow. The Arab communities had always hated their Portuguese masters and there were several revolts which were sternly repressed. But the serious, and in the end fatal, challenge came from the Omani of the Arabian coast. After intermittent hostilities that lasted many years the Portuguese were finally driven out of the whole of the northern part of East Africa. By 1740 they retained only the southern strip, now the coast of their present colony of Portuguese East Africa, while the old and now decayed Arab settlements in the north came under the control of Oman.

The Dutch in South Africa

On the 6th April 1652 Jan van Riebeeck, under instructions from the Dutch East India Company to establish a revictualling station at the Cape of Good Hope for ships plying to and from the Indies, dropped anchor in Table Bay. He was to build a fort sufficient for eighty men, to plant a garden, and to obtain cattle by trading with the natives. His instructions were quite plain: the place was simply to be 'a depot of provisions for the ships' and nothing else.

Van Riebeeck found two native races in occupation of the surrounding countryside, the Bushmen and the Hottentots. Only the latter had cattle and it was with them that he had to do business. Trade with the tribes in the immediate vicinity was not altogether satisfactory, and in order to find fresh meat which he simply had to have in order to fulfil his duty of victualling the ships, van Riebeeck was constrained to send exploratory parties further and further inland. Thus in 1655 Dutch expansion in South Africa had already begun. In 1657 the Dutch East India Company—still for the purpose of ensuring supplies for ships—planted a few farmers near the settlement. They were to be free (that is to say they were not servants of the Company) but they were subject to various controls which considerably curtailed their independence. These so-called 'free burghers' were intended merely to be purveyors to the Company. It was not until twenty years later that the Company, hitherto on the whole opposed to immigration, made any real effort to encourage immigration and settlement. In 1679 and in the following years farms were given out in full ownership, the village of Stellenbosch was founded, local government instituted, young women were imported to provide colonists with wives, a group of French Huguenots arrived and were gradually absorbed in the Dutch population, and by the beginning of the eighteenth century there were about 1,700 Europeans, men, women and children. As early as 1657 van Riebeeck had tried to meet the demand for labour by importing slaves and in succeeding years the number of slaves owned by the 'free burghers' increased considerably. In 1717 the decision was deliberately taken to develop the colony with slaves rather than with free white labour. This decision was a fateful one and had far reaching consequences.[1] Meanwhile the demand for cattle encouraged cattle farming and as this is an occupation requiring much land the colonists had to spread out to find it. Land was unlimited then, the only obstacle to its peaceful occupation being the Bushmen who were soon either killed or driven away. By the end of the eighteenth century the 'refreshment station' at the Cape had grown into a colony extending over a sizeable part of the modern Cape Province with a population consisting of Europeans, 'coloured', as people of mixed descent were called, and an assortment of other races at Cape Town; a number of settled farmers cultivating vines and corn with slave labour in the neighbourhood of the capital; beyond them the cattle farmers or Trek Boers, wandering further and further afield in search of grazing and water and game, with their families and their cattle and their Hottentot herdsmen.

These Trek Boers were a peculiar people. They were of Calvinist stock, like the other South African Dutch, and their religion derived more from the Old Testament than from the New. They came to compare their own wanderings with those of the Children of Israel and hence to look upon themselves in some sort as a Chosen People, while the African tribes with whom they came into conflict fell quite naturally into the category of Amalekites and Amorites and all the other *ites* whom the Israelites in their various

[1] pp. 72-3.

4

aggressions ousted from the Promised Land. They admitted no kind of equality with the coloured races, whom they regarded as classified by Providence to be servants for ever. Living a poor, hard, isolated life remote from towns, self-sufficient to a fault and masters of their own rugged environment, the Trek Boers resented any form of government control. All they asked was to be plentifully supplied with ammunition, otherwise to be left alone. These were the people who in due course came up against the Bantu tribes pressing south. It should here be noted that in many parts of South Africa the Bantu occupation is hardly older than that of the Europeans and in some parts more recent. The contact between Bantu and Boer had several important consequences. The first was that the old custom of roaming at will was checked. The Bantu were also farmers and the Trek Boers, who had long held the belief that all free men had a right to as much land as they needed, found that beyond a certain point any more land had to be fought for. This led to raids, counter-raids and wars, which had unhappy consequences not only immediate but also remote. For it is not too much to say that many of the racial complications from which South Africa now suffers can be traced back to the frontier conditions of a hundred and fifty years ago.

In 1795 the French revolutionary armies invaded Holland and Great Britain occupied Cape Town by arrangement with the Dutch King. This occupation came to an end in 1802. Four years later, Great Britain, at war with Napoleon and fearing lest the key to the sea route to India should fall into enemy hands, occupied the colony again, this time for good.

The Slave Trade

It seems that slave-trading is endemic in Africa. The author of the *Periplus* tells us that slaves 'of the better sort' were exported to Egypt from Ras Hafun[1] and slaves were an important element in the Moorish trade between West and North Africa across the Sahara. They also made a large contribution to the prosperity of the Arab settlements in East |Africa in medieval times. In the seventeenth and eighteenth centuries European trade with the west coast of Africa was practically synonymous with slaving. The Portuguese began it, but other European nations soon followed suit and in 1652 the British joined in when Sir John Hawkins sold 300 Negroes from West Africa to Spaniards in the West Indies. From

---

[1] On the eastern coast of Somaliland.

then on British participation grew under the highest auspices and by 1770 the British were carrying about half the total number of slaves taken across the Atlantic.

The sufferings of these unfortunate Negroes during the process of transportation were appalling. The direct route to the West Indies, the Middle Passage as it was called, lay wholly within the tropical belt, and the slaves were confined in a narrow space below deck in stifling heat, squeezed together like sardines, with bad food, and of course with no proper sanitation. Numbers of them died, and all arrived in a most miserable condition, only about 50 per cent of those transported being fit for effective work.

Nor were these poor wretches the only ones to suffer. One of the ways in which slaves were obtained was by inducing native chiefs to make raids into one another's country in order to take prisoners. This added the horrors of inter-tribal war to a trade that was already bad enough. During the slaving season the whole coast was a scene of terror and violence and devastation. It is curious that so loathsome a traffic should so long have passed uncensured. There were several reasons for this. One, of course, was that the ordinary Englishman knew very little about it. Africa and the West Indies were a long way away, and those who ran the Trade were at no great pains to give publicity to the detail of their proceedings. The good people of those days had more excuse for their ignorance of colonial affairs than we have for ours. Then, the Trade paid very well and was an important part of our maritime commerce. Not for the first time, nor for the last, was immorality justified by economic and political necessity. Finally, the people interested in the Trade were a powerful caucus, not lightly to be challenged.

Still there were protests, chiefly at first from Quakers and other religious people. In 1761 American Quakers went so far as to disown all Friends who continued to take part in the Trade. But the first really important victory for the Abolitionists was the judgment given in 1772 by Chief Justice Mansfield in the case of James Somerset, brought at the instance of Granville Sharp. The effect of Mansfield's judgment was that as soon as a slave set foot on the soil of the British Isles he became free. This was all very well for slaves who were able to reach England, but it did nothing to help those shipped direct across the Atlantic from Africa. Abolition of the Trade in British dependencies was due mainly to the efforts of Thomas Clarkson (1760–1846), William Wilberforce (1759–1833) and a small band of associates. Their task was a long and uphill one, for there was much prejudice to combat, strong potential allies to persuade, powerful interests to overcome. Victory came in 1807 when a Bill was passed which 'utterly abolished, prohibited and declared to be unlawful' any dealing in slaves among British subjects and in British ships.[1] In 1811 slave-trading became a felony punishable with transportation, and in 1833 the institution of slavery itself was abolished in all British colonies.

The abolition of the British Slave Trade and of British slavery did not destroy the whole of the system everywhere. It continued to exist not only in Africa and Asia but also in parts of the world ruled by Europeans,[2] in the Portuguese, Spanish and French colonies, in the southern states of America and in South America. It is true that all the nations formerly engaged in the Trade passed laws and made treaties for its abolition. But these engagements existed only on paper, and violations were frequent and regular. An Englishman may claim with pride that it was largely due to British interference with the shipping of other nations (to a degree far beyond international usage) that the Trade was finally stopped. The last bastions fell when slavery itself was abolished in the United States in 1863, in Cuba between 1880 and 1886, and in Brazil between 1883 and 1888. The abolition of Arab slaving from East Africa will be dealt with in a later section.

West Africa in the nineteenth century

One of the results of the campaign against the Slave Trade was the founding of the British colony of Sierra Leone. This was originally a settlement sponsored by the Abolitionists of slaves freed in England by the Mansfield judgment and of American Negroes who had fought on the British side in the War of Independence. The first expedition, made up of Negroes and white prostitutes, failed for lack of organization but the second, conducted under the auspices of a company floated by the Abolitionists, was far better managed. A settlement was founded on the present site of Freetown and continued under considerable difficulties until 1808 when it was taken over by the British Government as the Crown Colony of Sierra Leone.

The Republic of Liberia owes its origin to a somewhat similar enterprise on the part of Americans. In 1821 the American

---

[1] The honour of being the first to abolish the Trade among their own nationals belongs however to the Danes, whose abolition law became effective in 1804.
[2] The word is used here in the racial and not the geographical sense.

Colonization Society obtained land at Cape Mesurado which became the site of Monrovia, and planted there and at other places on the coast numbers of free Negroes from the southern states of America. The Republic was constituted in 1847. Although the government at Monrovia claimed to rule the indigenous people on the coast and for some distance inland, it had in fact for many years practically no control over any but the coastal areas.

At the beginning of the nineteenth century there were three British settlements on the west coast. These were the Crown Colony of Sierra Leone, constituted in 1808, and the forts on the Gold Coast and the Gambia, administered by a company called the Company of Merchants Trading to West Africa. This company was wound up in 1821, and the Gambia and Gold Coast establishments taken over by the British Government to be administered by the government of Sierra Leone. From 1828 to 1843 they were again placed under a committee of merchants, whose representative, Captain George Maclean, was a man of outstanding character. Although his political authority did not extend beyond the coastal settlements, his reputation for wisdom and honesty enabled him to extend British ideas of justice over a wide area, thus bringing some order and stability to a much troubled country. The British Crown resumed control of the settlements in 1843, Maclean being made Judicial Commissioner, that is Chief Justice with a special responsibility for the administration of justice among the local tribes. The jurisdiction which had grown up under Maclean's influence was then confirmed and defined in a celebrated treaty with the local chiefs known as the Bond of 1844, in which the chiefs recognized that the first object of the law was to protect individuals and property, declared human sacrifices and other barbarous customs to be against the law, and agreed that crimes such as murder and robbery should be tried by British judges sitting with the chiefs, 'moulding the customs of the country to the general principles of British law'. In 1850 the British bought the Danish forts and in 1871 also bought out the remaining Dutch, thereby becoming possessors of Elmina, the fortress originally founded by the Portuguese.

From the early days of the century the European settlements and the coastal tribes around them had lain under the threat of the great Ashanti kingdom in the interior. Attacks by the Ashanti were frequent throughout the century until 1873, when an Ashanti army invading the British sphere was defeated, driven back, and followed up the next year to Kumasi, the Ashanti capital, by a British army commanded by Sir Garnet Wolseley. The Ashanti agreed to renounce far reaching territorial claims, to keep the road to Kumasi open to trade, to pay a substantial indemnity and to abandon human sacrifice.

Further west along the coast the British in 1861 annexed the island of Lagos, whose chief, though friendly enough, was unable to prevent his country from being used as a base for slave raiding. In 1885, at the height of the Scramble for Africa,[1] the belt of thickly populated forest country between Lagos and the Cameroons was declared to be a British protectorate in order to forestall the Germans. This so-called Oil Rivers Protectorate, later the Niger Coast Protectorate, together with the Colony of Lagos, formed the narrow foothold from which the British presently advanced inland and created modern Nigeria.

The Napoleonic wars were not long over before French activity in West Africa began to revive. In 1817 France was able to regain some of her lost influence north of Sierra Leone. French merchants then turned their attention towards the south and from about 1838 onwards displayed considerable activity in those parts of the Guinea Coast which were not already under British influence. With the accession of Napoleon III in 1848 the French Government decided to develop the trade of the Senegal, and this policy found active expression from 1854 when French influence and power was extended up the Senegal River into the western Sudan. The Franco-German War of 1870–71 put a stop to the colonial expansion of France. This stop, as we shall see, was only temporary.

The Exploration of Africa

The nineteenth century was for Africa the century of discovery. When it opened, the Mediterranean coast was still largely the haunt of corsairs, a collection of closed little despotisms. Further east Nelson had destroyed the French fleet in the Battle of the Nile in 1798 and thereby foiled Napoleon's attempt to conquer Egypt. By 1801 the Turks, with British help, were again in control of Egypt, but their hold was precarious and did not last long. On the west coast the Slave Trade continued though its end was in sight, but several European nations maintained settlements on the coast for trading in other goods. On the east coast the Arabs were back in occupation of the northern part of their old empire. Ever since the Portuguese had been driven out the Omani Sultans of Muscat had

[1] pp. 52–3.

claimed overlordship of all these Arab settlements, but their dominion was still intermittent and shadowy. Though the nations of Europe had abandoned, or were about to abandon the Slave Trade, it remained an important occupation for Arabs, and Zanzibar was a vast entrepôt for the buying of slaves from the mainland and dispatch to Arabia and India. In South Africa the British were in Cape Town, and there were a number of settlements extending for some distance inland but the band of western civilization was still a narrow one. The interior of the continent was not of course entirely unknown. Ethiopia, the Blue Nile, the Senegal, the Libyan desert, the Congo, Angola, Mashonaland had all been visited at some time or other, in some cases as early as the fifteenth century, by European travellers, many of them Roman Catholic priests. Still further south, Dutch and English travellers knew the basin of the Orange River fairly well, and some had pushed beyond it. But there had been nothing in the nature of systematic exploration. This did not begin until 1788, with the founding in that year by the British of the African Association. The Association set itself to attack the problem of the Niger and sponsored several expeditions to that river from the north and from the west, of which the most notable were those of the heroic and ill-fated Mungo Park. Following the African Association, the British Government took up the quest and also sent expeditions, the most fruitful being that of Lander, the servant of an explorer named Hugh Clapperton who had died on a previous journey in Northern Nigeria. In 1830 Lander traced the Niger down to the ocean, thus solving the chief problem connected with that river. Further attempts to explore the Niger and its tributary the Benue followed, but met with little success until the expedition of Dr. W. B. Baikie in 1854. Meanwhile Major Gordon Laing reached Timbuktu from Tripoli in August 1826 but was murdered shortly after his arrival. Soon afterwards the Frenchman René Caillié performed the remarkable feat of reaching Timbuktu from the west, accompanying a caravan and disguised as a native. He continued his journey to Tangier where he arrived safely after extreme hardships. In 1850–55 the German Heinrich Barth, travelling under the auspices of the British Government with two companions who died during the journey, added enormously to current knowledge of the central Sudan. Other explorers, mostly French and English, penetrated inland from a number of points along the coast between the Gambia and Calabar, and some years later, in 1855 and again in

1863, the French-American Paul du Chaillu made important expeditions further south in the region of the Ogowe River.

The first half of the nineteenth century saw a considerable advance in the exploration of the Nile. The Scotsman James Bruce had lived adventurously in Ethiopia in 1769–72 and had seen the source of the Blue Nile. In 1821 the Frenchmen Cailliaud and Letorzek reached the confluence of the White and Blue Niles, to be followed in 1827 by Linant de Bellefonds, an emissary of the African Association. The German Rüppell visited Kordofan and travelled in the region of the Blue Nile between 1837 and 1839. Meanwhile explorers of various nationalities had been active in Ethiopia where by 1848 extensive triangulation had been done by the French brothers d'Abbadie, thus providing the basis for accurate maps. In the region of the Upper Nile an expedition mounted by Mohamed Ali in 1841 had pushed south to Gondokoro where in 1850 a permanent station was founded by Austrian missionaries.

The eastern side of Africa remained closed to European exploration a little longer than the rest of the continent, possibly owing to the fact that the coastal belt was already in the occupation of Arab colonists. In 1849 Dr. J. L. Krapf of the Church Missionary Society sighted Mount Kenya and in the same year his colleague Rebmann saw Mount Kilimanjaro. Rebmann's sight of Kilimanjaro, with Arab stories of great lakes inland, opened the possibility of a great field of exploration. The Royal Geographical Society sent first Burton and Speke (1856–59) then Speke and Grant (1860–63) inland from the coast opposite Zanzibar. The first of these two expeditions reached Tanganyika, Speke making a flying visit to the southern end of Lake Victoria; the second passed west of Lake Victoria, continued through Uganda, and at Gondokoro, on the way home by the Nile Valley, met Samuel Baker, who discovered Lake Albert, thus completing the broad outlines of the geography of the Nile. Meanwhile, further south, two German travellers came to unhappy ends: Albrecht Roscher was murdered in 1860 near Lake Nyasa, and Baron Karl von der Decken, after an unsuccessful expedition to Kilwa and a more rewarding one to Kilimanjaro, was murdered by Somali on the Juba River in 1865.

David Livingstone discovered Lake Ngami in 1849, reached the Zambezi in 1851, and in 1853 began a great journey that led him first to the west coast at Luanda then back across Africa. At about the same time Africa south of the Zambezi was attacked from the south-west by the Englishman Francis Galton and the Swede C. J.

Andersson, and later by Andersson alone. Other travellers in these regions were the trader James Chapman, the artist Thomas Baines, and the German geologist Carl Mauch, whose discovery of gold in the Tati area in 1866 caused a small gold rush. Livingstone's achievements received a most enthusiastic reception in England, and the British Government organized an expedition under him with the purpose of opening up the country to commerce in order to check the Slave Trade which still flourished under Arab auspices. The expedition lasted from 1858 to 1864 and though it was not by any means a complete success it added much to the current knowledge of the Nyasa area, and by underlining the evils of the Slave Trade contributed in some measure to its ultimate disappearance. Livingstone went back to Africa in 1866 and struck inland from the east coast at Mikindani. In the following years, with dwindling resources and none but his African porters and servants for company, often hungry and often ill, but sustained by his faith and by his consciousness of divine guidance, he explored the country between the coast and Lake Tanganyika with wonderful courage and determination. He was very near the end of his tether when, on 10 November 1871, Stanley found him at Ujiji. Stanley had left the coast at Bagamoyo on 21 March and by ruthlessly driving his men arrived at Tabora on 21 June, both his European companions, Farquhar and Shaw, having died on the way. He found the countryside round Tabora disturbed by war between the native chief Mirambo and the Arabs, joined in on the Arab side and took advantage of a lull in the fighting to slip away and reach Ujiji by forced marches. His arrival with plentiful supplies gave Livingstone sorely needed relief, and these two men so dissimilar in character then spent some months together, even engaging in a joint exploration of the northern end of Lake Tanganyika. Had Livingstone returned to the coast with Stanley on 14 March 1872 it is possible that he might have lived. As it was he was determined to complete his exploration of the river system south and west of Lake Tanganyika. He parted from Stanley at Tabora and struck southwards down the eastern side of the Lake, his first goal being Katanga. But the effort proved too much for his ravaged constitution and on the morning of 1 May 1873[1] his servants found him dead in his shelter near Lake Bangweulu in an attitude of prayer.

[1] This is believed to be the right date, but it is not quite certain. The last entry in his journal is dated 27 April.

A government expedition for the relief of Livingstone had been organized and was assembling at Zanzibar when Stanley arrived at the coast. Whereupon, since it appeared that Livingstone had already been relieved, the expedition returned to England. But a second relief expedition under Lieutenant Lovett Cameron started from Zanzibar on 2 February 1873 and at Tabora met Chuma, one of Livingstone's servants, who, with his companions, was carrying his master's body to the coast. Cameron decided nevertheless to push on to Ujiji, where he mapped the greater part of Lake Tanganyika, and then crossed to the Atlantic coast near Benguela where he arrived in November 1875. Stanley's great journey in 1874-7 finally confirmed that the great river system which Livingstone had suspected was that of the Nile was really that of the Congo.

The Great Trek of the Boers

The British Government, which ruled in Cape Town from 1806 onwards, was not popular with the Boers. These were people who were not amenable to government in any form, and this government had shown unmistakably that it meant to govern, and on new lines. Moreover, it was a government that tended more and more to come under the influence of the humanitarians. These were the people engaged in abolishing the Slave Trade and in preaching doctrines of native rights which to the Boers, who held as an article of faith that there was a gulf divinely fixed between the natives and themselves, was destructive of all security. Yet a third cause of restlessness was that even in the vast hinterland which the Boers at that time occupied, land in the quantities that they considered necessary for their well-being was no longer quite so freely available as before. One of the reasons for this was that the wars of the Zulu tyrant Shaka, like a stone thrown into a pond, had caused waves of Bantu migration in all directions, whole tribes being forced to flee to seek homes and land elsewhere. The competition between Boers and Bantu in the eastern borderlands of the Cape led to the so-called Kaffir Wars in which the British Government became automatically involved as the governing power, incurring great expense and considerable unpopularity. About 1835 these discontents came to a head and the Boers resolved to remove themselves from the reach of the British Government. By 1836 the Great Trek, which was to carry the European to the remotest confines of present South Africa and beyond, was in full swing. With all their possessions loaded on ox-wagons, women and children on the wagons and the men usually on horseback, the Boers trekked away to the Promised Land in the north. In the years that followed the trekkers spilled over the Vaal River into the Magaliesberg and Zoutspansberg, over into Zululand where one of their leaders, Piet Retief, was murdered with many of his followers by Chief Dingaan—the massacre was later amply avenged in the battle of the Blood River—up to the borders of Swaziland and of Portuguese East Africa. Thus in a very short time southern Africa became known as far north as the easterly bend of the Limpopo River. (*Plate* 9)

The Boers did not find the field entirely untenanted. There were already a considerable number of native tribes in most of these areas, sadly disorganized by the wars of the Zulus. There were also the Matabele, led by a dissident captain of Shaka named Mzilikazi, who had to be overcome before the trekkers could enter into enjoyment of the great plains that stretched between the Vaal and the Limpopo. Finally, there were the missionaries of the London Missionary Society, who had founded their mission at Kuruman in southern Bechuanaland in 1817, and had already, through David Livingstone, extended their influence at least as far north as the trekkers had extended theirs, and who, in the long run, were to become the most formidable opponents of all.

*　　*　　*　　*　　*

By the 'seventies all the great geographical problems of Africa had been solved, though there were still many blanks on the map. The course of the more important rivers and many of their tributaries had been traced; the great lakes were known; vast areas of land had been crossed and re-crossed by European explorers and mapped; there was a considerable body of knowledge about the inhabitants, climate, vegetation, fauna and natural features; there was already a considerable amount of literature about Africa, not of hunters' tales and travellers' fantasies, but sober accounts of people and places based on observed facts. About this time too, one kind of exploration came to an end. It was that prompted only by scientific curiosity, the passion for discovery for its own sake. With Stanley's journey down the Congo in 1874 there began the phase of political exploration which grew into the Scramble for Africa and ended in the partition of the continent between the Powers of Europe.

The French in North Africa

Before European penetration of Africa became competitive—the Scramble began in the early 'eighties—there had been a substantial advance of Europeans in North and South Africa. By 1840, as we have seen, the Boers were across the Vaal and spreading about the high veld. During the following decade the French established themselves in North Africa.

Algiers was long the headquarters of the Barbary corsairs, who preyed on the shipping of every nation. By the beginning of the nineteenth century the former Turkish sovereignty had vanished and the coast was studded with a number of small principalities always on the verge of anarchy, with no resources other than the proceeds of piracy. Numbers of expeditions, English, Dutch, French, Spanish and American, tried unsuccessfully at various times to check piracy until 1830, when the French fleet bombarded Algiers into submission and the French occupied the town. They were not, however, able to assert their authority over the rest of the country until 1847, after a long war with the gallant and skilful Abd el Kader. So began the great French Empire in Africa.

Egypt from the Middle Ages to modern times

The history of Egypt from the Arab invasions to modern times contains more than a fair share of unrest, assassination and massacre. The country was ruled at first by governors appointed by successive caliphs. During this early period the character of the Moslem occupation changed. The intention had originally been simply to establish garrisons but it was not long before the country was being systematically colonized. This period was also marked by a number of revolts by the Copts, all of which were suppressed, and by the spread of Arab speech at the expense of Greek. From 1352 to 1517 was the era of the Mamelukes, so-called because the sultans were drawn from the enfranchised slaves who officered the army. They made way for the Turks and Egypt became a dependency of the Porte. But the power of the Mamelukes was by no means destroyed and they were still in the ascendant when Napoleon invaded Egypt in 1798.

With the ejection of the French by the British and Turks in 1801 there began a bloody struggle for power between Turks, Mamelukes and Albanian soldiers, from which Mohamed Ali, an Albanian commander, emerged victorious. He killed off the Mamelukes, defeated a small British force and by about 1807 was the undisputed ruler of Egypt; though acknowledging Turkish sovereignty, he was virtually independent. He campaigned in Arabia, Greece and the Sudan, organized a strong but oppressive administration in Egypt itself, carried out public works at the cost of considerable suffering to the people, and started and encouraged the cotton trade. He died in 1849 and was succeeded by his grandson Abbas I who was murdered in 1854. Next came Said, a son of Mohamed, who in 1856 gave Ferdinand de Lesseps a concession for the construction of the Suez Canal. Said's successor Ismail was in some ways a progressive ruler, and did something to restore the administrative system, which since Mohamed Ali's death had fallen into anarchy. But the money and labour for carrying out the considerable public works which he put in hand were ruthlessly wrung from the miserable peasants to the point where there was nothing more to be got from them, while Ismail's own credit was so bad that he could not raise loans on the international market.

In 1875, to meet his needs, Ismail sold his shares in the Suez Canal Company to the British Government for four million pounds. Henceforward he found himself compelled to submit more and more to European control. Some of the courts of justice became international and finance came under the dual control of France and England. In 1878 Ismail made an attempt to return to his old autocratic ways but was immediately dismissed by the Turkish Government and replaced by Tewfik. In 1882 a programme of rehabilitation and reform begun by the British and the French was interrupted by the revolt of Arabi Pasha. This was put down by the British alone, the Sultan of Turkey having declined to suppress it and the French and Italians refusing to co-operate. Sir Evelyn Baring, later Lord Cromer, became British consul-general in Egypt in 1883 and instituted a series of reforms designed to introduce order and prosperity, and the elements of an independent, liberal government. Baring's appointment coincided with a successful revolt against Egyptian rule in the Sudan.

Egypt in the Sudan—the Mahdi—Gordon at Khartoum

In 1820 Mohamed Ali ordered that Nubia, northern part of the Sudan, should be conquered, and this was accomplished in the following two years in the face of strong resistance from the Nubians. Having taken Nubia, also Sennar and Kordofan, the Egyptians set up a civil government which was unbelievably oppressive and corrupt. The Sudanese were plundered by their rulers,

intolerable taxes were imposed on them and the Slave Trade became
the country's chief industry, in which the government itself took an
active part. In 1870 things took a turn for the better when Sir
Samuel Baker arrived at Gondokoro as governor of the equatorial
provinces under the Egyptian Government. He was succeeded in
1874 by Colonel ('Chinese') Gordon. Baker and Gordon both made
strenuous attempts to stop the Slave Trade, but the authorities in
Khartoum were inactive and gave them little effective support.
Gordon left the Sudan in 1876 but in the following year he was
given the governorship of the Egyptian provinces outside Egypt.
He waged unceasing war on the slave raiders and in 1879, when his
subordinate Gessi caught and executed Suleman Zobeir and other
ringleaders, no less than 10,000 captives were released. But when
Gordon left in 1879 all the old evils of Egyptian administration,
weakness and corruption at the centre, extortion and venality on
the periphery, returned with his successor Raouf Pasha. In 1881
Mohamed Ahmed, a man of Dongola, proclaimed himself to be
the long-awaited Mahdi (guide) of Islam. The Sudanese, weary of
Egyptian misrule, flocked to his standards.

By the beginning of 1884 the Mahdi was well on his way to
becoming master of the Sudan. Alarmed by the annihilation in
November 1883 of an Egyptian Army under Hicks Pasha, the
British Government sent Gordon to effect the withdrawal of the
Egyptian garrisons. Whether Gordon went beyond his instructions
and attempted not an evacuation but a re-occupation is a matter of
controversy.[1] However that may be, the situation worsened, Gordon
was shut up in Khartoum with no chance of escape, and on
26 January 1885 Khartoum fell to the Mahdist host and Gordon
was killed. A relief expedition under Lord Wolseley was too late to
save him. The Mahdi died in the same year, having completely
destroyed Egyptian power in the Sudan, and was succeeded by the
Khalifa (Caliph) Abdulla, a military autocrat who ruled by fear.
Public anger in England at the government's failure to save Gordon
contributed to the fall of the Gladstone Administration in 1885.

Arabs and British on the East Coast

The Arab Slave Trade on the east coast reproduced all the dismal
features of the Afro-European trade from West Africa. The whole
wretched process was repeated here, the raids, the inter-tribal

---

[1] The exact scope of his instructions has been the subject of discussion (see e.g.
J. S. R. Duncan, *The Sudan*, pp. 34–7).

wars, the treachery, the massacres. The captives also suffered appallingly on their long march to the coast. Roped together and shackled to a beam, many of them died on the way and those who fell out were left to die. On arrival at the coast they were shipped in dhows to Zanzibar thence on to their further destination in conditions of hideous discomfort and squalor. 'The sights I have seen, though common incidents of the traffic, are so nauseous that I always strive to drive them from memory.' The words are Livingstone's and it was Livingstone who forced the horrors of the Trade on to the conscience of his countrymen in a crusade which began on his return from his crossing of Africa in 1857. His personality, the prestige of his achievement, his heroic, dedicated life, kindled the imagination of the British people. There was no need for a campaign such as Wilberforce had been compelled to conduct to win popular support. When the British Government set about to eradicate the Trade in the Indian Ocean it had the full weight of public opinion behind it.

During the first half of the nineteenth century the grip of the Arabs of Muscat had been much tightened by Said bin Sultan, or Sayyed Said, who, after usurping the sovereignity of Muscat and devoting the first half of his reign to establishing himself firmly there, spent the second in building up a strong political and economic position in East Africa. In 1840 he went so far as to move his seat of government from Muscat to Zanzibar, from whence he exercised sovereignty over the mainland. This sovereignty was fairly firm at the coast but shadowy up-country. Said died in 1856 and was succeeded in Zanzibar by his son Majid, a shifty weakling, who, after a troubled reign of fourteen years, died and was followed by a younger brother named Barghash, a bold and resolute man, who had plotted against Majid almost since the latter's accession.

Great Britain was fortunate in having in Zanzibar a succession of brave and able consuls, men of the calibre of Hamerton, Rigby and especially John Kirk. It was to them that fell the difficult and delicate task of stopping the Slave Trade. The first policy was one of restriction, slavery being limited to the dominions of the Sultan of Zanzibar and export forbidden. From 1873 onwards the aim became total abolition and this was practically attained in the surprisingly short space of three years. By 1877 the inspiration of Livingstone, the combined efforts of the British consuls, the British Navy, and also, in the last phases, of Barghash himself, had brought the Trade in East Africa virtually to an end.

The Scramble for Africa

In the early 1880s there began a brisk international competition for colonies of which one aspect was the so-called Scramble for Africa. Hitherto rivalry in Africa had been primarily commercial, each nation striving to oust others from the trade of this area or that, and only rarely to impose an alien government on countries not suitable for white setttlement. This form of competition suited Great Britain very well. Her industries were second to none, her navy the best in the world, her merchants enterprising and ubiquitous. All that seemed to be necessary was the possession of a few forts and bases here and there to bolster commerce and suppress the Slave Trade; for the rest it was accepted that the unappropriated parts of the world would remain open to legitimate British trade indefinitely. The emergence of Germany as a world Power and France's recovery from her defeat of 1871 shattered these illusions. These two nations embarked on a purposeful career of overseas expansion, and it soon became clear that they intended to reserve the trade of their new dominions to themselves. At the same time the King of the Belgians set about to carve himself a private domain out of the Congo basin and Italy secured her first foothold in Africa at Assab on the Red Sea coast and from this small beginning developed an empire in the Horn of Africa. Great Britain, naturally averse to expansion, was compelled to join in, and through the agency of a number of brilliant individuals rather than by any vigorous action on the part of her government managed in the end to secure a substantial empire in Africa. Britain's participation was also determined by motives other than imperialist and commercial. The travels of missionaries and explorers had revealed not only the splendours of Africa but also its horrors. The opening up of Africa by the missionary, the soldier, the administrator and the trader went hand in hand with the abolition of the Slave Trade, the suppression of tribal war and the alleviation of much human misery.

The Scramble for Africa was marked by two important international conventions. The first was the General Act of a conference of Powers held in Berlin in 1884–85. This provided *inter alia* for freedom of trade in the Congo basin and for free navigation of the Congo and the Niger Rivers. The second was the Act of the Brussels Conference of 1889–90 which dealt mainly with slavery and the liquor traffic.

The Scramble lasted a little more than a decade. By the early 'nineties most of Africa had been divided among the Powers, and the map of the continent drawn largely as it remained until 1914. It was still a map lacking in detail, and in the following period several important changes were made, as well as many comparatively small adjustments to territorial boundaries. Perhaps the most important was the reconquest of the Sudan by the British and the establishment of an Anglo-Egyptian condominium over that territory. This coincided with the arrival at Fashoda on the Nile of Major Marchand at the head of a French colonial force, the spearhead of a thrust eastwards from Equatorial Africa. After much friction an Anglo-French agreement of March 1899 definitely excluded the French from the Nile basin and barred them from any further advance from west to east. Other important arrangements were those that took place in 1911–12, which resulted in a French protectorate over Morocco, the cession by France to Germany of a slice of Equatorial Africa which was added to the German Cameroons, and the definition of the respective zones and interests of Germany and France in and near Morocco. The final act of the partition of Africa was when Italy, whose attempt to conquer Ethiopia in 1906 had been bloodily repulsed at Adwa,[1] comparatively easily possessed herself of Tripolitania and Cyrenaica in 1911–12.

Christian Missions

Africa is to all intents and purposes a modern mission field. North Africa, land of Tertullian, St. Cyprian and St. Augustine, has long been part of the world of Islam, and Christian evangelism there is weak. Except for the valiant exertions of Portuguese priests in the Zambezi and Congo fields, missionary activity did not begin in Africa south of the Sahara until the middle of the eighteenth century.[2] From that time it steadily expanded, with periods of especially rapid growth in the 1880s and after World War I, until now there are few parts of Africa without a mission belonging to one or other of the Christian creeds. Indeed there are sometimes so many different missions in a comparatively small area as to create an impression of rivalry.

While the primary purpose of Christian missions is, and must be, to bring men to the Faith of Christ, Africa is indebted to them and

[1] See p. 147 fn.
[2] The Moravians started work in South Africa in 1737 but the Dutch stopped them.

to their supporters for immense services of an incidental kind. As pressure groups or as individuals they have fought tyranny and oppression, roused public opinion against scandals and abuses, and stimulated valuable reforms. In the earlier days of European expansion in Africa they provided the only social services that there were. The only schools were mission schools, and the only European medicine was that provided by the missionary, doing his best with plenty of hot water and a few simple drugs. With the expansion of government departments the missionaries are no longer the only teachers and doctors, but their educational institutions are still exceedingly important, and mission hospitals are in many places a valuable part of the medical organization of the country. Christian missionaries have also made a quite exceptional contribution to African studies. They were often the first to record the customs of the people among whom they lived, to learn African languages and reduce them to writing. If against these services we set some insensitivity to the value of harmless and ancient customs, too rigid an attachment to the forms of nineteenth-century Christianity, a tendency to quarrel among themselves, and, occasionally, political activities of a somewhat disingenuous kind, the balance of Christian missions in Africa is still weighted very heavily on the credit side.

Colonial Africa

The history of the various parts of Africa after the Scramble will be roughed out in the regional chapters, but in order to save repetition later it is opportune at this stage to make a few points of fairly general application.

The various Powers adopted very different political and social aims in the administration of their dependencies. The British, with a long tradition of devolution and disengagement, made it their aim to train the colonial peoples for self-government. Tolerant in religion and politics and respectful of tradition they found no better framework of government than that provided by Africans themselves. Purged of abuses, educated to meet the complex needs of the modern world, African institutions would provide the basis of future African self-government.

The French philosophy of colonial rule never included the concept of local autonomy. On the contrary, the underlying assumption was that the colonies were actually or potentially part of France, their people actual or potential Frenchmen. This principle was not easily applicable to the extensive, remote and primitive territories acquired by France in the late nineteenth century and the French were often driven to practices reminiscent of those adopted by the British. Nevertheless the theory of 'assimilation' was not until very recently abandoned and it was still the basis of the constitution of 1958 which gave a new definition to the relations between France and her overseas territories.

The Belgians placed no emphasis on political objectives, and appear to have followed the belief that the less the general public had to do with politics the better. Government was paternalistic and neither Europeans nor Africans had any franchise rights at all. On the other hand great importance was attached to economic development and the Africans were given considerable encouragement to participate in industry at comparatively high technical levels.

The Portuguese, like the French, dismiss the concept of autonomy but insist on that of 'identity'. There is close integration between the overseas territories and the metropolis, no colour bar, while Africans who fulfil certain qualifications become *assimilados* and acquire the status of Portuguese citizens of European birth. Unhappily the lack of facilities for higher education make those qualifications hard to acquire and the number of *assimilados* remains small.

The Germans appear to have entered on their overseas career with no colonial philosophy but that of direct rule through European administrators on simple forceful lines. Many of these administrators were inexperienced and of poor calibre, and their excesses led to several rebellions, of which the Herero rising in South West Africa was the best known example. These rebellions were repressed with great ferocity. Thereafter there were genuine attempts at reform which were interrupted by the 1914–18 war before their fruits could be known.

In the early days following the partition of Africa economic development was slow. All the facilities were lacking, labour was scarce and the distances enormous. In some colonies development was entrusted to monopoly companies who were granted powers of administration, in others very large blocks of land were given to planters, in others again the European trader provided the capital and organization necessary to foster peasant industries and bring their products on to the world's markets. It was not until after the Second World War that the conception of state initiative in planning and financing the development of backward areas was fully recognized. The result was that all colonial Powers launched development schemes designed to improve the economic position of their dependencies. The earlier British schemes laid no little emphasis on the promotion of 'welfare' and it soon became clear that the recurrent cost of numerous welfare projects would very soon cause such expenditure on welfare services as the local budgets would be unable to meet. In the last few years welfare has been played down and emphasis is now on promotion of those services best calculated to create economies capable of bearing services of their own.

In considering the policies and plans of the various colonial Powers it is important to remember that many of the people for whom the future had thus been mapped have already become independent. Some reference to the phenomenon of African nationalism will be made in a later chapter. Meanwhile it is sufficient to note that Africa is in rapid transition and that schemes that are being operated today may be on the scrap heap tomorrow. It is impossible to foresee how an independent Congo or Somalia will arrange its economics and politics, but one must assume that African leaders will recognize the deficiencies which present rulers are striving to remedy and will make plans of their own if they do not consider existing ones to be suitable. However that may be, the author of a book like this can only describe things as they are and hope that the foundations now being laid will prove to be sound, and acceptable to successor governments.

PART II

REGIONAL

Southern Africa
Central Africa
East Africa
The Horn of Africa
The Nile Valley
Mediterranean Africa
West Africa
Equatoria
Small Islands

SOUTHERN AFRICA

SOUTHERN Africa for our purpose includes the new Republic of South Africa, until 1961 a dominion of the British Commonwealth; South West Africa, formerly a German colony and now administered by the Republic; and the three territories of Basutoland, the Bechuanaland Protectorate and Swaziland, directly dependent on Great Britain.

The region is physically a plateau with an average height of four thousand to six thousand feet, enclosed by a great escarpment, tilting upwards on the eastern side and falling gradually away to the west. On the east and south-east the Drakensberg mountains represent the highest point of the escarpment, reaching an altitude of eleven thousand feet. In the west the edge is less distinct and the elevation only occasionally reaches six thousand feet. The plateau sinks west of centre to form the depression of the Kalahari, in altitude between two and three thousand feet, surrounded on all sides except the northern by a borderland rising to five thousand feet.

Between the escarpment and the sea the land drops in a series of terraces of varying width separated by mountain ranges running roughly parallel to the coast. These terraces are most clearly marked in the south, and form the Great and Little Karroo. The coastal plain is generally a narrow one except in the north-east where it widens out into Portuguese East Africa. The eastern coastal belt is well watered and in places supports a luxuriant vegetation. On the Atlantic side the dry Namib desert, varying in width from thirty to eighty miles, stretches up the coast for 850 miles between the Orange and Kunene Rivers.

No mere physical description can do justice to the grandeur of southern Africa. From the hills and valleys of Natal, with their productive gardens, gracious towns and splendid beaches, to the Cape, with its immense coastline and wooded, fertile hinterland, the country is one of spectacular beauty; even the monotonous downlands of Pondoland and the Transkei, the bare treeless plain of the Orange Free State, and the rolling steppes of the Kalahari and the Karroo, while not beautiful, have the majesty of unlimited space.

The climate varies throughout the region. On the east coast conditions are tropical, with a fairly high temperature and a rainfall heavy for this side of Africa (Durban receives over forty inches of rain a year). But at Cape Town the climate is of the Mediterranean type, with mild winters and no more than warm summers. This is undoubtedly the most agreeable climate in Africa south of the Sahara. Unlike tropical Natal and the temperate Cape the plateau is a zone of extremes. The summers are hot and the winters chilly. Rain is heaviest on the eastern, up-tilted side and dwindles in the west, where droughts are by no means uncommon. The rains are of short duration and fall in heavy showers. There are often violent thunderstorms and at certain seasons high winds sweep across the bare dusty plains. These conditions account for much of the prevailing soil erosion.

The whole region has an area of over one million square miles. Of this area the Republic occupies just under a half, and is geographically, economically and politically the heart and backbone of the region.

REPUBLIC OF SOUTH AFRICA

History

The British Government's policy in South Africa from the time of the Great Trek almost to the end of the nineteenth century gives an impression of timidity and vacillation. On the one hand there was reluctance to extend imperial responsibilities or to incur distant and expensive commitments. On the other, the circumstances of a large and warlike native population, a wandering body of land hungry farmers, and in consequence a restless and turbulent frontier, made impossible the favoured solution which was to withdraw and leave the colonists to sort things out for themselves. Efforts to compromise between the two extremes only bred chronic hesitation and uncertainty which persisted until the time of the Scramble for Africa, when Great Britain was forced by international considerations to take a more forceful line and to embark, still rather reluctantly, on a policy of expansion.

The two dominant personalities in South Africa during the last two decades of the nineteenth century were Paul Kruger and Cecil John Rhodes. Kruger, President of the Transvaal, was the epitome of the Boer frontiersman, powerful, simple and frugal in his habits, religious, xenophobic, narrow, conservative and shrewd. Rhodes was a manipulator and an amalgamator, a politician with a politician's standards of honesty, yet withal a man with a mission, placing all his wealth and power at the service of South African unity and the expansion of the British Empire in Africa. When gold was found on the Witwatersrand Kruger's rustic kingdom was invaded by gold-seeking foreigners or *Uitlanders* who demanded civic rights and seemed to Kruger to constitute a real threat to his government. To Rhodes, however, obsessed with his dream of South African unity, the *Uitlanders* were the instrument with which the unaccommodating Boer régime might be overthrown and the Transvaal brought into the comity of South African states. A force under Rhodes's henchman Jameson was assembled on the Transvaal border, a revolutionary conspiracy was fomented in Johannesburg, and on the night of 29–30 December 1895 Jameson set forth to march on Johannesburg at the head of his men. As everybody knows the Raid failed ignominiously, but its effects were nevertheless disastrous. The Boers were confirmed in their opinion that British imperialism meant to crush them and was prepared to resort to any means in order to do so;[1] British public opinion, in whose eyes Jameson was a hero, already suspicious of German manœuvres in South Africa, was further exacerbated by a telegram of congratulation which the Kaiser sent to Kruger. The Jameson Raid heightened tensions that were already high enough and increased the likelihood of the explosion that took place four years later.

The causes of the Boer War have been much debated and its course may be found in any book of South African history. To the modern Englishman, who has managed since then to struggle through two wars infinitely more bloody and more far-reaching, the Boer War, if he remembers it at all, seems little more than an affair of manœuvres with live ammunition. But it is deeply imprinted on the consciousness of South Africans of Boer descent and with the Trek is an important element in their lives.

Whatever the dispute about the origins and conduct of the war, it is generally agreed that the peace of Vereeniging, concluded between Great Britain and the defeated republics on 31 May 1902, was a generous one. Responsible government was promised as soon as conditions had become settled; the Dutch language was recognized as being equal with English, and Great Britain agreed to help in the reconstruction of the country. The ultimate flaw in the Treaty was

[1] The complicity of Joseph Chamberlain, British Colonial Secretary, has been much discussed but never proved.

that the native question was explicitly shelved until after the grant of responsible government. However, insistence on a liberal native policy at that stage would have probably caused a hitch and even a breakdown in the peace discussions, and experience has since shown that in any case the most firmly entrenched constitutional arrangements can be by-passed or abrogated.

The British undertakings were most faithfully observed, and Lord Milner, the High Commissioner, whose actions have been criticized as contributory causes of the war, found in post-war reconstruction a field for his great ability.

In 1910, after some two years of negotiations, the four colonies of South Africa, the Transvaal, the Orange Free State, Natal and the Cape Colony were formed into the single Union of South Africa. In 1931 the Statute of Westminster conferred on South Africa, as on other dominions, virtual independence within the Empire.

Since the Act of Union South Africa has fought by the side of Britain in two world wars, and the personality of Jan Smuts, in his younger days a commando leader against the British, and later a British field-marshal and world statesman, kept the Union generally in tune with the rest of the British Empire, though there were even then admittedly some discordant notes. Since Smuts's fall from office in 1948 and his death two years later, South Africa has been governed by Nationalists, modern representatives of the Boers who were defeated in 1902, and now called Afrikaners.

In October 1960 a referendum promoted by the South African Government gave a narrow majority in favour of turning South Africa into a republic. At the Commonwealth Conference in April 1961 the South African Prime Minister announced that on becoming a republic his country would withdraw from the Commonwealth. At the end of May 1961 South Africa accordingly became a republic outside the Commonwealth.

The People

The history of South Africa is one of conflict and though the country is now a political unity and has been so for fifty years, these discords between the different elements persist, and time has done nothing to mitigate them. It is impossible to speak of 'the people of South Africa' with any implication of common citizenship or of any community of thought and outlook. There are several 'peoples of South Africa', racially distinguished from one another and each too often bitterly antagonistic to the others. They cannot therefore be considered under one comprehensive heading but must be described separately. The term European, while perhaps not strictly applicable to people whose homeland is Africa, will be used in the racial sense to describe South African whites.

Europeans

At the end of 1960 the white population was estimated to be something over three million[1] and 70 per cent live in towns. It is divided into two main sections, the Afrikaners and the English-speaking South Africans. What makes an Afrikaner is not easy to say, but generally speaking he may be regarded as the modern representative of the Boer, who speaks Afrikaans as his mother tongue. Afrikaans is derived from the Dutch of the original European settlers. It now shares with English the status of official language and indeed tends to become the dominant one. Official notices are printed in both languages, both languages are taught in the schools, and bi-lingualism is a necessity in any public appointment and a considerable asset in any other employment. Until the last twenty or thirty years the Afrikaners constituted the rural part of the population and the English-speaking South Africans the urban. This is no longer the case, as the Afrikaners have come into the towns and participate largely in urban industries.

Afrikaner farmers are hospitable, honest, thrifty, and conservative. As farmers the quality varies. Many of them are shrewd, hard-working and competent men, but there is a fairly large number who are not. The town Afrikaner of the upper or professional classes is able, urbane and cultured. The artisan, apart from politics, is like an artisan anywhere. Below the professional man and the artisan there is another class of urban Afrikaner drawn in part from unsuccessful farmers who have drifted to the towns and there become slowly industrialized. It is among these that many of the so-called 'poor whites' are found.

Most Afrikaners have considerable pride of race, of which one aspect is the conscious fostering of the Afrikaans language, culture and literature. The spirit of the Great Trek is very strong in them, and affects their whole emotional and cultural life. The 'kaffir', as the black man is still called, is usually an enemy, at best a problem, and the old intolerance of Natives, bred of frequent wars with Xosa, Zulus, Matabele and others, is now sharpened by fear of

[1] The results of the 1960 census were not known when this was written.

native competition, by anxiety lest the western way of life may be submerged in a rising tide of colour. Hence an uncompromising insistence on the colour bar and the rejection of any kind of equality between black and white. Almost all Afrikaners belong to one or other of the branches of the Dutch Reformed Church, which combines a sombre calvinistic theology with a taste for politics, into which too many *predikants* throw themselves with zest. His religion does nothing to mitigate the Afrikaner's intolerance in matters of colour.[1]

English-speaking South Africans are mainly townsmen and business men, engaged in industry, mining and in the professions. In Natal, however, and part of the Eastern Cape, the majority of farmers are English-speaking. It is largely to the English-speaking South African that the economic development of South Africa is due. 'The English-speaking South Africans were responsible for mining and industrial development, for railway construction, for the establishment of towns and cities, for commerce and banking, for shipping and for harbour construction—in fact, for changing South Africa from an agriculturally backward community into a semi-industrial modern state.'[2] They have also made a most important contribution to the educational and cultural capital of the country. Their attitude towards their African fellow-citizens, however, is much the same in essence as that of the Afrikaners, but they are more cautious than the latter in expressing their views.

Africans

The non-European population consists chiefly of Bantu Africans who number nearly twelve million. They are divided into four main ethnic groups, Nguni, Sotho, Shangana-Tonga and Venda. The Nguni group, which includes the important Zulu and Xosa tribes, has its home in the east and south-east, in Natal and in the eastern Cape Province; the Sotho stretch in a broad band from the Drakensberg across the Orange Free State and the Transvaal to Bechuanaland; the Venda live in the northern part of the Transvaal, and the Shangana-Tonga in the coastal areas on the southern border of Portuguese East Africa. It is, however, important to note that although we speak of the tribal home, only about a third of the African population lives in the native areas, or, as they are called,

---

[1] It must however be said that the Dutch Reformed Church is particularly active in missionary work among non-Europeans.
[2] Marquard, *The Peoples and Policies of South Africa*, p. 72.

reserves. The rest are to be found in towns and on European-owned farms outside the reserves, most of them in the employment of Europeans.

The Reserves

A 'native reserve' is an area set aside for African occupation and represents at any rate parts of those areas in which the tribes were originally settled before being conquered by Europeans. The policy of establishing reserves in which Africans could live freely without exploitation or molestation by Europeans, was in fact strongly advocated by the early missionaries and other humanitarians, and it is now, some hundred and thirty years later, an important part of the theory of *apartheid*, which we shall discuss below.

The reserves are under the control of the Department of Bantu Administration and Development, and the day to day administration of the tribes remains in the hands of traditional chiefs. Special mention should be made of the Transkei, where an elaborate system of district councils (not, by the way, based on hereditary principles) 'constitutes South Africa's most original contribution to the science of governing Africans'.[1]

It is the aim of the present government to strengthen the position of the tribal chiefs and to foster the power of the traditional authorities.

Africans outside the Reserves

Nearly six million Africans live outside the reserves, and they are to be found in every part of South Africa, usually, as has already been said, in European employment.[2] Most of these people live in towns, and the drift, perhaps one should say rush, from the country to the towns is the chief characteristic of the population trend in South Africa during the twentieth century, as it was in England during the nineteenth century. That these comparatively recent towns-men now live under bad conditions may not be altogether the fault of the authorities. The rush caught the latter by surprise, and although an ambitious and energetic housing programme was initiated there must be a substantial time-lag before the supply of houses can catch up with the demand. Furthermore, in South African political thinking the urban African is a transient, living within the town as

[1] Marquard: *op. cit.*, p. 110.
[2] This figure was calculated when the total African population was believed to be about 9½ million and not 11 million as at present estimated. A closer figure will no doubt emerge from the 1960 census.

long as he is useful, but not expected to take root there and make it his home. The fact remains that many Africans are still living, and living permanently, in overcrowded and insanitary shanty towns which are hotbeds of crime and disease. More fortunate ones find accommodation in controlled 'locations' and the luckiest of all are housed and fed by their employers. Some smaller towns have very good African housing, with well built houses, schools, recreation halls and other amenities. The worst conditions are in the great centres such as Durban and Johannesburg, where many Africans live under conditions of great misery and squalor.

A full third of the total African population is to be found on European farms, either as squatters or as labourers. Here, although conditions may vary according to the character and ability of the owner or employer, life is physically and morally healthier. Housing may be of a simple kind, but at least it is not cramped. The labourer is positively encouraged to bring his family, who also work when necessary. The farmers are usually kind and humane men who take an interest in their servants' affairs. These have someone who will listen to them, to go to when they are in difficulties and they are moreover protected from the tyranny of petty officialdom or the depredations and violence of criminals. On the other hand all the more civilized amenities are lacking, there are probably no educational facilities for the children, wages are low and the employment is usually such as to inculcate neither skill nor industry. Life in the towns may be dehumanizing, but at least some who find employment there learn new techniques and new skills that they can use to improve, within limits, their situation in life.

The Coloured People

Half-way between black and white, estimated at the end of 1960 to number nearly 1½ million, come the 'Coloured' people. They are of mixed race, descendants of marriages and less regular liaisons between Europeans and native Africans, Malgache, Cingalese and other eastern races. They are distributed over the country, but the great majority are in the Cape Province. They find employment as artisans in the building industry and to a very limited extent in other skilled trades, and in the professions as teachers and doctors. From 1853, when the Cape Colony first obtained representative government, to 1951, the Cape Coloured were on a common franchise roll with Europeans. In the latter year the Nationalist Government took them off, in defiance of one of the so-called 'entrenched clauses' in the South Africa Act of 1909. This cost the Coloureds considerable political influence. The Coloured vote was influential in many constituencies and decisive in several and would almost certainly be cast *against* the Nationalist party. Now the Coloured people can no longer take part in a general election, and whereas formerly they had a vote in a large number of Cape constituencies, they can now only elect four members. These measures aroused considerable anger in South Africa, not only among the Coloured people, whom it affected directly, but also among many Europeans, who thought that the Government had violated the constitution.

Though many Coloured people can aspire to situations in general beyond the reach of the black man, there is still much poverty among them and their housing is generally poor. Economically and politically poised as they are between the worlds of white and black, rejected by one and rejecting the other, they seem the more pathetic of the victims of racial separation.

It is perhaps convenient here to mention the Cape Malays, a group of about 40,000 Moslems whose ancestors came from the east, some as slaves but most of them as political exiles, intermarried with Europeans and others, but retained their religion. They are good craftsmen and shrewd business people and are therefore in fairly prosperous economic circumstances. Their religion, which encourages in its adherents a sense of superiority and exclusiveness, serves them as an armour against the colour bar.

Indians[1]

The first Indians in South Africa were the indentured labourers who came to work in the sugar plantations of Natal in the 'sixties, when the British settlers could not get enough local labour. They were joined by their families and friends, and the community multiplied as Indians do, so that when free immigration was prohibited in 1911 there was already a sizeable Indian population in the country. In 1960 there were about 477,000 Indians in South Africa, of whom about three-quarters lived in Natal and the rest in the Transvaal and the Cape. They are not allowed to live in the Orange Free State. The Indians are for the most part traders, and some are market gardeners. Being very hardworking and thrifty, they

---

[1] The word is used here to include all the people of the Indian sub-continent, whether Indians or Pakistanis. The more general term 'Asian', in the South African context, might cause confusion with other Asians, such as Malays.

are prosperous as a community and many individuals are wealthy. Socially, however, South African Indians are not readily assimilable, as they have a natural gift for overcrowding under any conditions and tend to create slums wherever they settle. In 1927 the South African and Indian Governments came to an agreement called the Cape Town Agreement to co-operate in an assisted emigration scheme for Indians who wished to return to India. By 1947 some 15,000 Indians had taken advantage of the scheme but it was then recognized that its possibilities were largely exhausted. The South African Government now looks to the Group Areas Act[1] to confine the Indians to specified areas. Outside the Cape Province, which has always been more indulgent on colour questions than the other provinces, the Indians have no political or municipal franchise.

ECONOMY

(i) *Mining*

South Africa is almost synonymous with minerals and of all South African minerals gold is pre-eminent. More than half the world's supply of gold comes from South Africa, and the greater part of this production is at present from the Transvaal. Gold was discovered on the Witwatersrand in 1886[2] and soon attracted large numbers of fortune hunters who built the village of Johannesburg on this bare and windy ridge. Johannesburg is now a populous city, centre of a great mining area which forms a crescent stretching a hundred miles east and a hundred miles west before turning south to run another hundred miles into the Orange Free State. Along this crescent there are seven goldfields with fifty-five mines actively producing and six mines still being developed. Three famous mines, Crown, City Deep and Robinson Deep, are within three or four miles of the Johannesburg City Hall. In some places the reef is being worked at most prodigious depths. E.R.P.M., 11,301 feet, is the deepest mine in the world. In 1960 the yield from the South African gold mines will be worth about £260 million.

Ninety-four years ago the little son of a farmer named Jacobs picked up a pebble on the banks of the Orange River. This pebble

---

[1] This Act, which was passed in 1950, empowers the Government to declare any area a group area for European, Coloured, African and Asian. The intention is that in due course the various racial groups will live in distinct areas, and property in those areas may not be acquired by any member of another group. The Act has most unfortunate possibilities for people like Indians who may be compelled to move from some place where they probably have a valuable and long-established business.

[2] This is the date of the discovery of the main reef on the farm Langlaagte. Fred Struben had found gold on the farm Wilgespruit in 1884.

1. TABLE MOUNTAIN. The flat-topped mountain (5,582 feet) which towers over Cape Town

2. JOHANNESBURG. An aerial view of the centre of the South African mining industry, which with over a million inhabitants is also the largest town in South Africa

3. VICTORIA FALLS. The greatest waterfall in the world. The falls are on the Zambezi and were discovered by David Livingstone in 1855. The road and railway bridge in the foreground crosses the chasm separating Northern and Southern Rhodesia.

4. KARIBA DAM. This dam is on the Zambezi downstream from the Victoria Falls. It will irrigate an area of 2,000 square miles and more than double the electricity production of the Federation of Rhodesia and Nyasaland

5. COMMISSIONER STREET IN 1888. In marked contrast to No. 2, this photograph shows a Johannesburg street a few years after gold had been discovered on the Witwatersrand.

6. BOSCHENDAL HOMESTEAD. This building at Groot Drakenstein in the Cape Province is a fine example of the Dutch colonial style

7–9. PEOPLES OF SOUTH AFRICA. A Bushman in the Kalahari (*top*); a Zulu boy (*bottom, left*); an Afrikaner farmer in Cape Province (*bottom, right*)

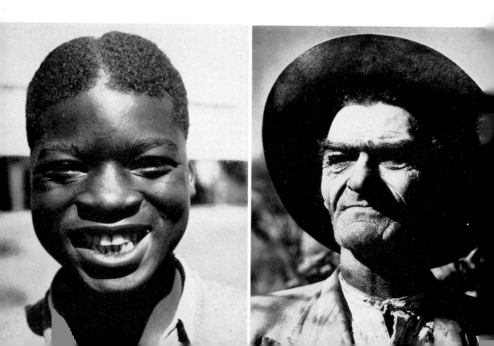

10–11. BASUTOLAND. A horseman at Mont-aux-Sources, 11,000 feet up in the Drakensberg Mountains (*above*), and a mother with her child (*below*)

12. BECHUANALAND. A camel patrol of the Bechuanaland Protectorate in the Kalahari

13. AFRICAN FARMER. Mr. Gristone Machingura on his 124-acre farm in the Msengezi Native Purchase Area near Hartley, Southern Rhodesia. He has frequently won prizes for having the best-kept farm in the area

14. ZIMBABWE. The ruins of a stone temple at Zimbabwe near Victoria, Southern Rhodesia

15. "THE WHITE LADY". This beautiful 15¾-inch painting of a young woman appears among the rock-friezes in the caves of the Brandberg, about 100 miles north of Walvis Bay in South West Africa. Its origin and subject have been much discussed

16–18. GOLD-MINING IN SOUTH AFRICA. A shaft-sinking crew at work, filling the kibbles with blasted rock before it is hoisted to the surface (*above*); white and black miners removing the loose overhanging rock at the working face before drilling (*right*); drilling the gold-bearing rock before blasting (*below*)

19–20. DIAMOND-MINING IN SOUTH AFRICA. White and black miners laying fuses in diamond-bearing blue ground at the Premier Diamond Mine (*right*); blue ground being loaded into trucks after blasting (*below*)

21–22. COPPER-MINING IN NORTHERN RHODESIA. Norrie Shaft at Chibuluma (*above*), and the Chingola open-cast pit at Nchanga (*below*)

23. TEA PLANTATION IN NYASA-
LAND. Tea was introduced into
Nyasaland in 1878 and has been
grown commercially since the
coffee crop failed in 1901. This
plantation is in one of the main
tea-growing areas, round the base
of Mlanje Mountain, seen in the
background

24. ALOES IN SOUTH AFRICA. A
plant native to South Africa
which yields drugs and fibres for
nets and cords

25. THE ZAMBEZI NEAR TETE. Evening on the great river about 300 miles from the coast in Portuguese East Africa

26. LUANDA WATERFRONT.
The new houses give an
almost Mediterranean air to
the capital of Angola

27. THE ANGOLAN 'PLAN-
ALTO'. The dramatic escarpment in western Angola as the
mountains drop down to the
sea

28. QUEEN ELIZABETH II OF THE CONGO IN ANGOLA. She is the descendant of a long line of rulers who were converted to Christianity by the Portuguese in the fifteenth century. Her silver crown was presented to one of her ancestors by the Pope in the eighteenth century

29–30. PEOPLE OF PORTUGUESE AFRICA. A girl from northern Mozambique has decorated her face with white chalk for ceremonial reasons (*above*); these two African girls of Angola show strong Portuguese influence in their dress (*right*)

31. CHILDREN OF ANGOLA. The little girl in the foreground shows clear signs of mixed ancestry

was found to be a 21¾ carat diamond.[1] Diamondiferous pipes were later found at Kimberley and the foundations were thus laid of an industry that provided the money for the conquest of Central Africa and for the development of the gold mines of the Witwatersrand. The principal diamond mines in South Africa are those round Kimberley, the Premier Mine near Pretoria, and Jagersfontein in the Orange Free State. Alluvial diamonds are found in or near the Vaal River west of Kimberley, in the south-west Transvaal, and at the Orange River mouth. The 'Cullinan', weighing about 1½ lb., and the largest white diamond ever discovered, was found in the Premier Mine in 1905. An alluvial stone, the 'Jonker' Diamond, 726 carats, about the size of a hen's egg, was found near the Premier Mine in 1934. The industry is very closely controlled in order to prevent a glut that would lower prices.

Apart from gold and diamonds South Africa exports a great variety of minerals. The year book specifically names forty-three in addition to a number included in the list as 'other'; there is also a small production of semi-precious stones. Gold is easily the most valuable mineral export. The runners-up are uranium, diamonds, copper, asbestos, manganese and chrome. It must be borne in mind that several minerals are extensively used in local manufactures. This applies particularly to coal and iron ore of which only a fraction of the output is exported.

Mining provides direct employment for half a million wage earners, but it is impossible to estimate how many people are indirectly affected by the industry. It is probably safe to say that in one way or another mining touches the life of almost everybody in South Africa, and that it will continue to do so for as long as we can foresee. (*Plates* 16–20)

(ii) *Manufactures*

The manufacturing industries of South Africa received a strong impetus during the Second World War when it became difficult, if not impossible, to obtain certain kinds of goods from overseas. The most important development is the steel industry. The government-sponsored ISCOR (Iron and Steel Industrial Corporation), which

[1] The official year book quotes a letter in the *Diamond News*, October 1956, which states that a Captain Richardson of the 86th Regiment, which was stationed at Cape Town in 1797, acquired a 56½ carat diamond for a guinea. In 1810 an Irish traveller, William Hume, purchased another Cape Diamond for £10. (*State of the Union, economic, financial and statistical yearbook for the Union of South Africa,* 1959/60, p. 169.)

uses local iron ore and coal, plans to produce 2,350,000 tons of steel annually by 1961. The textile industry is also an exceedingly flourishing one. Other important manufacturing industries are metal engineering, chemicals, printing, vehicle making, stonework, and the heat, light and power industries.

(iii) *Agriculture and Animal Husbandry*

The first European farmers in South Africa were agriculturalists who planted wheat and vines in or near the Cape Peninsula. Then, as settlement spread to regions too dry for agriculture, the pioneers took to cattle raising. The vine still dominates agriculture in certain areas of the Cape Province, and South Africa produces a variety of wines of good quality. There is also a fruit farming industry of comparatively recent growth but of considerable importance. Sugar cane production is a major industry in the coastal belt of Zululand and Natal. Tobacco is another successful economic crop, growing well round Rustenburg in the Transvaal. By far the most important cereal is maize, a most valuable staple food for the Africans. It is grown by both whites and blacks in the 'maize triangle' of the Transvaal and Orange Free State. Well behind maize come wheat, oats, sorghum, barley and rye. The cattle and dairy industry caters entirely for local consumption and there is no surplus for export. There are about 14 million cattle in the country in European and African hands. The basis of all beef and dairy stock is the Afrikander, a type evolved by selection from a native variety.

Of greater importance than cattle are sheep, which were first imported into South Africa from Holland in 1654. Eighty per cent of the sheep are now merinos which were found at the beginning of the nineteenth century to be well adapted to South African conditions. Wool is the most important agricultural product in South Africa and comes second only to gold as an export commodity. Most of the wool clip comes from the Cape Province, notably from the Great Karroo, which is particularly well adapted to sheep rearing.

Agriculture in the native reserves suffers from the usual defects of African agriculture, and production is lower than it need be. The staple crops are maize, millet, sorghum, beans, and sweet potatoes. Cattle are of considerable social and ceremonial importance and quantity is generally preferred to quality. As a result cattle are poor and small, though there are exceptions.

Taking it all round, South African farming does not present a very hopeful picture. Much of the country is arid and the soil is in many places of low quality. There is considerable erosion, not only in the reserves, but also on European farms. These unfavourable natural conditions are aggravated by the drift of the rural population to the towns, and by reluctance on the part of those who remain on the land to adopt new ideas and new methods. In this respect it is not only the Africans who are guilty of excessive conservatism.

(iv) *Communications*

South Africa has an even coastline and first-class harbours are consequently few. The river estuaries are almost all blocked by sand-bars and there is a dearth of sheltered bays. However, such harbours as do exist are very good. The two busiest are Cape Town and Durban and these are followed by Port Elizabeth, East London and Mossel Bay.

The discovery of diamonds and gold was quickly followed by extensive railway construction and South African Railways now link the interior to the ports and serve all the more important areas in the country. There is also a line from Cape Town through the Bechuanaland Protectorate to the Rhodesias and the Congo and Nyasaland. Good road transport services provide feeders to the railway in the rural areas. There is also a comprehensive system of air services which serves many important centres in the country and links South Africa with the outside world.

The Economy and The People

The economic development of South Africa springs in large part from the exploitation of minerals. Mining has led to the building of railways, the establishment of industries, the growth of towns, secure markets for the products of agriculture. The social effects have been no less dramatic. The countryman, both black and white, has come to the towns in great numbers. This has resulted, in the Native, in a decay of the old simple morality, and the loss of his tribal loyalties. Though this may also to some extent be true of the European it has also in his case had a further, political, effect. Whereas it was formerly broadly true that the Nationalist party was predominantly a rural party, relying for support on the Afrikaner farmers, this is no longer the case. The Afrikaner has invaded, and now threatens, the urban constituencies that the United Party once regarded as safely theirs. It is therefore probable that unless there is defection within their own ranks or serious civil commotion the

Nationalists will continue to govern the country for many years to come.

Of the half million Africans employed in the mining industry less than half come from the Republic. The others are from neighbouring territories. There are three forms of contract. Under the contract system proper the minimum period of engagement is 180 shifts. The prospective employees are medically examined and attested at some centre in their own country, and are then conducted to the mine of their choice at the expense of the industry. Here they are again medically examined, and those rejected are sent home, also at the industry's expense. The second form of contract is the 'assisted voluntary system', whereby men are accepted after a medical examination in the Republic or in the High Commission Territories and undertake to apply for employment at a mine within thirty days. They receive an advance of travelling expenses and they choose their own mine after a short initial period of engagement. Their travelling expenses are refunded to them if they complete a continuous working period of 180 shifts underground. Finally, men who make their own way to the mines are also engaged under the 'assisted voluntary system'. Many of those in the last category are employed on surface work. Life in the compounds is monastic, and, one would think, drab and dull, food is scientifically planned and well prepared, hygiene is carefully observed, and medical attention is very good. The compound managers are men especially chosen for their experience of Africans and knowledge of African languages, and are at pains to keep their charges in good heart and free from worries. The mine labourers are usually healthier at the end of their contract than at the beginning of it and the fact that they return to the mines time after time seems to show that the work is not uncongenial. About a quarter of a million Natives are in other industries. Here the wages are considerably higher than in mining, and the Native has some hope of attaining at any rate semi-skilled status in his employment. On the other hand conditions are not always so secure, and the employee may be put to many inconveniences, such, for instance, as difficulty in finding somewhere to live, that are absent from the mining industry.

With the importation of slaves for service with the early settlers, the Dutch East India Company laid the foundations of the South African labour system, wherein the heavy work is done by Natives. If at that time the decision had been taken to import and encourage white workmen, the southern tip of Africa might have become a white man's country, built, like Australia, Canada and New Zealand, by white men's hands. In South Africa the white man considers himself to be exempt from hard physical labour, this being regarded as the lot of the black. The South African industrial economy is thus divided in two horizontal layers, one on top of the other. From the head of some mining concern right down to the foreman controlling a small gang of 'boys', it is the white man who directs, and the black who does the physical work. In the trades the industrial colour bar operates to reserve skilled occupations to Europeans, and in spite of the economic disadvantages of this arrangement in the face of rising costs the European trades unions see to it that this remains so.

Problems of Race

The South African attitude towards colour is partly a product of history. The first Africans whom the early immigrants saw were Hottentots and Bushmen, and they recoiled from any suggestion (such as was made by the missionaries) that they could have anything in common with people such as these. The early period of settlement was followed by one of expansion, and in expanding, the settlers came into conflict with the Bantu tribes. There was hardly a time, up to quite late in the nineteenth century, when there was not a native war going on somewhere. Thus the African came to be regarded as the enemy, temporarily suppressed, no doubt, but only waiting his chance to follow a new Shaka, a new Dingaan, in a war against the whites. To the fear of rebellion and massacre must now be added that of economic and political competition. Admit the blacks to full commercial and political equality, say the whites, and they will swamp us by sheer weight of numbers. Finally there is the social fear reflected in the popular question 'How would you like your sister to marry a Negro?'

These factors have created a colour bar which excludes the non-white from all participation on equal terms in white society. Black may not live with white, nor eat and drink with him, nor study, work, play, bathe, or travel with him, or go to the same places of amusement, nor worship God with him, nor even shake him by the hand. The black man's only place in white society is that of a servant or an unskilled worker.

The policy of discrimination against people of colour has provoked much criticism in a world where the majority of people are coloured. Such criticism may come ill from some countries where conditions except among the ruling classes are much worse than in South Africa. Nevertheless many of the charges are well founded, and South Africa, quite convinced that she is the only one in step, has tended in reply to turn in more and more upon herself.

The theory of *apartheid*, which means 'separateness', is not, like the colour bar, in essence an assertion of superiority. It merely implies that white and black shall live apart. As the guide book blandly says, 'It is intended that as the non-Europeans develop their own residential areas, they will themselves staff their offices, schools, police force, hospitals, etc. with opportunities of advancement not hitherto open to them.'[1] Whereas the colour bar is designed to protect a privileged position, *apartheid* is a plan whereby two races may live beside each other without friction.

The Afrikaner is not naturally a good 'mixer' with other races, be they white or black, and *apartheid* is nothing new. It is clear that the Boers who trekked away from the Cape Colony in 1836 did their best at first to avoid entanglements with Africans. For a number of reasons they did not succeed, and even those who went furthest afield in their search for empty land soon found themselves in alliance or at odds with native tribes. If the Boers had been a nation of smallholders and South Africa had remained a poor agricultural and pastoral country, some kind of segregation might perhaps have been possible. As it was, every Boer regarded a farm of 6,000 acres at least as his birthright, and was bound therefore to enclose native holdings, whose original owners became dependants and squatters; and the revolution brought about by mining brought Africans in thousands, and then in millions, into the industrial areas to live cheek by jowl with the white man. *Apartheid* was designed to re-create segregation between the races and to arrest a process which South Africans consider demoralizing for the African and threatening to the European. The African's proper place is with his tribe in his reserve. His government is not parliamentary democracy, but traditional tribal government. He does not therefore need the franchise. Where African populations are unfortunately completely divorced from tribal life and have no other possible home but the town, arrangements will be made under the Group Areas Act,[2] for them to live in their own areas, some distance from those in which the European lives. Meanwhile—and this is no invention of the Nationalists—the Africans in towns are sub-

[1] *Year Book and Guide to Southern Africa, 1959* (Union Castle Line), p. 24.
[2] See p. 68 and fn.

ject to a number of petty restrictions, the most irksome of which are the pass laws. These involve Africans in frequent conflicts with the police, choke the courts with technical offenders and fill the gaols with people who are not really criminals.

Apartheid in its purest form is not an untenable racial theory. In fact it is quite arguable that the races would be considerably happier if they *were* separated, neither making demands on the other. Unfortunately that is just what they would do. The white man has by now become so used to the African as the very basis of his whole structure (witness the gold mines) that he cannot do without him. The African, on the other hand, could not fail to claim a substantial share of the things that the more ingenious white man would continue to create. Black and white are now so inextricably mixed that separation is no longer possible.

Apartheid is also precluded by physical conditions alone. The native reserves represent only 13 per cent of the land of the country and are overcrowded and eroded. To create Bantustan, in which the African could live as spaciously as he does, say, in Nigeria or Tanganyika, with his own government, his own schools, hospitals and services of all kinds, and with the resources to enable him to do so, it would be necessary to redraw the map of South Africa so as to provide him with land adequate to his needs, say about two-thirds of the total available, in homogeneous blocks and with proper safeguards against misuse. The transfer would not only involve bare acres but also economic assets, and it would have to be recognized that mines, ports and railways and so forth would be included and arrangements made to work them for the benefit of the new owners. European money, European brains, European techniques would be needed for years, but an African civil service could in time be built up, and the European staff would gradually fall away. Once the land transfer had taken place, the European would be at liberty to treat the remainder as white man's country, and work like almost everybody else works if he wants to get anything done, by the sweat of his own brow and without coloured labour. He would be all the better for it. That would be true *apartheid*, and it is inconceivable that any South African government could even propound the beginning of it and live.

Since *apartheid* is ruled out, what is left? Nothing but a revolution within the present structure. The races may remain where they are alongside each other, their lives inextricably intertwined, but two forms of colour bar at least must be abolished, the industrial

and the political. In industry, in the professions, the more efficient
Europeans will easily hold their own; but numbers of Africans have
it in them to reach high rungs of the ladder, and nothing should be
done to prevent them from doing so. Less efficient Europeans must
learn that the time is long past when prestige is to be gained by
refusing to wield a pick and shovel. As to politics there need not
necessarily be a common roll, but the African must be adequately
represented in Parliament and in local government by his own
people. A most necessary legislative reform is the abolition of the
pass laws, or else their application to everybody. In the social field
some form of residential zoning on racial lines is probably desirable.
This should be sympathetically devised and all zones should be
provided with proper services. Personal relations between the races
are largely a matter of habit and outlook and it is difficult to legislate for them. But some effort should be made to improve the
manners of the European man in the street towards his African
fellow-citizens. Words like kaffir, nigger, coon, coolie, should not
be regarded as part of the vocabulary of decent people, and hector-
ing and bullying should be frowned upon. Of all possible reforms,
this, a reform in behaviour, in its way the easiest, might be the most
effective of all.

The Republic

The referendum which turned the Union of South Africa into
a republic was for white people only, which means that over ten
million of Her Majesty's subjects were removed from their allegiance by the vote of less than a million others, without being heard
or else against their will. How much public support there was for
withdrawal from the Commonwealth it is impossible to say;
perhaps as much as there was for the Republic, perhaps less. It
must be said at once that the referendum turned far more on
domestic affairs than on the issue of monarchy or republic, and the
result may be read as a narrow vote of confidence for the government's native policy. Nevertheless it is unlikely that the change to a
republic will affect the African's condition since the power of the
British Government to influence South African native policy could
not be weaker than it already was. On the other hand a republic, so
far from making possible a united nation by removing the 'colonial'
loyalties of British South Africans, as the Nationalists promise, will
much more probably widen the rift between the two white sections.
Having swept away the last traces of British suzerainty the trium-

phant Nationalists are not likely to spare what remains of the English heritage. English-speaking South Africans may expect to see their language placed more and more at a disadvantage in comparison with Afrikaans, their opportunities to obtain posts in the public service diminish, their cherished links with Britain and the outside world harder to maintain. They may well react violently against this erosion of their position.

The future of South Africa as a republic outside the Commonwealth is obscure indeed. The idea that a small and divided community of Europeans in a strategic position at the southern end of Africa, surrounded and vastly outnumbered by African peoples, and practising policies that are anathema to Africans and to the rest of the world, could maintain its position in defiant isolation is pure illusion.

South West Africa

The Country

South West Africa has an area of some 320,000 square miles and occupies the drier side of the continent from the Kalahari to the Atlantic Ocean. Most of the country is plateau land with an average altitude of 3,600 feet, varied by a number of small mountain ranges. The coastal belt is the desert called Namib.[1] No permanent river flows through the territory, the only running streams being on the boundaries, the Orange River in the south and the Kunene and Okavango in the north. The rainfall is unreliable and droughts are of frequent occurrence. The zone of highest rainfall is the north-eastern corner, which is also the most densely populated part of the territory. The plateau round Windhoek, the capital, has extensive grasslands and is very good ranching country. The Caprivi Strip is a freakish tongue of land a hundred miles long by thirty wide running westwards from the north-eastern tip of the territory and separating Angola and part of Northern Rhodesia from the Bechuanaland Protectorate. It is generously watered by the Okavango, Kwando or Linyanti and Zambezi Rivers, and is not infrequently flooded in places.

German Colonization and After

In 1882 a German merchant named Franz Lüderitz purchased land round Angra Pequeña from the local chief. The British

[1] p. 59.

Government refused to take advantage of the opportunity offered to them by the German Chancellor Bismarck to act as the protecting power, with the result that in 1884 Bismarck himself, weary of protracted negotiations, assured Lüderitz and his associates of German protection. This led in due course to annexation by Germany of the settlements and the hinterland. In 1903 the Herero tribe rose against the Germans and the revolt was put down with such appalling ferocity that the tribe was reduced in numbers from eighty thousand to fifteen thousand. The Hottentots joined in the rebellion and it was not till 1908 that the authority of the Germans was re-established. Reforms in the German colonial system hardly had time to prove themselves before war broke out in 1914 and South West Africa was captured by South African forces. When the war ended the mandate to administer the territory on behalf of the League of Nations was conferred on South Africa. The mandated territory included the Caprivi Strip. Owing to the inaccessibility of the Strip and the consequent difficulty of controlling it from South West Africa, it was placed under the administration of the Union in 1939.

South West Africa is divided administratively into the Police Zone, which is generally the area conquered by the Germans, and the Tribal Area, which lies in the far north of the territory. Within the Police Zone the system of government is direct and based on European law. In the Tribal Area administration is left largely to the traditional authorities.

The Question of Status

At the end of the Second World War, South Africa, alone of the states still administering mandates, declined to place South West Africa under United Nations trusteeship on the grounds that U.N.O. was not legal heir to the defunct League and that the latter had no power to transfer its functions to any other organization. Moreover, pointing to the close associations between the two countries, South Africa proposed that South West Africa be incorporated in the Union as a fifth province, supporting this proposal with the statement that the majority of the natives were in favour of it.

In spite of much international pressure, South Africa, while affirming her intention to administer South West Africa in the spirit of the mandate, has persisted in her attitude towards the United Nations and the question remains unresolved. The demand for incorporation has not been pressed but it is to be noted that the two countries have been brought much closer together politically by the grant to South West Africa of comparatively strong representation (exclusively European of course) in the South African House of Assembly and Senate, and by a Citizenship Act (1949) which makes it possible for those ex-enemy aliens who were 'denaturalized' to apply once more for naturalization.

In 1958 a good offices committee of the United Nations, appointed to consult with the Union Government on a possible basis for agreement, suggested that South West Africa might be partitioned, the north, which holds most of the native population, to be administered by the Union as an integral part of the Union under United Nations trusteeship, the rest of the territory to be annexed to the Union. The Union Government announced itself willing to consider this suggestion if invited to do so by the United Nations but at the next session the latter rejected partition as a solution. Several nations have since expressed concern in South West African affairs and matters are not likely to be allowed to remain where they are.

The People

The Herero, almost exterminated by the Germans, are slowly regaining strength and in South West Africa have increased to 32,000. There are also well established colonies of Herero in the Bechuanaland Protectorate, descendants of people who fled from the Germans. They occupy a position of some prestige and do not appear likely to return to South West Africa. The Herero are a people of striking appearance whose tall, lanky build and straight narrow features have been ascribed to a Hamitic strain.[1] The Ovambo, an important tribe numbering about 200,000, have their home in the north in the country bordering on Angola. They were never subdued by the Germans but are law-abiding, peaceful and conservative in their habits. The Nama, of whom there are about 30,000 and who live in the south of the territory, are Hottentots in origin but are now almost completely detribalized. The Bergdama or Damara, a little-known people who number 25,000–30,000, live in small settlements in the north and centre of the territory. It seems that they are true Negroes[2] though they speak the language of the Nama Hottentots by whom they were captured and enslaved

[1] Seligman, *Races of Africa*, pp. 170–1.
[2] Seligman, *Races of Africa*, p. 82.

long ago. Their customs have also been influenced by the neighbouring Bantu. The oddly styled Bastards, who do not appear to
resent the name, are 'coloured' people, descendants of Europeans
and Hottentots, who form a community of about 8,900 people
centred on the town of Rehoboth. Finally there are something over
twenty thousand Bushmen (1953).[1] The Caprivi Strip has a population of riverain people who employ themselves in agriculture and
fishing.

The white population is about 70,000 and consists largely of
farmers, miners, traders, professional men, together of course with
a number of government officials and missionaries. It is not possible
at present to state in what proportions the various European races
occur, but some years ago, when the European population was
smaller than it is now, it was said to be made up of 30,000 Afrikaans
speakers, 15,000 German speakers and 5,000 English speakers.

Economy

The economy of South West Africa is one of the most vigorous
in southern Africa. Except in the north, agricultural conditions are
poor owing to scanty rainfall, and most of the territory is devoted to
stock raising both for dairying and for meat. In particular the
breeding of karakul sheep for pelts is a flourishing industry. There
has been a remarkable development in the fisheries of the Atlantic
coast and these are now an important factor in the economy. In
value of production the principal industry is mining. There are
extensive deposits of alluvial diamonds of high quality from the
mouth of the Orange River northwards to Conception Bay, a distance of 300 miles. Other minerals are copper, lead, vanadium, tin,
manganese, beryl, lithium and various semi-precious stones.

South West Africa is connected to the South African railway
system, and Windhoek has good air services. Walvis Bay and
Lüderitz Bay (former Angra Pequeña) are good natural harbours.

The White Lady of the Brandberg

Among the many fine Bushman paintings in the caves of the
Brandberg in the country north of Walvis Bay there is one that is of
very special interest. This is 'The White Lady of the Brandberg'.
It is a portrait of a young woman with attractive features and of slim
build, a net of pearls round her hair, her hips and breasts adorned

[1] P. V. Tobias, 'On the survival of the Bushmen' (*Africa*, Vol. XXVI, No. 2,
April 1956).

with ribbons and pearls. In her right hand she carries a cup and in her left a bow and four arrows. There are plumes in one armlet and she is wearing shoes. Her face and neck, and her body from well above the waist to her feet, are white. She gives a marvellous impression of youth and freshness and grace and not unnaturally has provoked much speculation and argument. Who was this White Lady? Was she a princess? Did she come from Egypt or North Africa? Or did she belong to some early race that is now extinct? A less romantic theory is that she was just a local woman whose face and body had been daubed with clay. Whoever she was, her portrait is the most important rock painting in Africa, and, with the exception of some in Spain, in the world.   (*Plate* 15)

THE HIGH COMMISSION TERRITORIES

Embedded in the Republic of South Africa are the three territories of Basutoland, the Bechuanaland Protectorate and Swaziland. They are in the Republic yet not of it for they are British dependencies and are governed by the High Commissioner for the United Kingdom in South Africa.[1] Bechuanaland and Swaziland are protectorates, Basutoland a colony, but the effective difference between a colony and a protectorate is small and for convenience they are often all three referred to as protectorates. Each territory has its own form of local government under a British resident commissioner, and the methods of administration are similar to those followed in the British tropical dependencies, emphasis being on native rights, dignity and freedom.

BASUTOLAND

History

The modern 'Basuto Nation' was founded about 1830 by a chief named Moshesh during the turmoil caused by the wars of the Zulu chief Shaka. Moshesh gathered round him the remnants of broken tribes and by wise statesmanship and clever diplomacy became the acknowledged leader of a large and expanding group of people who presently became known as Basotho, commonly and incorrectly Basuto.[2] With the arrival of white people in his country Moshesh

[1] As British diplomatic representative in South Africa he ceased to be High Commissioner on 31 May 1961 and became Ambassador to the new Republic. He continues to govern the three British territories as High Commissioner.
[2] The term Sotho is used by ethnologists and linguists to describe a large ethnic group in which the Basuto form the Southern Sotho sub-group (see p. 64).

came to the conclusion that the best guarantee of his people's future was British protection, and his policy was henceforward directed to this end. In 1868 Basutoland was declared British territory.

Moshesh died in 1870 and in the following year Basutoland was annexed to the Cape, a step taken without much consultation with the people. War between the Cape and Basutoland broke out in 1880 when the Cape Government tried to disarm the Basuto. The result was inconclusive and open war was followed by a period of great confusion. Finally the Cape asked the British Government to be relieved of the troublesome charge. The British Government, exceedingly tepid, eventually yielded and in 1884 the Basuto were once more taken over by the imperial authorities. Since this last annexation Basutoland has led the uneventful but not unhappy life of a small British dependency. In the 1914–18 war several thousand Basuto volunteered for service in the African Labour Corps, and in 1939–45 over twenty thousand enlisted in the Royal Pioneer Corps and saw service in North Africa, the Middle East and Italy. The territory has come into sinister prominence as the result of so-called 'ritual murders', a strange and horrible manifestation of superstition that one had hoped would not nowadays be possible. The parts of the victims are used for making medicines apparently designed to increase the political power and prestige of the person to whom they are administered. In the ten years 1947 to 1957 nearly one hundred such murders were reported to the police.

The Country

Basutoland is an island in South African territory, surrounded by the provinces of Natal, the Orange Free State and the Cape. It is a high mountainous country, and of the total area of 12,000 square miles, no less than two-thirds are at an altitude above sea-level of 6,000 ft. and more, rising to 11,000 ft. in the Drakensberg range. It is not without reason that it has been called 'the Switzerland of southern Africa'. Two of the largest rivers in South Africa, the Orange and the Tugela, have their source in Basutoland and the country is well watered by numerous streams that flow off the mountains. This country of mountains has no railway and most of the main roads are in the western lowlands. For the rest there are tracks and bridle paths which the people use to get from place to place.

The People and their Government

The Basuto, like most mountaineers, are a hardy, proud, independent people. They are ruled by a paramount chief and by a large number of lesser chiefs and headmen, most of whom belong to the family of Moshesh. British power is represented by the Resident Commissioner and by a cadre of administrative and technical officers and police. The British Administration and the chiefs combine fairly satisfactorily to govern the country. The day to day affairs of the people are managed by the chiefs, foreign affairs and domestic matters of the highest importance by the British authorities. Until recently the 'parliament' of Basutoland was the Basutoland Council, consisting of elected and nominated members, all Basuto. The Council's function was purely advisory, and in 1958 the Basuto asked that it be replaced by a legislative assembly. The British Government agreed and Basutoland thus took a big step towards responsible government.

Economy

The economy of Basutoland is based on agriculture and livestock and the people are a race of small peasant farmers. Pressure on available land is strong. The African population was about 642,000 in 1956, and the arable land only represents 12-13 per cent of the total area of the territory. The lowland areas are now full to saturation and population is spreading into the mountain areas, which until fairly recently were reserved for the grazing of stock. Since 1936 Administration and people have been fighting a gallant battle against soil erosion with the help of substantial grants from the British Government. The exports consist of wool and mohair, followed by wheat, sorghum and cattle. Basutoland has no industries to speak of, and has to import all consumer and capital goods, as well as some agricultural produce and livestock. Imports exceed exports in value, but this is offset by the 'export' of labour to the mines and industries of South Africa (about 60,000 go there to work every year), and by the consequent flow of money back to the territory.

BECHUANALAND

The Country

The Bechuanaland Protectorate has an area of 225,000 square miles,[1] and extends from the Molopo River, a tributary of the

[1] It was thought until recently to be considerably larger.

Orange River, in the south, to the Chobe River, which joins the
Zambezi, in the north. The eastern boundary is the Transvaal and
Southern Rhodesia, while on the west the boundary is South West
Africa. The Protectorate is thus surrounded by South Africa or by
South African-controlled territory except along the line where it
adjoins Southern Rhodesia.

Most of the Protectorate consists of the Kalahari desert, the home
of the Bushmen, not really a desert in the sense that the Sahara
is one, but rather a steppe, where grass does grow when it rains, and
where, if sweet underground water could be found—this is by no
means improbable—human and animal life could easily be sustained.

The eastern side of the Protectorate is quite hilly, and comparatively fertile. It is through this relatively pleasant country that the
railway from Cape Town to the Rhodesias goes.

The north-western corner of the Protectorate is called Ngamiland. This is the delta of the Okavango River, which rises in Angola
and after flowing into the Protectorate in a fine broad stream, presently spreads out in a vast swamp cut by narrow channels through
the reeds and papyrus. Apart from the Okavango system and its
northern neighbour the Chobe and a few unimportant streams on
the eastern side, there is no running water in the Protectorate. Real
forest is also very scarce and is represented almost exclusively by a
belt along the southern bank of the Chobe River. There are great
areas of *mopane* (Colophospermum Mopane) which might pass for
forest if one were not too particular, but for the rest the Protectorate
consists largely either of treeless steppe or of thorny scrub.

History

In 1817 the London Missionary Society established a station on
the Kuruman River in southern Bechuanaland 140 miles south of
the present British Protectorate. Under the direction of the great
Robert Moffat the Kuruman mission took a leading position among
the Protestant missions of South Africa. The mission's most famous
son was David Livingstone, who spent the first years of his ministry
in Bechuanaland. In 1836 the Great Trek brought the Boers to the
frontiers of Bechuanaland, which thereafter had to resist continuous
pressure from land-hungry trekkers. In 1884–5 the British Government, hitherto hesitant but now urged on by various motives, the
first of which was fear of German expansion from South West
Africa, took over most of Bechuanaland, annexed the southern

part as a colony under the name of British Bechuanaland and declared a protectorate over the country north of the Molopo River.[1] In 1895 British Bechuanaland was transferred to the Cape Colony and is now part of the Republic of South Africa, but the Protectorate, which had meanwhile been extended to the Zambezi, remained at the people's wish a direct responsibility of the British Government, which it is to this day.

The People

The African population of the Protectorate is less than 300,000 and consists of Bechuana (properly Batswana), who are Western Sotho, and a number of subordinate tribes. The greater part of the population, naturally enough, lives on the eastern side, but there are 30,000 people in Ngamiland in the north-west. The Bechuana, though not unique in this respect, differ from many African tribes in that they live in largish towns. Arable land and pastures are often at great distances from the towns, and the Bechuana spend a considerable part of the year away from home on their lands or at their cattle-posts.

Economy

Like the Basuto the Bechuana have long been accustomed to work in South African mines and industries, and it is fairly safe to say that nearly half the able-bodied manpower is absent from the Protectorate at any one time. In their own country the Bechuana are peasant farmers and their pursuits cattle raising and agriculture, with emphasis on the former. There are over a million cattle in the Protectorate and with the development of water resources the cattle population will in time rise even higher, especially if various surveys that have taken place with a view to utilization of the Kalahari ever come to anything. The Colonial Development Corporation has an abattoir and cold storage in the Protectorate. Carcasses and live cattle are exported mostly to South Africa, the Rhodesias and the Congo. Some beef from Bechuanaland has actually found its way to London. Unfortunately there is always the danger of foot and mouth disease. When this disease breaks out, export markets are closed.

Agricultural exports are considerably smaller since in cereals

---

[1] A protectorate was then a far more tenuous form of government than it later became.

the Protectorate is hardly self-sufficient, but large quantities of beans are exported in a good year.

The Protectorate is known to contain minerals though these have not yet been fully explored. The Monarch Mine in the Tati area is believed to be the oldest gold mine of the modern era in South Africa. There are also great quantities of coal. Other minerals include asbestos, manganese and copper.

SWAZILAND

The People and their Government

The Swazi belong to the Nguni branch of the Bantu family and are therefore akin to the Zulu and the Xosa. They number about 254,000 and their traditional government is that of a paramount chief acting with the help of two councils, one made up of chiefs and notables, the other a smaller one which advises him in personal and family matters. The Resident Commissioner has his headquarters at Mbabane on the western side of the Protectorate. He keeps in close contact with the Paramount Chief and is also advised by a European advisory council, drawn from a European population of about 8,700, most of whom, apart from officials, are farmers, miners, and people engaged on various development schemes.

The Country

Swaziland has an area of 6,700 square miles and like Bechuanaland is almost surrounded by South African territory, being bounded on the north, west and south by the Transvaal, and on the east by Tongaland in the province of Natal; but in the east it also has a common boundary with Portuguese East Africa, and the port of Lourenço Marques is easily accessible by road.

The country falls into three well-defined geographical divisions, roughly equal in size, which run from north to south and are known as the high-, middle-, and low- (or bush-) veld. It is on the whole a well-watered country and where rainfall fails, as it sometimes does, it will no doubt in due course be supplemented by irrigation from the several excellent rivers which the country is fortunate enough to possess.

History

The Swazi say that they originally lived in southern Tongaland, and that they migrated about 150 years ago to the country west of the Lebombo mountains, between the Pongola and Great Usutu

Rivers. About 1815 they were involved in a dispute with the Ndwandwe, another Nguni group which was ultimately absorbed by Shaka's Zulus. The Swazi fled to the site of present day Bremersdorp in the Eastern Transvaal under their chief Sobhuza or Somhlolo. Here they prospered and expanded. Under Sobhuza and his successor Mswazi they occupied the country right up to Barberton in the north and extending towards Carolina and Ermelo in the west. They also claim that the tribes living in the district now called Lydenburg gave allegiance to the Swazi chief. These wide dominions were later considerably reduced. In 1846 Mswazi ceded whatever rights he had round Lydenburg to the Lydenburg Republic. Then the Pretoria Convention of 1881, which defined the frontiers of the Transvaal, still further reduced the area over which the Swazi formerly held sway. All these modifications were made quite peaceably and the Swazi were never seriously disturbed by war after their original flight to the north from their home in Tongaland. They suffered occasional raids from the Zulus, which they always survived, and the Zulu chief Dingaan, Shaka's murderer and successor, was killed by the Swazi when he fled north for safety after his defeat by the Boers and his own brother Mpande. One Zulu raid took place in 1847, and in 1855 the Swazi ceded a narrow strip of land to the Boers along the northern bank of the Pongola River on purpose to put Europeans between the Zulus and themselves.

Apart from these mild diversions the Swazi seem to have weathered the nineteenth century fairly well. This may have been due to the fact that they were themselves of fighting stock and knew very well how to look after themselves. In addition they appear to have accommodated themselves more easily to Europeans than either the Basuto or the Bechuana. They were for a long time friends and allies of the Transvaalers, and they were also friends of the British. The Swazi managed to preserve a comfortable balance between the two until quite late in the century, though in the end they too became involved in the rivalry between Boer and Briton and in 1894 passed into the power of the South African Republic.

After the Boer War Swaziland was attached to the Commission of the Governor of the Transvaal and in 1906 was transferred to the High Commissioner for South Africa.

Land

The land question is complicated by the reckless concessions

given out by Mswazi's successor Mbandeni. This wretched chief
sold away every conceivable right until the whole of the country had
in fact been parcelled out to concessionaires. In 1907 one third was
expropriated and became available for the Natives and since then
other land has been bought by the government and the Paramount
Chief with the result that about one half of Swaziland is now available for native occupation.

Land distribution in Swaziland is a patchwork affair and European and African areas are much intermingled. It has been suggested that this situation, while increasing the difficulty of governing
the country, has the good effect of increasing understanding
between the two races and has also influenced the African to adopt
higher standards of housing and agriculture.

Economy

Swazi agriculture appears more or less to fulfil its object of providing the people with their staple foods. There is a cattle population of about half a million head (1958). Imports are mainly capital
goods of various kinds and general merchandise. Exports exceed
imports in value and the most important export is asbestos from
the Havelock mine, one of the five largest asbestos mines in the
world. Other minerals of importance to the Protectorate are barytes
and diaspore. There are several small manufacturing industries
mainly concerned with the processing of local products. The
Colonial Development Corporation has invested fairly heavily in
various schemes. Labour migration is not such a strong feature of
the economy as in Basutoland and Bechuanaland but some 6,000–
7,000 Swazi go to work in South Africa every year.

The Question of Incorporation

The author may be accused of devoting more space to the High
Commission Territories than their wealth and position warrant,
but comparatively obscure as they are, these countries have a
political significance that gives them a peculiar importance of their
own.

South Africans have long claimed that the High Commission
Territories should properly belong to them, and this question
of 'incorporation', as it is called, hangs like a question mark over
the future. It is one that cannot be dealt with exhaustively in this
book. The South African case is based on geographical, economic
and political grounds, some of which are very strong. The geo-

graphical and economic arguments can only with difficulty be answered, and the fact must be faced that the territories *are* practically surrounded by South Africa, and are economically largely dependent on it. The political arguments are more easily rebutted. But there are two overwhelming reasons against transfer of the territories to South Africa. One is that the people are resolutely opposed to it, and would resist it with all their strength; the second is that Great Britain is under the strongest obligations, both historical and moral, to continue directly to protect these people so long as protection is required. These reasons seem quite conclusive.[1]

But if we assume that the High Commission Territories remain British dependencies, there are lesser, but still important questions to be asked. Have these territories the means to provide their people with the richer, fuller life to which they have the right to aspire? Can they support those administrative and technical services which will enable them to live as reasonably viable modern African states? The answer at present is certainly no. On the other hand economic development, much of it financed, and all of it directed, by Great Britain, is going ahead, especially in Swaziland and Bechuanaland, as fast as manpower resources permit, and in 1959 a comprehensive survey of requirements and natural resources was conducted by an economic mission, from which results will doubtless emerge. Social services, not generous but in a limited way efficient, have been introduced and are growing. The people are prepared to bide their time and in any case would certainly prefer to remain under British protection than to be incorporated in South Africa, even if incorporation were to mean (as is by no means proved) increased material prosperity.

[1] Since these words were written South Africa has become a republic outside the Commonwealth and the prospect of 'incorporation' seems more than ever unlikely.

CHAPTER TWO

CENTRAL AFRICA

THIS region comprises the British territories of Northern and
Southern Rhodesia and Nyasaland, constituting the Federation of Rhodesia and Nyasaland, and the Portuguese colonies of
Mozambique (Portuguese East Africa) and Angola. It stretches in a
broad band across the continent and is bounded on the south by
Southern Africa and on the north by Tanganyika and the Congo.
Although it may be argued that the Portuguese colonies do not
properly belong to Central Africa there are nevertheless quite good
reasons for including them in this chapter. Angola lies roughly in
the same latitude as British Central Africa; it contains the upper
basin of the Zambezi River which is a dominant feature of Central
Africa; it also has strong and fairly recent historical associations
with the countries that later became Rhodesia and Nyasaland.[1] On
the other side of the continent Portuguese East Africa is clearly the
seaboard of Central Africa. It was for centuries the door in and out
of Zambezia (if one may so call the country through which that river
flows) and it is now the entrepôt for the trade of this region.

The Country

The region is flanked on either side by a coastal plain which rises
more or less steeply through an intermediate zone of irregular terraces to the great plateau which forms the backbone of Africa. In
Mozambique the littoral belt is widest in the south and narrows
towards the north. The coastal climate is tropical, rainfall fairly
abundant and vegetation luxuriant. The Mozambique plateau has a
mean altitude of 3,500 feet and is rimmed on the west by mountains. The temperature is reduced by altitude and rainfall shows a
decrease from the coast inland, increasing again in the highlands.
Mozambique has several important rivers, including the mighty
Zambezi which cuts the country in two, and the Limpopo which
rises in the Transvaal and runs into the Indian Ocean north of
Lourenço Marques. The natural vegetation is largely of the

[1] For instance, Livingstone's first journey; claims made by the Portuguese to
possession of a broad belt across Africa which included these territories; the trend
and direction of the Slave Trade.

90

savannah type but there is dense forest inland from Beira and fertile zones in the areas watered by the great rivers and in the uplands near the frontier of Tanganyika. Malaria is endemic on the coast and in low-lying areas; there is tsetse fly in many places and it is believed to be spreading. The total area of the territory is about 298,000 square miles.

In Angola the coastal plain is thirty to one hundred miles wide and is really nothing but the northerly extension of the South West African desert. The rainfall is low and the coast is only saved from complete aridity by the relative humidity of the atmosphere. The plateau has an altitude of four thousand to seven thousand feet and is a rolling well-watered tableland falling away in the east to the Congo and Zambezi basins and in the south to the South West African desert. Large numbers of streams and rivers, the most important of which is the Kwango, flow northwards off the plateau into the Kasai, one of the largest of the Congo's affluents, which in its upper course forms for three hundred miles the boundary between Angola and the land of the Congo. Other rivers rising on the plateau are the Kwanza and the Kunene which both flow westwards to the Atlantic, the latter in its lower course forming the boundary between Angola and South West Africa. The vegetation of Angola is savannah of various kinds and there is some forest along the larger rivers in the north. The area of the territory is nearly half a million square miles.

The three British territories all lie on the great African plateau. Southern Rhodesia has an area of about 150,000 square miles and consists of a belt of highland at a general level of something over 3,500 feet running through the middle of the country from the south-west to the mountainous eastern border, enclosed by the lowlands of the Zambezi and Limpopo Rivers and of Mozambique on the north, south and east. Rainfall averages 32 inches in the year and is more reliable on the eastern side than on the west, and the south-west of the country tends to be dry. The natural vegetation is savannah but there are considerable areas of open forest, and in the Zambezi lowlands denser forests where valuable timber is found.

Northern Rhodesia with an area of about 290,000 square miles is flat and undulating and lies between 3,000 and 4,000 feet, rising occasionally to 5,000 feet. There are individual mountain peaks of 8,000 feet. The area includes much of the watershed of the Zambezi and Congo Rivers. The rainfall varies between 50 inches in the north to 25 inches in the south and drought often occurs between

May and October. The vegetation is savannah merging into park-
land in areas of heavier rainfall. The climate is eminently bearable
except in the valleys of the Zambezi and Luangwa during the hot
and rainy seasons.

The key to the geography of Nyasaland is the Great Rift Valley,
which runs through the Protectorate from end to end and forms
the trough in which lies Lake Nyasa. The Protectorate consists of
the Lake itself and a narrow strip of land to the west of it. East and
west of the Rift the country is mountainous and precipitous. There
are high plateaux culminating south of the Lake in the mountain
masses of Zomba (7,000 feet) and Mlanje (10,000 feet) in the Shire
Highlands. At the other extreme, the Rift in the south is only 600
to 300 feet above sea-level. The Shire River flows from the south
end of the Lake and joins the Zambezi 250 miles from the Lake.
The climate varies with the altitude. On the Lake shore it is rather
hot and very humid and in the Shire Valley still hotter in some
months of the year. But in the highlands it is very pleasant and
healthy, and there are mists and cold nights, and fires are welcome
in the house. The rainy season lasts from November to April and the
rainfall varies from 30 to over 60 inches in the year. The total area
of Nyasaland is 46,000 square miles, including more than 9,000
square miles of water.

The People

Portuguese East Africa was inhabited from the earliest times by
people who have long disappeared but who have left evidence of
their existence in the form of implements and rock paintings.
There are also buildings of the Zimbabwe type indicating the
presence at one time of a superior race which may well have been
indigenous. The population today is overwhelmingly Bantu, but
there still survive remnants of an older, possibly pre-Bantu race of
whom the Chopi are an example. This ancient race did not know
iron, and was overpowered and subdued by the invading Bantu
tribes.[1] These invaders were probably the ancestors of the Tonga
people who now predominate in the country south of the Sabi
River.[2] Exactly when the invasion took place is by no means sure,
but it was certainly in fairly remote times. After living undisturbed

[1] Henry Ph. Junod, 'Notes on the ethnological situation in Portuguese East
Africa on the south of the Zambesi' (*Bantu Studies*, Vol. X, No. 3).
[2] Not to be confused with a small group of Tonga who live round Inhambane.
These, like the Chopi, are survivors of earlier inhabitants. There are Tonga in the
Northern Province of Nyasaland and two groups in Northern Rhodesia.

perhaps for several centuries, the Tonga themselves were invaded by Soshangane and his Nguni tribesmen, seeking an empire of their own. This they found in Gazaland, where they subdued the Tonga tribes in typical Zulu fashion, raiding, looting and incorporating the young men into their regiments. Many Tonga emigrated to the Transvaal, where they still are, usually as subjects of the local Sotho and Venda chiefs. After Soshangane's death his sons quarrelled over the succession and there was much fighting and insecurity. His grandson Ngungunyane was the last of the independent Nguni chiefs; after playing a part in Anglo-Portuguese rivalry he was subdued by the Portuguese in 1895.

The middle belt of the colony between the Sabi and Pungwe Rivers is occupied by a large tribe named Ndau which is connected with the people called Mashona on the eastern side of Southern Rhodesia.[1] North of the Pungwe there is a mixture of tribes, many of whom also have connections with the Mashona.[2] In the northern part of the territory the virile Yao occupy the north-west corner while east of them the Makua, a large group with many sub-tribes, stretch down from the Rovuma to the Zambezi delta. The African population of Mozambique is about six million, and in 1955 there were 66,000 Europeans, 17,000 Asians and 30,000 people of mixed race.

The ethnography of Angola is not at all well known. The tribes living in the northern coastal section appear to have cultural and linguistic affinities with their northerly neighbours in the Congo, though now of course they come under different political régimes.[3] The people in the south of the territory may be said to be Western Bantu, many of whom show signs of Hamitic admixture and others of Negrillo and Bushman blood.[4] The African population of Angola is about five million and there are also about 200,000 Europeans.

The population of the Federation of Rhodesia and Nyasaland is believed to be over eight million, including 297,000 Europeans, 25,000 Asians and 13,500 Coloured people. In Nyasaland and Southern Rhodesia the African population is edging towards three million in each territory. In Northern Rhodesia the number lies somewhere between $2\frac{1}{4}$ and $2\frac{1}{2}$ million. The Europeans are not so

---

[1] Junod, op. cit.
[2] Junod, 'A contribution to the study of Ndau demography, totemism and history, (*Bantu Studies*, Vol. VIII, No. 1).
[3] Baumann and Westermann (*Peuples et civilisations de l'Afrique*, p. 174) call them 'le groupe du bas Congo'.
[4] Baumann and Westermann, op. cit., p. 174.

evenly divided, over 70 per cent of the total being in Southern Rhodesia, 26 per cent in Northern Rhodesia and under 3 per cent in Nyasaland.

There is evidence that in the past the region was inhabited by a powerful people with a comparatively high standard of civilization. The ruins of Zimbabwe, a massive citadel built of many small blocks of granite skilfully laid without mortar, testify to a craftsmanship far superior to any that existed among the people living there in the nineteenth century. Buildings of a similar type, but simpler and smaller, are to be found in other parts of the region. As we have already noted, Zimbabwe is now generally held to be the work of a native race.[1]   (Plate 14)

From the earliest times of Portuguese settlement there had been tales of a great king in the interior whose name or title was Monomatapa and who ruled over a people called Makaranga. Indeed one Portuguese explorer, Antonio Fernandez, visited him at his capital north of the present site of Salisbury. The Portuguese accounts leave no doubt that there was such a powerful chief in the sixteenth and seventeenth centuries though it cannot be assumed that his people were the builders of Zimbabwe. One thing is certain, and that is that the old lords of the land mined for gold, for their workings are there for all to see. News of these workings filtered southwards and the chief attraction to European pioneers was the belief that the land that lay to the north of the Limpopo contained unlimited wealth in gold.

The modern African inhabitants of Southern Rhodesia are the Matabele in the west, and the Mashona cluster in the east. The latter are still sometimes called Makaranga, but the name properly applies only to one group of tribes in the cluster.[2] The Matabele are Nguni who seceded from Shaka's Zulu empire and then migrated under Boer pressure to the neighbourhood of modern Bulawayo. They were a warlike and bloodthirsty people, who established an empire of terror between the Zambezi and the Limpopo valleys and beyond. The Mashona were among the people whom they periodically raided for slaves and regarded as their subjects.

Like the Mashona and the people of the coastal plain, the tribes round Lake Nyasa were also to experience the effects of Zulu expansion. Yet another Nguni chieftain, Zwangendaba, in a migration that is surely one of the most remarkable in African history

---

[1] pp. 13–14.
[2] F. W. T. Posselt, *A survey of the Native Tribes of Southern Rhodesia.*

(there is yet another as remarkable, which will be described later), fought his way to the southern end of Lake Tanganyika. After the death of their leader his followers, who are now called Angoni,[1] split into several groups but all ultimately settled round and about Lake Nyasa, where they had no difficulty in establishing themselves among the comparatively peaceful people of the Lake, with whom they intermarried, and many of whom they incorporated into their own system. About the middle of the nineteenth century the country was also invaded by Yao from Portuguese East Africa. Today the native population of Nyasaland consists, as to just over three-quarters, of the original tribes and of people who have immigrated from Portuguese East Africa during the present century. The remainder, forming about 24 per cent of the whole, is made up of Yao and Angoni, the former rather the more numerous.[2]

Northern Rhodesia has seventy-three tribes speaking thirty different dialects falling into six main language groups. With few unimportant exceptions these tribes are descended from people who invaded the country, some from the direction of the Congo and some by a route east of Lake Tanganyika, not earlier than the beginning of the eighteenth century. Many of the tribes are small, many are disorganized, with little cohesion and without strong loyalties to any acknowledged authority. Tribal wars and the Slave Trade had already caused them to disintegrate before the coming of the Europeans. Some tribes have withstood these corrosive processes better than the others, for instance the Bemba in the north and the Barotse in the west. About 130 years ago Barotseland was invaded by a people of Sotho stock called Fokeng, who had been driven from the Orange River by tribal wars and arrived in the Zambezi valley after a journey fully comparable to that of Zwangendaba's Angoni. Under their chief Sebetwane, who became a friend of Livingstone, these Makololo, as they were called, prospered for a time in their new surroundings. They declined under his successors and in 1873, Sepopa, a chief of local ancestry, led a rebellion and annihilated all the male Makololo. The women passed to the conquerors, who also conserved the Sotho language which to this day is spoken in Barotseland.

---

[1] So spelt nowadays. It is obviously derived from the generic name Nguni.
[2] These figures are taken from Hailey, *Native Administration in the British African Territories*, Part II, pp. 24–25, quoting from the 1945 census. They are therefore fifteen years old, and the situation may have changed.

BRITISH CENTRAL AFRICA

Economy

No economy in Africa has expanded more rapidly than that of the Rhodesias. New buildings, new developments have sprung up as if by magic, and towns like Salisbury, Bulawayo, Lusaka and others have grown so as to become almost unrecognizable in little more than a decade. The shine wore off in the late 'fifties owing to the fall in the price of copper during 1956 and 1957. This was accompanied by a fall in price of other primary products and there was a general reduction in commercial activity. Despite this set-back the record of the Federation is one of growth, and viewed from the economic standpoint, long-term prospects are good.

Mining

The Copper Belt of Northern Rhodesia is the largest source of copper in the Commonwealth and the fourth largest in the world (1959). It was first explored in the early 1920s when it was trackless bush, and four of the present six mines were in operation by 1939. The economic outlook was immediately transformed and the budget rose from a mere half million pounds to ten million in a very few years. It is largely on copper that new schools, roads, hospitals and other consequences of increasing prosperity are founded. Townships have sprung up at each mine, and the mines employ 8,000 Europeans and 47,000 Africans. Other important minerals, all from Northern Rhodesia, are cobalt, zinc, lead and manganese. It must here be said that the two-tier industrial structure which we noted in South Africa also exists in Northern Rhodesia. Though the Belgians in Katanga next door long ago demonstrated that the African is capable of skilled industrial tasks, the European miner on the Copper Belt reserves the upper tier exclusively to himself. This is not the policy of the government nor that of the great mining companies, but the bar is jealously enforced by powerful trades unions dedicated to the maintenance of the European workers' position.[1]   (*Plates* 21–22)

Southern Rhodesia did not, after all, turn out to be the Eldorado that the pioneers expected. There was no large continuous reef as on the Rand, and mining was in the hands of small men, running small mines. Asbestos is now exported in greater value than gold,

---

[1] Recently (September–October 1960) there have been hopeful signs that the whites are willing to compromise.

and Southern Rhodesia is the leading world producer of the highest grade asbestos though third in total production. The Wankie Collieries have a capacity of 5 million tons of coal a year, chrome ore is a growing export and several other minerals are gaining in importance.

Nyasaland has a wide variety of minerals, but little mining has so far taken place.

Land and Agriculture

The only country of the Federation where significant land alienation has taken place is Southern Rhodesia. Here the agrarian situation is governed by two important pieces of legislation. The Land Apportionment Act of 1930 virtually divided the land of the colony between Europeans and Africans. The total available area is 96 million acres of which 21½ million were native reserves and 31 million alienated to Europeans before the Act was passed. The Act declared another 7½ million acres to be Native Purchase Areas in which Africans might hold land in individual right; another 17½ million were allotted for European purchase; and the balance, about 18 million acres, was not assigned. Since the original act was passed more land has been allocated to Africans from that which was left unassigned. The 'Purchase Areas' have been increased and in addition between nine and ten million acres have been declared to be 'Special Native Areas', in which occupation would be dependent on such farming standards as the government might impose.

The Land Apportionment Act is complemented by the Native Land Husbandry Act of 1951, which is designed to prevent the abuse of land and to improve African agriculture. This bold measure aims at nothing less than the complete individualization of native land tenure on the European pattern together with high standards of farm management. To meet the requirements of the law the African farmer will have to become a full-time, highly skilled professional.[1]

Alienation of land in Northern Rhodesia and Nyasaland, compared to the position in Southern Rhodesia, is almost negligible. The percentage in Northern Rhodesia is 2·5 and in Nyasaland 5·1.

Tobacco is the chief commercial crop of the Federation, as an export second only to copper and accounting for 12 per cent of the

---

[1] For a discussion of land matters in Southern Rhodesia, see Philip Mason's chapter on land policy in Gray, *The Two Nations*. For comment on the principle of individual tenure see pp. 133–4 below.

world's tobacco exports. It is grown by Europeans in Southern Rhodesia and by Europeans and Africans in Northern Rhodesia and Nyasaland. Maize is the most important grain crop. It is not only the staple food of the African but also, owing to increased production in recent years, an important export crop in the Rhodesias. Nyasaland is the leading African producer of tea, and also produces cotton, groundnuts and tung oil. Groundnuts are an important cash crop in Northern Rhodesia where production is expanding. Southern Rhodesia has recently begun to produce tea, and sugar is grown in the Zambezi valley.   (*Plate* 23)

About five-eighths of Northern Rhodesia is infested by tsetse fly, and the cattle industry therefore has very definite limits. There are however well over one million cattle in the territory, mostly African-owned. Nyasaland has a cattle population of about 350,000, and in Southern Rhodesia, where cattle ranching by Europeans is an important factor, there are 3,630,000 cattle, of which 1,553,000 are owned by Europeans and the rest by Africans.

Secondary Industry

Several influences have contributed towards the growth of secondary industry, perhaps the most important being the high cost of imported goods and the difficulty of obtaining them. Unprecedented immigration after the last war provided the manpower, and a whole variety of manufactures have now developed. These include iron and steel, textile and clothing, metal fabricating, engineering and many others. There is of course a question mark and that is whether the market can sustain much further expansion of secondary industry. There must surely be a limit to the rate at which the European population will increase, while the purchasing power of Africans is still fairly low. Nor does there appear to be much prospect of an export market for finished articles. Another limiting factor is the shortage of both skilled and unskilled labour. In short, the future of the secondary industries may well depend on raising the African standard of living so as to provide a good domestic market, increasing the number of African artisans, and controlling the present somewhat wasteful use of unskilled labour.

Migrant Labour

A dominant factor in the African economy of all three territories is work for wages either within the territory or outside it. In Nyasaland it was estimated that in 1958 no less than 169,000 men were away from the Protectorate at work in other countries. At times of peak employment 160,000 are employed in the Protectorate. In Northern Rhodesia in 1958 there were about 323,000 men in paid employment including about 18,000 aliens who had come in from outside. Owing to the strong attraction of the Copper Belt most Northern Rhodesians work inside the territory, only about 12,000 having emigrated to work in other countries in 1958.

Southern Rhodesia is in somewhat different case. Of the total African population of 2,590,000 (1958) well over 600,000 are in paid employment within the colony. Even these do not suffice to meet the needs of the numerous industries, and there is a strong market for immigrant labour. But the effects of wage labour may not be the same here as in Nyasaland because of the growing cleavage in Southern Rhodesia between the agricultural and industrial populations. If the Native Land Husbandry Act does what is expected of it, the African will no longer be able to divide his time between temporary employment in the city and inefficient cultivation in season of a small plot in the reserve. He will be compelled to choose between agriculture and industry and there will thus grow up, as in more advanced countries, permanent and separate urban and rural communities. Although a great deal of emphasis has rightly been laid on the education of the farmer and the improvement of agriculture, too little has yet been done for the permanent town dweller, and one aspect of the profound and on the whole salutary change which the present policy will bring about has thus not been squarely faced. In 1958 a commission specially appointed to inquire into the life of Africans in towns presented the Plewman Report, which contained sensible and helpful recommendations. This report was shelved and the opportunity to deal with the problem early and in a realistic way was lost.[1]

Power

The Federation has coalfields the exact extent of which is unknown, but which must be enormous. Mention has already been made of the Wankie Collieries: these are estimated to possess reserves of 5,200 million tons of bituminous coal, much of which is coking coal. There are also large coalfields of varying quality in the north-west and north-east of Southern Rhodesia, in Nyasaland and in Northern Rhodesia. The Wankie field is the only one in production.

The Federation does not rely for energy only on coal. Hydro-

[1] Philip Mason, *Year of Decision*, pp. 189 *et seq.*

electricity is another most important potential source of power. The Kariba Gorge project on the Zambezi will more than double the Federation's capacity for producing electricity. Other rivers of the Federation might also be used for this purpose. The Kafue was at one time considered, before Kariba, as a first choice, the Shire in Nyasaland is another possibility, the Chambezi in Northern Rhodesia yet another. Meanwhile there are several generating stations in the Federation which supply power to the towns and to the Copper Belt and whose capacity has recently been increased. Finally the presence of uranium ores in various places conjures up visions of plants for the production of nuclear power. Altogether the fuel and power potential of the Federation is a very satisfactory one.   (*Plate* 4)

Transport

The first railway to serve Rhodesia was built by the British South Africa Company from Vryburg in British Bechuanaland through the Bechuanaland Protectorate and reached Bulawayo in 1897. The line from Beira to Salisbury through Umtali was opened in 1899, and Salisbury and Bulawayo were joined in 1902. From Bulawayo the line reached the Victoria Falls in 1904. From there it was continued across Northern Rhodesia to the Congo, where it arrived in 1909. Now the Federation has 2,400 miles of railway forming part of a continuous network through the Congo, Portuguese East Africa, the Bechuanaland Protectorate, the Union of South Africa and South West Africa to ports on the east, south and south-west coasts of Africa. There was formerly much congestion at the port of Beira but the opening in 1955 of a new railway between Southern Rhodesia and Lourenço Marques gave much relief both to the railways and to the port of Beira.

The main trunk roads of the Rhodesias run parallel to the railway lines, with very many branches. In general the roads are of earth and of a fairly low standard but they are improving. There are a few hundred miles of really first-class road, especially in Southern Rhodesia, and in Southern Rhodesia again there are many so-called strip roads, which consist of two parallel strips of tar macadam some feet apart, and which enable traffic to move at times when all-earth roads may be impassable. Nyasaland roads are mostly of earth and though some may be considered to be 'all weather', most of them are at the mercy of the season.

The Federation also has some by no means negligible waterways.

Lake Nyasa carries a certain amount of traffic by railway steamers; the Zambezi is navigable for short stretches; Lake Bangweulu carries local traffic; and there is some waterborne trade from the Abercorn area by Lake Tanganyika to the Tanganyika Central Line.

Central African Airways was established in 1946 and provides services to a great many places in the Federation. C.A.A. also operates services to East and South Africa and to London. A number of international airlines link the Federation with other territories and there are also several air charter firms. In addition to the main international airport at Salisbury there are major airports at Livingstone, Bulawayo, Lusaka and Ndola.

*   *   *   *   *

The above picture of a buoyant economy is marred by grave politico-social doubts and fears. If these could be overcome and confidence restored, the economic future of this area would be a hopeful one.

SOUTHERN RHODESIA

History

In 1888 three emissaries of Cecil Rhodes, C. D. Rudd, J. R. Maguire and F. Thompson, extracted a mineral concession from Lobengula, chief of the Matabele. This was the Rudd Concession. The British South Africa Company, formed by Rhodes the following year with the Rudd Concession as its foundation stone, was granted a Royal Charter which gave the company the right to acquire very full powers of administration in an extensive 'field of operations'. In 1890 a band of pioneers entered Mashonaland and proceeded to make farms for themselves and to look for gold.

Inevitably there was friction with the Matabele, who looked upon the Mashona as their subjects and Mashonaland as within their territory. Lobengula himself, though he had never intended that the Rudd Concession should lead to outright occupation of land which he regarded as his, did his best to keep the peace. But hostilities broke out in 1893 when a raiding party of Matabele entered the settled area in order, so they said, to punish some delinquent Mashona. They were driven out with losses, and a force of pioneers, supported by the Bechuanaland Border Police, invaded Matabeleland. Lobengula's army was smashed in two battles, the chief himself fled and some weeks later died, all resistance

8

collapsed, and the pioneers began to measure out farms and gold claims in Matabeleland. The Matabele, their spirit by no means crushed, rose in rebellion in 1896. The situation was complicated by a rising among the Mashona, hitherto believed to be timid and peace loving people. By negotiations with the chiefs, conducted with considerable courage, Rhodes persuaded the Matabele to lay down their arms. The Mashona rebellion dragged on far into 1897, when it came to an end with the capture or surrender of the leaders. Southern Rhodesia, uniting Matabeleland and Mashonaland, was constituted in 1898.

The history of Southern Rhodesia has been one of steady, and lately, spectacular growth as a colony of settlement. In the early days of the century there was much discussion as to the country's future. There had grown considerable discontent with Company rule and the settlers now discussed alternative forms of government. The issues narrowed themselves to two: whether the territory should have its own government, or whether it should join the Union of South Africa. A referendum held in 1922 decided on the former, and in 1923 Southern Rhodesia became a British colony with responsible government. Southern Rhodesia made an outstanding contribution towards the British cause in the war of 1939–45. Rhodesians served on all fronts with all the services and took part in some of the fiercest battles of the war. The Colony also became an important part of the Empire Air Training scheme, and thousands of airmen were trained for the Royal Air Force at the Rhodesian training centres.

NORTHERN RHODESIA AND NYASALAND

The Portuguese, with their settlements on the east coast, had long regarded the Zambezi valley as properly theirs. On the other hand these claims were not supported by any solid or consistent attempts at settlement, and they were challenged by British missionaries and explorers long before the Scramble for Africa began. Livingstone landed at the mouth of the Zambezi in 1858 and discovered Lake Nyasa in the following year. The Universities Mission to Central Africa, which came out to exploit this new field, began badly with the death of several of its members, including Bishop Mackenzie, and then retreated to Zanzibar in order to prepare a more gradual and better planned advance. Inspired by Livingstone's life and death the Free Church of Scotland founded the Livingstonia Mission in 1875 and in the following year the Church of Scotland established the mission at Blantyre. In 1878 the brothers Moir arrived to start the African Lakes Company, which was to work in close co-operation with the missionaries. In 1886 Portugal tried to counter these first British steps in Central Africa by making comprehensive treaties with France and Germany in which those powers recognized a Portuguese claim to all the territory between Portuguese East Africa and Angola. This would have had the effect of giving Portugal a broad belt right across Africa, thus barring the British advance from the south. The British Government protested and the claim came to nothing, but meanwhile, as Cecil Rhodes prepared to occupy Mashonaland, three most enterprising men, Harry Johnston, British Consul in Mozambique, Alfred Sharpe and Joseph Thomson, negotiated treaties favourable to the British with chiefs from Lake Nyasa across to the Congo Free State in the very territory claimed by the Portuguese, while Lochner, a servant of the British South Africa Company, concluded a treaty with the King of Barotseland. In 1890-91 the Scramble for Africa resolved itself into a series of agreements between the European powers. The agreement with Portugal assured Nyasaland and Mashonaland to Great Britain. The convention also, incidentally, put a stop to a spirited attempt by the British South Africa Company to obtain possession of Gazaland, which was adjudged to be within the Portuguese sphere. An agreement with Germany fixed the boundary between the British sphere and German East Africa. In 1891 Nyasaland, as that country is now called, became a British protectorate, and the country west of it, now Northern Rhodesia, passed under the administration of the British South Africa Company.

Once the international and constitutional position had been settled, it became possible to deal with the Arab slave traders who preyed on the weaker tribes round the north of Lake Nyasa. The African Lakes Company with the aid of European volunteers had for some time waged war against the slavers, but with only moderate success. Harry Johnston, now Commissioner for the British Protectorate, set himself to exterminate the pests with meagre forces but with unlimited energy and this he practically succeeded in doing by 1896 when ill health compelled him to go home. In addition he set up the beginnings of an administration within the Protectorate, concluded a land settlement and introduced a system of taxation. It was a remarkable feat by a remarkable man.

From the end of the Slave Trade until quite recent times the history of Nyasaland was a peaceful one. The position at the beginning of the 1914–18 war was hazardous, owing to the common border with German East Africa, but the immediate danger over, the country made a notable contribution to the forces that fought the East African campaign. It was during this war that John Chilembwe, an African minister partly educated in the United States, encouraged by the Germans, rose with his followers in the Blantyre district and murdered several Europeans. Chilembwe himself was killed and the rebellion fizzled out. During the 1939–45 war 30,000 Nyasalanders, including a high proportion of the small European population, served in the forces.

In the British South Africa Company's territory north of the Zambezi it was not possible at first to do more than keep open communications and fight the Slave Trade. However, in 1899 and 1900 the territory was divided for the purpose of administration into two parts, North-western and North-eastern Rhodesia, but the two territories came together again in 1911 under the name of Northern Rhodesia. Meanwhile Europeans had entered the country and demanded representation. This they got in 1918 in the form of an Advisory Council. The question of amalgamation with Southern Rhodesia, and then, perhaps, with South Africa, was one that was frequently canvassed during the early years of European settlement. A large body of opinion in both countries declared itself against amalgamation of the Rhodesias, without which any closer connection between Northern Rhodesia and South Africa was hardly possible. Moreover European opinion in Northern Rhodesia was alarmed by expressions of Afrikaner nationalism, both in South Africa and among some of the settlers themselves, and also by the way the South African Government handled labour troubles among white workers. By the end of the First World War the Europeans were disenchanted with the Company itself and were actually looking to the Colonial Office to take the country over. In 1919 all the leading Europeans demanded that Northern Rhodesia should become a crown colony with proper unofficial representation. In 1924 Company rule was brought to an end, a Legislative Council was established, and Northern Rhodesia became an imperial protectorate.

Federation

Although early suggestions for the amalgamation of the Rhodesias had not borne fruit, it remained true that there was a strong and

growing community of interests between the three British territories. The question of closer association did not therefore die away
but on the contrary became the subject of inquiry by a commission
under Lord Bledisloe in 1938. The Commission reported against
immediate amalgamation, and recommended instead the creation
of an inter-territorial body to co-ordinate various common services.
Nothing was done during the war years but in 1945 the Commission's recommendation was implemented by the establishment of
the Central African Council, a consultative body with a
permanent secretariat but, unlike its counterpart in East Africa,
with no central legislative assembly. Pressure for a closer connection continued and in 1950 a committee of officials was set up to
consider the question. There followed lengthy discussions which
ended in the summer of 1953 in the establishment of the Federation of Rhodesia and Nyasaland. The federal constitution is
elaborate. A Governor-General represents the Queen and there
is a cabinet presided over by the Federal Prime Minister. The
members of the cabinet are drawn from the Federal Assembly,
and this assembly has fifty-nine members. Of these forty-four are
elected, twenty-four from Southern Rhodesia, fourteen from
Northern Rhodesia and six from Nyasaland. Then there are eight
African members of whom four come from Southern Rhodesia
and two each from Northern Rhodesia and Nyasaland. There are
three European members specially charged with responsibility for
African interests of whom one is elected in Southern Rhodesia
and the other two are appointed, one each by the Governors of
Northern Rhodesia and Nyasaland. Finally there are four specially
elected African members, two each from Northern Rhodesia and
Nyasaland. It must be explained that fifty-three of the fifty-nine
members are chosen by an electorate which is at present overwhelmingly European, only four, the specially elected Africans,
being incontestably chosen by Africans.

The question of safeguarding African interests was anxiously
discussed, and the solution finally adopted was a standing committee
of the Assembly, called the African Affairs Board, and consisting
of three European members representing African interests and one
of the elected African members from each territory. The general
function of the Board is 'to make such representations to the
Government, in relation to any Federal matter, as the Board may
consider desirable in the interests of Africans, and, if a Territorial
Government so requests, to assist that Government in the study of

matters affecting Africans'. The particular function of the Board is to 'draw attention' to any Federal legislation, if in their opinion, 'such legislation constitutes a differentiating measure', that is to say a measure which inflicts on Africans restrictions and disabilities to which Europeans are not also liable.

The Federation has exclusive powers of legislation in a wide range of subjects, particularly external affairs and defence, many aspects of finance and commerce, inter-territorial and international communications and all higher education. There are also a number of subjects on which territorial governments may legislate concurrently with the federal, federal law prevailing in case of conflict, while territorial governments remain in control of their own domestic affairs, in particular those having a specially close relation to the day to day life of the African peoples.

To an outsider the Federation is a rather puzzling affair. By no means all Europeans concerned approved of it, and many Africans capable of forming an opinion were actively opposed to it. Against the undoubted advantages of unity as a source of economic strength and of power to resist the southward pull of the Union of South Africa must be set the disparate nature of the elements which it was proposed to unify: on the one hand a self-governing colony with a large European ruling class holding most of the power and half the land; on the other, two predominantly African protectorates, one rich, one poor, governed from London on traditional colonial lines.[1] In February and March 1959 there was rioting and bloodshed in Nyasaland due apparently to distrust of the Federation and to the fear that the policies of Southern Rhodesia, in which Europeans predominate, would be extended to Nyasaland. It is not enough now to affirm that these fears are groundless and that federation has on the other hand brought, to Nyasaland especially, financial benefits that would have otherwise been quite out of her reach. The damage is done and the very word 'federation' has become a sort of symbol to Africans of their grievances, the epitome of their fears and the obstacle to their hopes. It is a bogey that will not easily be exorcized.

As to the Europeans, it must here be explained that the people from whom Sir Roy Welensky, Prime Minister of the Federation and its foremost champion, draws his strength are not in origin a landed aristocracy such as that which has in the past created oppo-

[1] It should however be remembered that Northern Rhodesia has a strong and self-assertive European population.

sition to liberal reforms in countries like the West Indies or the southern states of America. Sir Roy himself is a man of the people and if his lot had been cast in England might easily have become a trades union leader or a socialist politician. Similarly, his supporters, especially in Southern Rhodesia, are artisans, clerks, minor civil servants, recent immigrants many of whom might have been expected to stand well to the left in an English election. Now in post-war Southern Rhodesia they enjoy an exceedingly high standard of living and all the privileges of a ruling class. They may not feel very deeply about federation, but they are determined to keep their present social, economic and political position. Native riots and agitations will cause them to rally behind any leader who appears to stand for the defence of white interests.

The Constitution of the Federation provides that it should be reviewed not less than seven nor more than nine years from the date of its coming into force and the troubles of 1959 showed that it was in any case high time to take another look at the whole thing. A commission under the chairmanship of Lord Monckton was appointed 'to advise the five governments, in preparation for the 1960 Review, on the constitutional programme and framework best suited to the achievement of the objects contained in the Constitution of 1953. . . .' The report of the Commission, presented in October 1960,[1] recommends a number of very important changes. These involve reconstruction of the Federal Government so as to secure much greater African representation, transfer to the territories of a number of important functions, leaving only defence, foreign affairs and regulation of the economy to the Federal Government, new constitutional safeguards and the abolition of racial discrimination, and finally the grant of the right to secede from the Federation after the new arrangements have had a fair trial. This last recommendation will be the most controversial of all. The pro-Federationists will say that secession will sabotage the Federation; the African extremists will say that they want secession not in the future but now. Neither attitude is altogether reasonable. Many of the advantages of Federation might well be retained by some looser form of association. On the other hand it would be a pity to dismantle an elaborate and in many ways effective machine before all safeguards against its abuse had been fully tried.

It should be noted that controversy has lately tended to shift

[1] Report of the Advisory Commission on the Review of the Constitution of Rhodesia and Nyasaland (H.M.S.O. Cmd. 1148).

from the issue of Federation itself to that of African political advancement within the countries that constitute the Federation.

THE PORTUGUESE TERRITORIES

History

MOZAMBIQUE

The Portuguese have been a long time in their present East African colony, longer certainly than some of the Bantu tribes who now people the hinterland. When their empire included the whole of the East African coast, they had treated with the Monomatapa and traded for gold up the Zambezi. In 1531 a trading post had been established at Sena, about 100 miles up the river and another at Tete a few years later. In 1572 Francisco Barreto ascended the Zambezi with twenty-two ships and a thousand men, and when he, and most of his expedition with him, died of fever, his successor Homem again pushed inland, establishing a trading post as far up the Zambezi as Chicora and others on the Mazoe, and reached the Manica gold field by way of the Revue. No permanent occupation of the interior was contemplated and the up-country tribes were as little affected by the coming of the Portuguese as they had been by the Arabs. Some attempt was made by Christian missions to proselytize the people of the interior. In 1560 the Jesuits undertook an expedition which got beyond Manica, but which was withdrawn in 1562 after the leader had been murdered. The Dominicans succeeded in establishing stations on the coast and up the Zambezi valley. The missionaries showed courage and endurance, but the impression that they made was negligible.

During the second half of the seventeenth century the Portuguese empire in East Africa wilted under the Arab assault and soon nothing was left but the settlements south of Cape Delgado which as the years passed sank deeper and deeper in squalor and decay, saved only from extinction by the active participation of the colonists (including high officials) in the Slave Trade.

At the time of Livingstone's Zambezi expedition in 1858 the Portuguese still claimed sovereignty of indefinite extent over the interior, but could do nothing to clothe those claims in substance. At any distance from the coast conditions were anarchic. Slave raiding by the Yao at the instigation of Portuguese and Arabs was endemic, and in the neighbourhood of Lake Nyasa the country had been swept clean by a fierce tribe called the Mazitu. 'The borders of this land,' wrote Kirk, 'are deserts. All the people have been killed and it has been a dreadful slaughter, for the shores are covered with skulls, and where a foraging party has passed fresh bodies beginning to decompose lie scattered on the sand.'[1] Some years passed before anything was done to stop these horrors and to stifle the Slave Trade at this source. Apart from sponsoring Livingstone's expedition the British Government manifested no interest in the hinterland of Portuguese East Africa until about 1877, when Consul Frederick Elton from Mozambique visited the Nyasa country. Thereafter Central Africa became the scene of considerable tensions between the British and Portuguese which were only resolved in 1891 by the agreement which became the basis of all future Anglo-Portuguese relations in Africa.[2]

To develop the territories now recognized as theirs, the Portuguese, like the British in Rhodesia, chose the device of the chartered company. Two such companies, the Mozambique and the Nyasa, received charters to develop and also to administer the very large areas within their respective concessions. The Mozambique Company was to a great extent independent of the government, with a governor and a civil service of its own, the government retaining only the administration of justice, defence and foreign policy. The concession expired in 1941 and the company was wound up in the following year. The Nyasa Company came to an end in 1929. Yet a third company, the Zambezia, had rights in large areas, including some of the most fertile in the country, but did not possess the same administrative powers as the two chartered companies. Several years passed before the Portuguese succeeded in asserting their authority over the whole territory. It was not, in fact, until 1912 that Mataka, last of the chiefs still unsubdued, was forced to fly across the Rovuma into German territory, and the way was clear for the development of the interior.

ANGOLA

Diego Cão discovered the Congo River in 1482 and erected a stone pillar at the river mouth. He sent an embassy of four of his men to the chief who lived some distance inland, and discovering on his return from his explorations further south that his envoys had been detained at the chief's town, seized four Africans and took them with him back to Portugal. The King of Portugal treated the

---

[1] R. Coupland, *Kirk on the Zambesi*, p. 205.
[2] p. 103.

four hostages as honoured guests, caused them to be instructed in the Christian faith, and himself acted as godfather when they were baptized. When therefore Diego Cão took them back to their home in 1484 or 1485 these messengers of goodwill paved the way for excellent relations with the Manicongo, or King of the Congo, as the chief was called, which led in 1490 to a Portuguese expedition with priests, skilled workers and a number of christianized Africans. This expedition had as its object the conversion of the chief to Christianity and the creation under him of a civilized state in friendly alliance with Portugal. It is sad, but hardly in the circumstances surprising, that this brave attempt to bring western civilization to Africa should have failed. It is, however, worth remembering as an enlightened experiment in race relations.

The next important Portuguese expedition to Angola was of quite a different kind. In 1574 Paulo Dias de Novais sailed from Lisbon armed with a *donataria* to a large area south of the Kwanza River. A *donataria* is a form of territorial proprietorship subject to certain development conditions and corresponds in some sort to the charters granted to British companies centuries later. Dias was not able to make any headway against native opposition, and when he died in 1589 hardly anything had been done to fulfil the conditions of the donation. When Portugal was joined with Spain under the Spanish Crown in 1581, the Dutch, in prosecution of their war against Spain, took Luanda and then Benguela. The Portuguese came back in 1648 and were kept busy for several years in reasserting their position in the country. When finally they succeeded in re-establishing themselves in the very small area in which they had a foothold it was not to initiate a vigorous programme of development. The attention of Portugal had long since been diverted from Angola to the glittering possibilities of Brazil, where untold wealth waited to be exploited by the exertions of sturdy blacks. In 1500 or thereabouts the raffish inhabitants of St. Thomas had turned their island into a great slave centre, and Angola had become a hunting ground for rival factions of slavers early in the sixteenth century. The trade was so profitable and called for so little expenditure of money or energy on the part of those engaged in it that it soon replaced all the more exacting occupations. No further attempt was made to develop agriculture and mining and the possibilities of the country were entirely neglected. The rulers became corrupt, there were abuses in the public administration, the old missionary ideals decayed, and the country fell into a condition of stagnation from which, in spite of the efforts of individual governors, it did not really emerge until the twentieth century.

The Scramble for Africa left Portugal secure in the possession of Angola. She had consistently asked for considerably more, including the whole of the Congo River mouth, but these wider claims were opposed by Great Britain, whose particular concern in these parts was the suppression of the Slave Trade. In 1884 Great Britain and Portugal signed a treaty which in fact recognized Portuguese claims on the coast, including the river mouth and some distance inland, but provided for free navigation of the river, which was placed under an Anglo-Portuguese commission. This treaty roused a storm of protest and the Portuguese, recognizing that it would have to be abandoned, now turned to Germany and France and proposed an international conference. This proposal led to the Conference of Berlin of 1884–5.[1] Subsequent negotiations and agreements fixed the northern boundary of Angola at the southern bank of the Congo River and also gave the Portuguese the Kabinda enclave, which lies north, but not immediately north of the Congo River mouth.

Economy

Since 1938 there have been a series of plans aimed at the development in Portuguese overseas possessions of an economy complementary to that of the mother country. In Mozambique the schemes include rail and port development; improvement in public health; township development; establishment of power and light supplies; development of the cotton industry. There has been considerable alienation of land by way of concessions, that is to say temporary grants of land which are confirmed on the fulfilment of certain development conditions. Some of the concessions are very large, the maximum area of a single concession being as high as 125,000 acres, though in some districts the limit is fixed at 25,000 acres. The principal European export crops are sugar, tea, copra, sisal and cotton. There is a growing export of timber. Europeans also grow maize and a wide variety of lesser crops. Native production, in addition to locally consumed foodstuffs, also includes export crops such as cotton, groundnuts and cashew nuts.

Though various minerals are known to exist in the territory only coal has attained any importance. A number of processing industries have grown up on a basis of local raw materials. The more important

[1] p. 52.

of these are sugar milling, the distillation of power alcohol, the manufacture of cement and asbestos products, soap making, cotton ginning, flour milling and tobacco production.

Stock raising is restricted by tsetse fly, but there are about 800,000 head of cattle in the country altogether, of which about 150,000 are in the hands of Europeans. The latter maintain the greater part of the meat and milk supply.

Portuguese East Africa has a number of good ports, of which the most important are Lourenço Marques, the outlet for the Transvaal, and Beira, which serves the Rhodesias, Nyasaland and Katanga. The transit trade through these ports is a most important feature of the economic life of the territory. There are twelve railway lines running inland from the ports. Of these, three are of outstanding importance; that running from Lourenço Marques to Ressano Garcia where it joins the South African Railway to Johannesburg; the line from Lourenço Marques to Malvernia where it joins the Southern Rhodesia Railway to Bulawayo; and third, the Beira–Machipanda line, which joins the Southern Rhodesia Railway to Salisbury.

With considerable natural resources, a rising population, improving communications and good harbours, the economic prospects seem good. The main difficulties appear to be financial. Plans for development are ambitious and expensive, and it seems doubtful whether there is sufficient public or private capital available to meet requirements.

The economic picture of Angola is not an impressive one. The Africans concentrate on subsistence farming, the collection of tree crops and beeswax and in some places they cultivate coffee and cotton. European colonists on the plateau grow cereals and other simple crops of high bulk but of low value and all more cheaply produced by Africans. A number of plantations produce economic crops such as coffee, sugar, sisal, tobacco, fibres, palm oil and palm kernels. The most valuable export is coffee which in 1957 represented 45 per cent of Angola's exports. Large quantities of maize are grown for local consumption and for export. The fishing industry is an important economic activity and fish products account for about 12 per cent of the exports. There are believed to be about 1·2 million head of cattle in the country but the industry has not been extensively developed. Mineral possibilities are believed to be very good but comparatively little is known about them. However, diamonds represent about 12 per cent of the total exports, and several other minerals are exported, including salt, copper and especially manganese. High hopes are pinned on the discovery of oil and experimental wells are in operation near Luanda. The yield is said to be promising.

Angola has four railway lines. Easily the most important is the Benguela Railway, which connects the port of Lobito with Dilolo on the borders of the Congo and so provides the mines of Katanga with an outlet to the Atlantic Ocean. The other lines run inland from the ports of Luanda, Mossamedes and Amboin.

Development plans envisage the improvement of ports, railways, aerodromes, roads and bridges, the development of hydro-electric schemes, agricultural resettlement and assistance, and geological survey.

In the first half of 1961 there was a rising in Angola, with the murder of Europeans by Africans and fierce military reprisals. In June there was still no sign of an end to hostilities. Available information is scanty but it is clear that the situation has the character of a civil war, with excess on both sides and much loss of innocent life.

MADAGASCAR AND THE COMORO ISLANDS

Madagascar—Country and People

The island of Madagascar is nearly one thousand miles long and 360 miles across at its greatest breadth. It is the fourth largest island in the world which is not also a continent. It lies opposite Portuguese East Africa, from which it is separated by the Mozambique Channel at an average distance of 250 miles. The physical appearance is not unlike that of the African continent of which it was a part in very remote times. That is to say, a plateau with an elevation of about 4,000 feet runs down the middle of the island and is flanked on either side by a coastal plain. The 'backbone' is much nearer to the east than to the west, with the result that the eastern plain is narrow and the rise to the plateau abrupt, whereas the western plain is fairly broad and in consequence the slope is more gradual. In the south the slope from the coastal plain to the plateau is also gradual. The east coast is almost a straight line and Tamatave, the principal harbour, is protected only by coral reefs. In the extreme north-east there is one very large indentation, the bay of Diego-Suarez, which is one of the finest harbours in the world. There are several good estuaries on the west coast and a good harbour at

Tulear. The capital of Madagascar is Antananarivo, situated on the plateau and splendidly sited on a rocky ridge which towers over the surrounding rice-fields.

The eastern side of the island is hot and wet and rain falls throughout the year. The rainiest period is from December to July, but it is never really dry, and nearly 4 inches fall in October, which is the driest month of the year. The east coast is also subject to cyclones. The west coast has well marked wet and dry seasons. The wet season, which is also hot, occurs between October and April; the dry cool season is from May to September. The plateau is fairly cool and drops to nearly freezing point in the dry season between May and September. During the rest of the year it is warm to temperate. The annual rainfall, most of which occurs between December and March, is 54 inches. There are no arid districts on the island except the southerly tip and the extreme south-west.

There are two substantial massifs on the plateau, both of volcanic origin, that of Tsaratanana (9,450 feet) in the north and that of Ankaratra (8,575 feet) in the centre of the island. The eastern side of the island, where the gradients are steep and rainfall constant, is cut by the gorges of perennial streams. On the more gently sloping western side, where the rains are seasonal, the smaller rivers only flow during the rainy season. The largest river on the island is the Betsiboka, which runs into the sea on the north-west coast. Other rivers on the west side are the Mania, the Mangoky and the Onilahy. The most important rivers flowing eastwards are the Mangoro and the Maningory. In the south the Mananara drains a substantial area. Madagascar has no really large lakes. The largest, Alaotra, is twenty-five miles long but in the remote past was considerably larger.

Vegetation follows the climatic zones. Hot and wet conditions on the eastern side have favoured the growth of evergreen forest, much of which unfortunately has been destroyed by fire or by clearance for agriculture. The plateau, with high winds and poor soil, is mainly grassland and savannah. The western side, with a seasonal rainfall, has deciduous forest. The vegetation in the dry south and south-west is sparse and semi-desertic. There are mangrove swamps in the estuaries of the western rivers.

That Madagascar became separated from the African continent in very remote ages is illustrated by the great differences between the plant life of the island and that of the mainland. Equally significant is the fact that many African animals, such as the anthropoid apes and the larger ungulates and carnivores, are absent from Madagascar. On the other hand the island has many small animals which are almost peculiar to it, and the fauna generally is marked by a strong individuality which it owes to long isolation from other zoological regions. There are no less than thirty-nine species of lemur, some of them very highly specialized; a great number of different chameleons; several animals belonging to the civets, the largest of which, *Cryptoprocta ferox*, forms a genus and a family to itself; and many birds, insects and fish. It is noteworthy that the fauna has Asian rather than African affinities, giving support to the theory that Madagascar, while once part of Africa, was also physically connected with Asia.

Certainly the population is not African in origin. The Malagasy, as they are collectively called, are in fact basically of Malayo-Polynesian and Melanesian stock, resembling the people of the Indian and Pacific archipelagos in appearance, customs and especially in their language. There is an African admixture, par-ticularly among the western tribes, and there are several Arab colonies. There are also Indians and Chinese, and 54,000 French by birth. The total population is 5–5½ million.

The most important native people, as well as the most numerous and advanced, are the Merina or Ambaniandro, commonly called Hova,[1] whose homeland is Imerina on the plateau near Antana-narivo. The Sakalava occupy most of the western side of the island and the Betsimisaraka a considerable stretch along the eastern seaboard. South of the Hova on the plateau are the Betsileo round Fianarantsoa. Other important tribes are the Antaimoro, whose chiefs are of Arab origin and who still use Arabic script, the Antaisaka, the Antanosy and the Bara. The most backward tribes of the island are the Mahafaly and the Antandroy in the extreme south.

History

The first European to see Madagascar was a Portuguese sea captain named Diego Diaz, who sighted the east coast on 10 August 1500. Because that day was the Feast of St. Lawrence, Diaz named his discovery 'Isle of St. Lawrence'. During the seventeenth and eighteenth centuries the French tried to establish posts on the

---

[1] Strictly speaking 'Hova' applies only to one class of Merina society, the middle class or freemen. The nobles are Andriana and the slaves Andevo. Now the whole tribe is called 'Hova'.

island but usually failed owing to resistance on the part of the
natives. The island was in those days a notorious haunt for the
pirates who infested the Indian Ocean. The people of the island
were apparently divided into small tribes until quite modern times.
The seventeenth century, however, witnessed the growth of the
Sakalava kingdom which at its zenith occupied half the island.
When this empire declined it was succeeded by that of the Merina
under King Andrianampoinimerina and then under King Radama
(1810–28), the latter a particularly able ruler who made Imerina
a progressive and expansive kingdom. During his reign the
London Missionary Society began work at Antananarivo, the
language was reduced to writing, the Scriptures translated, and
schools established. Radama's wife and successor Ranavalona I
(1828–61) fiercely opposed foreign influences and undid much of
the work of her predecessor, and her son Radama II was assassinated after a short and not very promising reign. However, the two
succeeding monarchs, Queen Rasoherina (1863–68) and Queen
Ranavalona II (1868–83), the latter married to an able prime
minister, both proved to be competent rulers who reformed and
reorganized the administration, encouraged Christianity and education, and established diplomatic relations with Britain, France
and the United States, who all posted consuls to Madagascar.

In 1883 differences arose between the Malagasy and the French
and the latter occupied Tamatave and Majunga. In 1885 a French
protectorate was accepted by Queen Ranavalona III, but after a
period of strained relations lasting some ten years a French expedition occupied Tamatave and in 1896 Madagascar was annexed to
France. The royal power was abolished and in 1897 Ranavalona
was sent into exile first to Réunion, then to Algiers. The task of
pacifying the new colony and establishing French authority was
entrusted to the humane, energetic and far-sighted Gallieni, who,
with the possible exception of Lyautey—at one time one of his
subordinates—was the most remarkable of the French administrators of the nineteenth and twentieth centuries.

In 1942 Madagascar was occupied by the British to forestall a
possible Japanese occupation and in the following year handed to
the Free French. In 1947 there was a serious rebellion which was
only suppressed with difficulty. Like other French colonies
Madagascar made very fast political advances in the following
decade and under the name Malagasy Republic is now an autonomous republic within the French community.

32–34. Views of Mount Kilimanjaro. The highest mountain in Africa (19,340 feet), with a perpetual cap of snow, Kilimanjaro is on the frontier between Kenya and Tanganyika, 170 miles from the coast and 210 miles south of the Equator. The view from the air (*above*) shows the Kibo and Mawenzi peaks on the right and left, with Mount Meru in the background to the south-west. The views from the trees (*right*) and a cross-roads (*below*) show the mountain as it appears in the distance

35. Lake Tanganyika. A view from Kigoma of the 400-mile long lake in the western arm of the Rift Valley between Tanganyika and the Congo

36. Great Rift Valley
A mail train climbs the
valley about 40 miles from
Nairobi; the mountain in
the background is the ex-
tinct volcano Longonot

37. FALLS ON THE ABBAI. The Abbai or Blue Nile rises in Lake Tsana in Ethiopia and runs south, west and then north to its confluence with the White Nile at Khartoum

38. CAPE GUARDAFUI. A nineteenth-century print showing the steep headland at the north-east tip of the Horn of Africa

39. THE TREE OF PARTING. This tree in western Tanganyika is near the place where Stanley and Livingstone parted in 1871, Stanley going to the coast and Livingstone to his death on his last expedition

40. LIONS IN KENYA. A lion and lioness happily lolling in the Nairobi National Park

41–42. GIRAFFE AND ELEPHANT IN EAST AFRICA. A reticulated giraffe in the Meru Game Reserve, Kenya (*above*), and a bull elephant in the acacia bush country of northern Tanganyika (*below*)

43. CAIRO. A view of the minarets towering over the rooftops of the older eastern part of the city

44. MOMBASA HARBOUR. The old harbour of the main seaport of Kenya

45–46. EGYPTIAN ANTIQUITIES. The 200-foot Step Pyramid of Saqqara is the oldest known stone building in the world—it was constructed for King Zoser nearly 5,000 years ago (*above*); this relief from the Temple of Montu at Tôd, showing part of a procession with the bull-god Montu followed by his soul in the form of a bird, is only about 2,000 years old, but it is unmistakably in the tradition of the ancient Egyptian inscriptions (*below*)

47–48. ETHIOPIAN ARCHITECTURE. The old castle of Gondar, 30 miles north of Lake Tsana, which is not unlike medieval European castles of the same period (*above*); and one of the rock-monasteries of Lalibala, 100 miles east of Lake Tsana, which are the most remarkable examples of Ethiopian architecture (*below*)

49-51. PEOPLES OF EAST AFRICA AND
THE HORN. Masai dancers in Tanganyika (*above*); two Somali elders
(*left*); mother and child, Uganda
(*below*)

52. Dhow off Mombasa
The typical sea-vessel of
East Africa

53. A Fishing Fleet, Kisumu. Boats setting out from Kisumu on Lake Victoria, the largest inland sea in Africa and the third largest in the world (over 26,000 square miles), and also the main source of the Nile

54-55. DAGAA FISHING. The dagaa (*left*) is a small sardine-like fish considered a delicacy in East Africa which can be caught by lamplight during the night (*below*)

56. EUROPEAN FARM IN KENYA. This farm is in the Solai valley north of Nakuru

57–58. PLANTATIONS IN EAST AFRICA. A pyrethrum plantation at Mologo in northern Tanganyika (*above*), and a clove plantation at the Kizimbani Experimental Station in Zanzibar (*below*)

59–60. GUM ARABIC IN THE SUDAN. The acacia bark being tapped to collect the gum (*above*), and a Government gum auction in progress at El Obeid (*below*)

61–62. WATER STORAGE IN THE SUDAN. The hollow trunk of a baobab tree is used for keeping water (*above*); the Sennar Dam on the Blue Nile, 160 miles south-east of Khartoum (*below*)

63–64. AGRICULTURE IN THE SUDAN. Members of the Khogalab Irrigation Co-operative Society ploughing their land (*above*), and a peasant pausing by a canal on his way home with some millet (*below*)

65–66. THE TSETSE FLY. A fly half an inch in length (*above*), and an immunized Ankole cow being used as a bait for flies in Uganda (*below*)

Economy

The most important cereal crop is rice, which is grown both by the Malagasy peasants and by European planters. It is the principal food crop and is cultivated in all parts of the island except in the arid areas of the south. Enough is grown to provide a surplus for export. Next in importance is cassava, from which tapioca is derived. Maize, beans and sweet potatoes are also important crops, cotton and tobacco are produced for local consumption, sugar cane is grown under irrigation, coffee is cultivated on the eastern slopes of the central uplands, considerable attention has been given to the production of essential oils, and there are coconut plantations in the north-west which provide a small export of copra. Vanilla has been introduced from Réunion and cloves are grown on St. Mary's Island off the east coast and on the neighbouring mainland. Mention must also be made of sisal and the castor oil plant. Cocoa has not been very successful but has given results round Tamatave.

On the plateau stock rearing constitutes the backbone of the native economy. The cattle are of the Zebu type and are not of high quality, but there is an export to Réunion and Mauritius and a meat packing industry on the island. The cattle population is about seven million; there are also about 400,000 fat-tailed sheep and about the same number of goats and pigs. Skins and hides form a valuable export.

Minerals are fairly plentiful. The most important is graphite, of which Madagascar is one of the largest producers in the world. Other important minerals are gold, coal, mica, and semi-precious stones.

Good roads connect the larger towns and there is a network of earth roads passable in the dry weather. There are four railway lines. The main line runs from Tamatave through Moramanga to Antananarivo. From Moramanga there is a line to the great rice-growing area round Lake Alaotra. Another runs south from Antananarivo to the town of Antsirabé, and Fianarantsoa, centre of the Betsileo, is joined to the coast by a line to Manakara. Some of the rivers, especially on the western side, are to some extent navigable and on the east a chain of lagoons connected by canals, called the Pangalanes, runs down the coast for about 400 miles and carries traffic. There are air services to France from Antananarivo.

When the British troops occupied Madagascar in 1942 they found that the islanders, in defiance of a fairly tight blockade, were

9

living without too much discomfort on local resources. Bread was
made from rice flour, there seemed to be plenty of vegetables,
meat and fats, and fuel alcohol was made from sugar cane. Public
services were in operation, markets were open and communications
well maintained. The only real hardship was a shortage of clothes.
Much of the island's self-sufficiency was no doubt due to French
ingenuity, but this could not have found such effective expression
unless materials were plentiful and varied. It therefore seems to the
writer that Madagascar has an economy at least as well balanced as
any of the newly independent states in and around Africa.

*   *   *   *   *

The Comoro islands lie in the Mozambique Channel 300 miles
off the coast of Madagascar and 200 miles from the east coast of
Africa. The group consists of four principal islands: Mayotte,
Anjouan or Johanna, Moheli and Grand Comoro. The population
of about 180,000 is of mixed Malagasy, Negro and Arab blood. The
Arab influence is an old one and most of the people are Moslems.

The French took possession of Mayotte in 1843 and French
protection was extended to the other three islands in 1886. In 1908
the group was attached to Madagascar for purposes of administration and was declared a French colony in 1912, this declaration
being ratified in 1914. The islands now have the status of a French
overseas territory.

The soil of the Comoros is fertile, food grows plentifully and
exports include copra, coco fibre, sugar, vanilla, sisal, wild pepper
and essential oils. There are only a limited number of cattle owing
to the mountainous nature of the islands. It remains to add that the
climate is very pleasant and that there are no poisonous snakes.[1]

---

[1] The authority for this excursion into herpetology is *La France de l'Océan
Indien* (Terres Lointaines, Vol. VIII).

CHAPTER THREE

EAST AFRICA

The Country

THIS is the region comprising the British and former German territories in East Africa and so includes Kenya, Uganda and Tanganyika, the island of Zanzibar with Pemba, and the Belgian trust territory of Ruanda-Urundi. The region is bounded on the north by Ethiopia and the Sudan, on the west by the Congo and Lake Tanganyika, on the south by Northern Rhodesia, Nyasaland and Portuguese East Africa, and on the east by the Indian Ocean. The north-eastern tip of Kenya is separated from the sea by the southerly projection of the Somali Republic. The principal towns are Nairobi and Mombasa in Kenya, Kampala, Entebbe and Jinja in Uganda, Dar-es-Salaam, Tanga and Tabora in Tanganyika, Usumbura in Ruanda-Urundi, and Zanzibar town. The total area is about 704,000 square miles and the estimated population just over twenty-seven million.[1]

The coastal plain is rather narrow, varying in width from about ten to forty miles, and stretches from the Somali border in the north to Portuguese East Africa in the south. It is fringed with coral reefs through which there are occasional deep water inlets, but natural protected harbours suitable for large ocean-going vessels are few. The climate is warm and the atmosphere humid. The average rainfall is 45–47 inches in the central part, considerably less in the north and south. The rains fall in well-defined seasons, the long rains in April and May, the short, lighter rains in November and December. There are great mangrove swamps in the river deltas and these are backed by a thin cultivated palm belt which soon gives way to tree savannah and in places to bush considerably thicker than the savannah further inland.

Behind the coastal plain there is an extensive low plateau called the 'nyika', an area of poor light soils except on the banks of rivers, with a rainfall ranging from five inches to thirty inches, broken by

[1] The distribution is as follows:

		Area				Pop.	
Kenya		224,960	sq. mls.				6,450,000
Uganda	,,	93,981	,,	,,		,,	6,536,000
Tanganyika	,,	362,688	,,	,,		,,	9,000,000
Ruanda-Urundi	,,	20,575	,,	,,		,,	4,860,000
Zanzibar	,,	1,020	,,	,,		,,	300,000

occasional outcrops of high ground and ranges of hills. The 'nyika', which has been compared in shape to an hour-glass,[1] bulges in the north to cover most of the Northern Frontier Province of Kenya, and in the south to include the whole of the Southern Province of Tanganyika. The neck is about 100 miles wide inland from Tanga.

West of the 'nyika' the ground rises gradually to the great continental plateau which in East Africa lies between 4,000 and 10,000 feet. Through the plateau, roughly in a north-south direction, run the two arms of the Rift Valley. The eastern arm is a deep trough, in some places forty miles wide and 3,000 feet below the level of the surrounding country, its floor dotted with lakes and extinct volcanoes. The western arm contains Lakes Tanganyika, Kivu, Edward and Albert. Between the two arms is the depression which contains Lake Victoria and the drainage system of the Nile.

The plateau is dominated almost throughout its length by a number of mountain masses. Of these the most important are the Kenya ranges, the Ruwenzori range on the borders of Uganda and the Congo,[2] and the mountains of northern and southern Tanganyika. The highest individual mountains are Kilimanjaro (19,340 feet), Kenya (17,040 feet) and Mount Stanley in the Ruwenzori range (16,791 feet). All except the last are extinct volcanoes, and Kilimanjaro, which is also the highest mountain in Africa, has in its higher peak, Kibo, an almost perfect crater.   (*Plate* 100)

The climate of the plateau is exceedingly varied and depends much on altitude. The rainfall ranges from 100 inches in the north-west corner of Lake Victoria to 20 inches in central Tanganyika. The higher parts have a cold bracing climate exceedingly congenial to Europeans. At lower altitudes, under say 5,000 feet, it can be very hot, but the atmosphere is not excessively humid, and the hot days give way to cold nights. Many a traveller in these parts has welcomed a good log fire at night.

Vegetation is as diverse as climate. Huge areas of the plateau, especially towards the south, consist of savannah, with low trees and shrubs which give the country a parklike appearance. Some of the dryer parts produce little more than thornbush and scrub, but the mountainous areas of high reliable rainfall still have large blocks of fine natural forest and formerly had much more. The high mountains have a vegetation of particular interest; characteristic

[1] *East Africa Royal Commission 1953–1955 Report* (H.M.S.O., Cmd. 9457), p. 7.
[2] The Ruwenzori range is also part of the western rim of the Congo basin.

features are the forests of tree groundsels and giant species of lobelia.

Two great rivers and several lesser ones run through the southerly part of the region. The Rovuma forms the boundary with Portuguese East Africa, and the Rufiji flows into the sea in a broad delta some eighty miles south of Dar-es-Salaam. Other rivers are the Ruvu and the Pangani, flowing into the Indian Ocean, and the Malagarasi, which feeds Lake Tanganyika. In the more northerly part the rivers are fewer and smaller. The Tana flows into the Indian Ocean not far south of Lamu on the Kenya coast. The Kagera between Tanganyika and Uganda has an importance of its own: it is the chief feeder of Lake Victoria and may thus be said to be the beginning of the greatest, in length at least, of all African rivers, the Nile. There are, of course, innumerable lesser streams throughout the region, but they are almost entirely seasonal and only flow during and shortly after the rains.

The island of Zanzibar is in the Indian Ocean at a distance of twenty-two and a half miles from the coast of Tanganyika, with its dependency Pemba lying about twenty-five miles to the north-east. Two-thirds of Zanzibar consists of low-lying coral country, though there is one ridge rising to 390 feet above sea-level on the western side. On the other hand Pemba is for the most part rich, fertile country. Its highest point is 311 feet above sea-level. Climatic conditions are very much the same as on the coast of the mainland, except that the rainfall is heavier and the heat is often mitigated by a sea breeze. The heavier rainfall is responsible for a more luxuriant vegetation than is to be found on the mainland, and both islands were formerly covered with forest, but this has now been almost entirely cleared for agriculture.

East Africa is the home of innumerable wild animals, though certainly not as many as before. The growth of the population and its spread under more peaceful and prosperous conditions into areas hitherto uninhabited, economic development and more intensive cultivation, indiscriminate killing for meat or for valuable trophies, all these factors have brought about a reduction in the animal population and even when animals have survived they have retreated to more inaccessible areas. The East African governments are concerned to ensure the survival of animals to the greatest extent compatible with human needs and every effort is made to balance the interests of the African with game preservation by appropriate legislation and the creation of game reserves and national parks.

Tsetse Fly

East Africa, especially at the lower altitudes, has its fair share of
the pests that threaten animal and human health in one way or
another, but the most injurious and so far the most intractable is
probably the tsetse fly, which causes trypanosomiasis in humans and
in cattle. Ways and means have now been found of exterminating
the malarial mosquito, formerly the most dangerous enemy of man
in the tropics, but all efforts to exterminate the tsetse have proved
ineffective, and even the methods of control so far devised are
chancy, arduous and expensive. Happily the human form of trypanosomiasis is curable and can of course be avoided by keeping out
of a fly-infested area. But to cure animal trypanosamiasis in all the
animals that might contract it is too vast and expensive a proposi-
tion to be practicable in African conditions. The territory most
seriously affected is Tanganyika, where about two-thirds of the
total area is infested with tsetse, which is steadily spreading. Kenya
and Uganda both have wide areas of infestation, but less than
Tanganyika. The tsetse has far-reaching demographic and economic consequences. Infested country may not be uninhabitable but
it certainly tends to cause concentration of people in the areas that
are less heavily infested. Huge areas are as it were sterilized against
human occupation. The presence of tsetse also makes the keeping
of cattle impossible. Thus the people living within the area are not
able to practice a balanced economy by a combination of agriculture and cattle-rearing.   (*Plates* 65–66)

THE PEOPLE

Europeans

Europeans have lived in Kenya for nearly three generations and
in the course of time have created out of virgin country a civilized
landscape of remarkable beauty, with good houses and pretty
gardens, orderly plantations, well tended farms, and towns with a
good number of fine buildings. They are not only farmers; in fact
the farmers are the smaller part of the European population. There
is a large business and professional community, miners, artisans,
tradesmen and shop assistants, and of course government officials
of every kind and missionaries. There are 66,400 Europeans in
Kenya, and these are mostly British. In Tanganyika Europeans number about 23,000 and they are a more varied community. There
are of course the British, who form nearly 70 per cent of the

European population, but there are also Greeks, Italians, Dutch, Germans, Swiss, Americans and others. About half the Europeans of Tanganyika live in towns and are engaged in the usual professional and commercial occupations. Most of the others are farmers, miners, plantation managers and overseers, government officials or missionaries and are scattered round the territory, many of them in the Tanga, Northern and Southern Highlands Provinces. Uganda has 11,000 Europeans, the great majority of whom, in this predominantly African country, are of the official and managerial classes. The European population of Zanzibar, mostly government officials and traders, is small.

Asians

The connection between the Indian sub-continent and East Africa is an ancient one and there are now 300,000–400,000 Indians and Pakistanis in the three British mainland territories, representing a domiciled rather than an immigrant population. The two principal divisions are Moslems and Hindus but there are also Sikhs, who are usually artisans, and Goans from Portuguese India. Asians now practically monopolize petty trade and control a high proportion of the import and export trade; they predominate as artisans; the cotton ginning industry and the sugar plantations of Uganda were largely developed by them, and their hold on these is only now being challenged by Africans. They are law-abiding, industrious and commercially competitive. One such community in particular, the Ismailis, who are Moslems and followers of the Aga Khan, is extremely well organized, having central direction, wide international contacts, and elaborate arrangements for education, insurance, banking and housing. Other communities, though perhaps less highly organized, are notably self-sufficient and capable of dealing with their own affairs.

Arabs

These former masters of the East African coast now live in somewhat diminished state, but they still enjoy considerable prestige among Africans. Through them the religion of Islam has become firmly established on the mainland coast and in those inland towns where Arabs settled in numbers. The Arabs have retained a certain prominence in public life on the coast of Kenya while in Zanzibar the Sultan is of course an Arab, as are at present most of the people of importance and authority on the island.

Africans

The African population of East Africa consists largely of Bantu peoples, with enclaves of Hamites and Nilotes. It represents many different stages of culture, from the advanced and politically highly organized Baganda to the primitive Watindiga of Tanganyika, who are hardly a degree above the South African Bushmen. It includes people as different as the quick-witted Chagga of Kilimanjaro, who have readily adopted certain aspects of western life, and the aloof and dignified Masai, who cling tenaciously to their own ways. There are nomads, and semi-nomads, cattle people and people with no cattle, farmers and hunters, cultivators of coffee or cotton, and people who cultivate practically nothing at all. Similarly, there are tribes with well established constitutions, an official hierarchy, a respected, semi-sacrosanct chief. Others may not recognize any more complicated authority than the head of the family. In a study of this scope it is impossible to do more than to take a few examples at various points in the scale.

The Baganda are probably the most highly developed people in East Africa. They live in the kingdom of Buganda, which is one of the four provinces in the Uganda Protectorate.[1] In fact Buganda was formerly merely a part of the empire of Bunyoro, but at the time of the first European explorers it had risen to the dominant position in the region. The kingdom of Buganda was the end-product of Hamitic immigration which had placed an alien aristocracy, the Bahima, with an elaborate 'king ritual', on the lacustrine Bantu peoples.[2] As Bunyoro declined in strength, so did Buganda grow and the Europeans found it a compact, despotic state centralized on the king, or, as he is called, the Kabaka, with a powerful and efficient hierarchy of chiefs appointed by him and holding office at his discretion. Buganda is now a country of landowners, tenants and landless labourers, many of the latter immigrants who have become permanent residents. The Kabaka presides over a well-developed system of government and is assisted by ministers and by a council formerly almost entirely selected by him but now tending to become more representative. The country is divided into counties, sub-counties, and parishes, each in charge of a chief or headman of appropriate status. The people are quick-witted, intelligent,

[1] Bu and U are different prefixes of the same noun class. Buganda and Uganda are therefore the same word in different languages, though geographically they now have different meanings.
[2] p. 10

sensitive, colourful, with some instinct for commerce and a taste for politics. They have taken with great zest to western gadgets, bicycles, cars, gramophones, radios, and in due course they will no doubt buy television sets. The women are among the most emancipated in Africa.

In Ruanda-Urundi a pastoral aristocracy of Hamitic origin, the Watusi, occupy a position analogous to that of the Bahima in Uganda. They are traditionally believed to have come from the north-east some 500 years ago, bringing with them cattle which are distinguished by horns of extraordinary length. They have mingled less with the local Bantu arable farmers, the Bahutu, than the Bahima have done in Uganda and have retained their physical characteristics in notable measure. These are a long head, fine features and exceptionally tall build, many Watusi reaching a height of 6 feet 6 inches and 7 feet.

As we move eastwards we come to the Chagga who live on the slopes of Mount Kilimanjaro, highly intelligent farmers who grow coffee and sell it through their own co-operative society, with an outlook at least as up-to-date as the Baganda and with more push and go.

The Kikuyu, or Agikuyu as they call themselves, are the biggest and most important tribe of Kenya. According to their own tradition they started as a tribe in the area of the present Fort Hall district, the exact place of origin being a large *Mukuruwe* (acacia) tree. Owing to pressure of an increasing population they moved southwards about the sixteenth century into Kiambu, then occupied by a tribe of hunters and honey collectors called Wandorobo. The Kikuyu bought land from the Wandorobo by very complicated processes in which religious rites played an essential part. A piece of land so bought was called a *githaka*, and there developed from this system of land acquisition a real landowning class, which is a rare thing in Africa. Each *githaka* also had its quota of tenants, and in the course of several centuries the Kiambu district became very well populated and prosperous. At about the same time as they came down into Kiambu the Kikuyu also moved up to the foothills of Mount Kenya.

At the end of the nineteenth century four major disasters ravaged this part of Africa. A great smallpox epidemic, a great rinderpest outbreak, a drought with consequent famine and a plague of locusts. Although these disasters were not confined to Kikuyuland they had here certain peculiar indirect effects which will be described later.

The social organization of the Kikuyu is exceedingly complex
and cannot be given in detail here. It comprises two distinct
aspects: on the one hand there is a patriarchal sub-clan system
closely linked with land ownership; on the other an organization
based on certain territorial units, the word for which means
'ridges'. Traditionally the Kikuyu have no chiefs in the sense that
Europeans understand the word. Authority formerly resided in the
councils of elders evolved from the twin aspects of their social
system. The chiefs whom the Kikuyu have today are largely the
creation of the European administration.

The Kikuyu are in a sense the most active and progressive people
in East Africa. 'Among the most noticeable characteristics of the
Kikuyu today are a strong instinct for trading and profit making, an
intense land-consciousness, a great propensity for litigation, and an
insatiable desire for education.'[1] They are also very active politically, with a bias against the government and against Europeans.
This bias found its most extreme and fanatical form in the Mau
Mau movement[2] but it is shared by many Kikuyu who opposed
and even fought against Mau Mau. With the Luo from the neighbourhood of Lake Victoria, the Kikuyu are the dominant element in
African nationalism in Kenya.

The Masai are pastoral Nilo-Hamites who live on the plains of
Kenya and Tanganyika. Tall, elegant, red-skinned, hair in a pigtail,
a toga-like cloth negligently draped over the body, spear in hand,
they watch their cattle, until recently secure in their sense of
superiority and remote from the conflicts that racked the rest of the
African world. They have now apparently become conscious of the
nationalist pretensions of the Kikuyu and apprehensive lest all
power in an independent Kenya be engrossed by that tribe. In the
face of this danger they seem to have come to a sort of understanding
with other Nilo-Hamites like the Nandi with a view to protecting
the interests of the so-called Kalenjin peoples.[3]

---

[1] *Report on Kenya Land Tribunals* by A. Phillips, 1945, quoted by Lord Hailey,
Native Administration in the British African Territories, Part I, p. 121.

[2] pp. 131–2.

[3] Professor A. N. Tucker has kindly supplied information on the word Kalenjin.
It seems to be an ethno-political name of recent origin which covers all people who
speak languages of the Nandi sub-group. Its meaning in Nandi is 'We have told
you'. It does *not* apply to the Masai, or to the Teso-Turkana-Karamojong people,
so cannot be equated with Nilo-Hamites on the linguistic side or with K.A.D.U.
on the political side (K.A.D.U. is the party now in power in Kenya and is opposed
by the essentially Luo-Kikuyu party K.A.N.U.). Although the Masai are not
strictly Kalenjin, one must suppose that they would act generally in sympathy
with other Nilo-Hamites, as indeed present trends seem to indicate.

Poles apart from the Kikuyu on the one hand and the Masai on the other are the Swahili. These are the African people of the coast and of Zanzibar, Bantu with a more or less strong admixture of Arab blood but more often of Arab culture. They are all, nominally at least, Moslems. Their language, an admirably flexible instrument of Bantu origin with many Arabic and other foreign words, is the *lingua franca* of East Africa and is even spoken in the Congo. The Swahili are worldly, witty and polite. They have an ancient poetic tradition and theirs is the only truly East African literature. They are shrewd in matters of trade and commerce. The more sophisticated have about them a not unattractive decadence peculiar to the old Arab civilization of the coast.

There is thus no *type* of East African. Instead, there are a large number of different people at different stages of civilization and representative of different cultures, each following a way of life differing in some way from the others, all with different ambitions and aspirations, and with different material and mental equipment wherewith to attain them.

History

The Scramble for Africa ended in the recognition by Germany of the British protectorate over Zanzibar and in the division of the mainland between Germany and Great Britain, Germany taking the southern part and Great Britain the northern. In their first attempts to colonize East Africa, both Germany and Great Britain relied on the device of a commercial company endowed with powers of administration. In 1884 the German explorer Karl Peters founded the Union for German Colonization, and the British Government, always anxious to avoid expense, were delighted to entrust the new territories to Sir William Mackinnon's Imperial British East Africa Company. The early years of European occupation were very turbulent. The German company met with bitter resistance from the Arabs and was quite unable to deal with an uprising led by one Bushiri and hence called the Bushiri Rebellion. So ineffective was the Company that the German Government took over and a protectorate was declared in 1891. Internal troubles continued, however, for many years and there were many tribal risings, all ruthlessly suppressed. The most serious was the so-called Maji Maji Rebellion, which occurred in 1905–6 and involved the whole of the south-eastern part of the territory.

In the British sphere missionaries had been at work in Uganda since 1877, first the Protestants and then the Roman Catholics, known respectively to the natives, quite accurately , as 'Waingereza' (English) and 'Wafaransa' (French). The Kabaka of Buganda, Mwanga, under Arab influence, caused Bishop Hannington to be murdered as he set foot in the country, and then instituted a savage persecution of the Christians, many of whom died martyrs' deaths in circumstances of great heroism. In this anarchic situation Captain Lugard, representative of the Imperial British East Africa Company, was hard put to it to keep any sort of order, and indeed fighting broke out from time to time until 1892.

The Company's means were quite inadequate to deal with a situation of this kind, and there was a serious danger that all British authority would be withdrawn. After much hesitation the British Government stepped in, relieved the Company of all its responsibilities west of Lake Naivasha and declared a protectorate over the kingdom of Buganda in 1894. Other parts were added later. In the following year the government bought the Company out of the remainder of the British sphere and the territory from Naivasha to the coast became the East Africa Protectorate and later, Kenya. In 1902 the Eastern Province of Uganda was added to it, to be followed by the Rudolph Province in 1926. In Uganda the brief era of peace that followed the declaration of 1894 was broken by a mutiny of Sudanese troops in 1897, which became a rebellion when Mwanga, declaring himself a Moslem, and Kabarega, chief of Bunyoro, joined in. Peace was not restored until 1899, when Mwanga and Kabarega were captured and removed to the Seychelles. In 1900 Sir Harry Johnston, Special Commissioner for the Protectorate, negotiated with regents on behalf of the infant Kabaka an agreement whereby Buganda, while ranking as a province of the Protectorate, retained extensive powers of self-administration and in which the Kabaka's high position was recognized.

The Maji Maji Rebellion came as a shock to public opinion in Germany where it was realized that incessant native troubles pointed to something seriously wrong in the administration of German East Africa. Colonial affairs, which had hitherto been the concern of a sub-department of the Chancellor's office, were transferred to a newly created ministry, and Bernard Dernburg, the first Colonial Secretary, began to introduce some very badly needed reforms. Dernburg was succeeded in 1911 by Wilhelm Solf, who did much to further the policy of his predecessor, but the intentions of these two well-meaning men were frustrated by the 1914–18 war.

After a long campaign, in which the German commander von Lettow-Vorbeck manœuvred with much skill against heavy odds, German East Africa was taken by British and Belgian troops. After the war the greater part was awarded to Great Britain to administer under mandate from the League of Nations. The districts of Ruanda and Urundi fell to Belgium under the same conditions. These mandates became U.N.O. trusteeships after the 1939–45 war.

Although Kenya, Uganda and Tanganyika have all been administered by Great Britain for a long time, the two former since the 1890s and the latter since 1918, their evolution has differed considerably. Uganda has never been other than an African territory, owned and to an increasing extent administered by Africans. This characteristic is reflected in the history of Uganda under British rule. Despite excitements now and then this has been an era of progress and increasing prosperity for the African. Kenya, on the other hand, soon became a colony of settlement with a strong and energetic resident European community. Although generalizations of this kind are dangerous, nevertheless it might be argued that the history of Kenya until the Second World War is largely concerned with the efforts of these Europeans to establish a home in Kenya and to assure conditions such as would in their opinion make their own community permanent and prosperous.

Tanganyika is largely an African territory and the emphasis has been chiefly on African interests. There are islands of European settlement in the north and in the south, while the lead in economic matters has in the main been taken by Europeans and Asians. But the energies of the British administration since its inception have been almost exclusively devoted, directly or indirectly, to the economic and social advance of the African, while the training of the people to govern themselves has been steadily kept in view, though the methods have changed and the tempo has increased considerably in recent years.

In Ruanda-Urundi the Belgians followed very much the same policy as the British in Uganda. There was some non-native immigration, but the aim was to foster and improve indigenous institutions, and to preserve and develop the territory as an African country.

Of Zanzibar in its heyday it was said 'When you play the flute at Zanzibar, all Africa, as far as the Lakes, dances',[1] but with the

---

[1] This is the version given by W. H. Ingrams in *Zanzibar, its history and its people*.

establishment of European protectorates on the mainland the political importance of the island fell away. The slave market was closed in 1873 and the disappearance of the slave traffic was soon followed by a slump in the entrepôt trade in other goods as Europeans established ports on the mainland. Nevertheless the social and cultural influence of Zanzibar persists, and it remains what it has always been, a meeting place of Asia and Africa.

With the Italians in Ethiopia and the Japanese in the Indian Ocean the 1939–45 war came very close to the East African territories, and all played an active and useful part in the war effort. Large numbers of Africans and, proportionately, of Europeans, served in the forces that took Ethiopia and subsequently moved on to other theatres of war, and those who remained at home concentrated on the production of food and materials so as to make the region as far as possible independent of imports from other countries. Large numbers of prisoners of war, internees, and refugees from central Europe spent the war years in East Africa, and the region also lay right along the lines of communication between North and South Africa.

The end of the war found East Africa, as a producer of primary materials in short supply, on the eve of a period of great prosperity, and bold plans were made for economic development. It is to this era that belongs the notorious Tanganyika Groundnut Scheme, an operation directed not by the Colonial Office but by the Ministry of Food, and by no means typical of the realistic and well integrated programmes that were also planned and carried out. This was the time too when it was realized that constitutional advance must be hastened to meet pressing demands from the Africans, and when self-government came to be regarded not as an ultimate aim but as a goal that must be reached in the near future.

In 1953 a speech by the Secretary of State for the Colonies roused fierce suspicions in Uganda that the country might be federated with the other East African territories against its will. Reassuring statements by the Colonial Office and the Governor went some way to allay public excitement but did not satisfy the Kabaka of Buganda, who argued that the reassurances were not so strong as others that had gone before, and went on to make new demands which, if accepted, would have nullified the British policy of developing Uganda, including the kingdom of Buganda, as a unitary state. After much discussion the Kabaka accepted the reassurances but refused to abandon the additional demands, whereupon the Governor withdrew British recognition of him and deported him forthwith to England. This step, designed to remove an obstacle to the policy of building a strong, independent, democratic, united Uganda, caused such a furore among the Baganda as to make it impossible to pursue any policy at all. Eventually both the Baganda and the British Government accepted the compromise proposals of a specially appointed constitutional committee, and the Kabaka was restored to his throne.

Unfortunately the matter does not end there. The issue in Uganda is in essence a clash of opinion among Africans as to who shall inherit the power now wielded by the colonial authorities. The 'new men', radical nationalist politicians, representative of an up and coming middle class, see the future in terms of a unitary state in which they shall constitute the governing class. The traditionalists, mainly centred on the Kabaka and his parliamentary assembly the Lukiko, conscious of the eclipse of the aristocracy in other parts of Africa, reject the unitary state, in which they suspect that the traditional power would be weakened and destroyed. Instead they want a federation in which the kingdom of Buganda would be allowed to develop separately and the traditional authorities enabled to retain their powers undiminished. The traditionalists can claim with some justice to be at least as well qualified as the politicians, if not better, to fill the role of successor government. They have a civil service in being, age-old experience of administration at a level suited to existing African standards, and they, especially the Kabaka, enjoy the respect, indeed the reverence, of a large part of the population. It must also be admitted that so-called democratic politicians elsewhere, equipped in preparation for independence with the most elaborate parliamentary institutions, have managed in a very short time to become as authoritarian as any African monarch. It is fortunately not the task of the author of this book to solve problems to which statesmen and administrators have still not found the answer. One might however suggest that a too rigid attachment to the idea of unity should not preclude the examination, or even the trial, of more elastic arrangements, and that at the same time the Kabaka's government might do more than it has done till now to reach an accommodation with the rest of Uganda.

This historical sketch ends on a sombre note. Shortly after the Second World War there began in Kenya a movement called Mau Mau. It was confined almost exclusively to the Kikuyu and its

origins appear to have lain in land shortage, various social and
political grievances, and more generally in a profound unease
generated by the sudden impact of an alien civilization. The movement was assiduously fanned by a number of desperadoes, twisted
into a grisly brotherhood by pseudo-religious sanctions, and
equipped with oath-taking ceremonies of a most terrifying and
bestial nature. In due course the movement broke out into murder
and terrorism on a grand scale. Though primarily xenophobic Mau
Mau killed many more Africans than it did Europeans. Fortunately
the greater number of Kikuyu did not join in and many fought
against the terrorists. Nevertheless, it took a small army of troops
and police and a great number of irregulars to suppress the movement,[1] and it was not until January 1960 that the state of emergency
officially came to an end. During 1960 there were reports that the
Mau Mau oath was again being administered, and the Government
took precautions against another outbreak.

Land

There is no subject on which Africans are more sensitive than
land, which plays a critical part in East African controversies,
particularly in Kenya.

European settlers acquired land in the highlands by purchase
from chiefs or from the Imperial British East Africa Company
before the East Africa Protectorate was declared in 1895, but it
was not until the turn of the century, when the cost of maintaining
the Uganda railway through empty country made it imperative to
find a source of revenue, that the British Government committed
itself to a steady policy of European settlement. The climate of the
highlands seemed to be well suited to Europeans and great areas
moreover seemed to be unoccupied. The great pasture lands on
the high plateau appeared to have no native tenants at all. We
know now that this situation was only temporary and that a series
of natural catastrophes[2] had so scattered and reduced the human
and cattle population as to create an impression of emptiness that
was not normal. The entry of Europeans into Kenya thus coincided

---

[1] General Lathbury, who took over command in 1955, says that he then had at his
disposal three brigades of infantry, a reconnaissance squadron, an artillery battery,
a regiment of Royal Engineers and a company of the Kenya Regiment. The Kenya
Police were fully deployed, and there was a force of 9,000 tribal police. These
ground forces were supported by the Royal Air Force and the Kenya Police Air
Wing. ('The Security Forces in the Kenya Emergency', *Rhodesia and East Africa*,
p. 36.)

[2] p. 125.

with a period of unusual depopulation. This coincidence, combined with ignorance of the nature of African land tenure, weakness in the face of settler demands, and indecision on the part of the British Government, led to alienation in a manner and on a scale which has left the tribes of Kenya with an abiding grievance. This was not alleviated by subsequent demarcation of reserves to be 'set aside for the benefit of the Native tribes for ever', and was positively accentuated by the virtual exclusion of the highlands to any but white settlement. The belief that land shortage was due to the alienation of land to Europeans was one of the causes of Mau Mau. In 1953 a Royal Commission under the chairmanship of Sir Hugh Dow was appointed with terms of reference amounting to a mandate 'to examine all possible measures to achieve improved standards of living, having regard to possible increases in the population and to the present congestion of African population in certain areas'. The Commission's report, a cardinal document in East African history, was presented in 1955[1] and is too detailed and exhaustive to be analysed here. It must however be noted that the most important and far-reaching recommendations are those relating to land: 'Throughout our Report we insist that the approach on a tribal basis to questions of land tenure and land use is incompatible with the development of a modern economy, and this applies equally to a purely racial approach to the Highlands question . . . we recommend that though there should be no disturbance of existing titles to land except in circumstances, clearly defined in the law, which are designed to meet the national interest, there should be machinery established which will permit the leasing of land free from restrictions imposed by tribal or racial reservations.' The consequences of these recommendations are twofold. First, the policy of the 'White Highlands' can clearly no longer be maintained; and most people would agree that in the present climate of opinion the Commission only anticipates a process that was inevitable, if only for political reasons. The second consequence is that tribal or communal occupation of land must give way to individual tenure, and here the issue is more debatable. The old form of tenure is deeply rooted in African society, and many Africans regard it as a protection of their rights in land. Moreover, as has often been said in the past, individual tenure is not without its dangers in comparatively unsophisticated communities. However, the Commission does not underrate the

[1] *East Africa Royal Commission 1953–1955 Report* (H.M.S.O., Cmd. 9475).

difficulties that lie in the way of the proposed change, and the Report sets out very fully the arguments for it, and the safeguards that should accompany it.

In Uganda and to a great extent in Tanganyika the land question has not been complicated by a policy of European colonization. In Uganda all land outside towns and trading centres, and in Buganda all land whatsoever, is regarded as being held by government in trust for the native population, while in Tanganyika the whole of the land, except that already alienated in German times, is held by the government to be administered for the common benefit of the people of the territory. In effect this means that land cannot be alienated to non-Africans unless it is not likely to be required for African use in the foreseeable future. In Zanzibar all waste and unoccupied land and all land occupied in accordance with local and tribal custom is vested in the Sultan. However, large estates have come into the possession of Arabs in various ways under conditions equivalent to freehold though not defined by law. In order to prevent Arab and African land from passing into the hands of non-Natives, the attachment of this land or its produce for debt is forbidden and all alienation is subject to the control of a Board appointed by the British Resident.

Economy

The East African mainland is a major producer of sisal, tea, coffee and cotton. Other important agricultural products are groundnuts, copra, tobacco, pyrethrum and wattle extract. Industries such as sisal production, requiring heavy machinery and a large labour force, are in European or Asian hands, as also is tea farming and to a large extent the more complicated and expensive forms of processing. But the most significant factor in recent economic development is the growth in the trade in African cash crops. While remaining a peasant farmer, concerned primarily with growing food crops such as maize, millet, pulses and roots for his own consumption, the African has turned with considerable success to the production of cash crops such as coffee, cotton, groundnuts, tobacco and rice and there is a growing tendency, encouraged by the administration, towards African ownership of plant and machinery. The co-operative movement has been fostered and extended, the most important societies being the Cotton Marketing Union in Uganda and the Kilimanjaro Native Co-operative Union in Tanganyika. The East African Co-operative Training Centre at

Kabete in Kenya receives students from the other territories.

Cattle play a most important part in the economic life of East Africa, and most Africans look upon them as the most desirable form of wealth. Yet the distribution of cattle is exceedingly uneven owing to the climate and the tsetse fly and other pests. Nevertheless, most African families keep a few head of stock when they can, and those who cannot usually manage to have a few goats. Among the Masai, on the other hand, cattle represent almost the sole wealth of the tribe, because the Masai do not cultivate. In tribes with a mixed economy cattle still fill a most important role, and provide meat, milk and money when it is required.

In some areas African stock owners have developed a thriving manufacture of ghee (clarified butter), and in spite of a bias among Africans against selling cattle, East Africa exports increasing quantities of meat, meat products, hides and skins.

The European farmers raise very good cattle from imported stock and Kenya has a thriving meat and dairy industry.

Most of the world's supply of cloves comes from Zanzibar and Pemba and there are believed to be four million trees in bearing on the two islands. The clove was probably brought to Zanzibar from Mauritius early in the nineteenth century and was cultivated compulsorily by order of Sultan Sayyed Said. It is liable to three deadly diseases of which only one has so far yielded to control, so that an economy based on this crop alone might be regarded as precarious, especially as the French in Madagascar have encouraged clove production. Fortunately there is an alternative in the coconut and Zanzibar is a considerable exporter of copra and coconut oil.   (*Plate* 58)

The coastal and lacustrine peoples of East Africa have engaged in fishing since time immemorial and dried fish, both from the sea and the lakes, has always been an article of trade. Surveys of both inland and coastal fishing grounds have been conducted and the development of fisheries will supply the people with much needed protein. The potentialities are very great.

Neither Kenya nor Uganda are great mineral producers. Large deposits of soda are worked at Magadi in Kenya, and Uganda exports tin, copper, wolfram and small quantities of other minerals. The minerals of Tanganyika are probably considerable and are only now beginning to be properly developed. The most spectacular are the diamonds of the Mwadui deposits owned by Williamson Diamonds Ltd., but the country also contains lead, gold, tin, mica,

silver, tungsten, salt, copper and several other minerals of lesser
importance in addition to great quantities of coal and iron.

Transport

The main railway lines run, as might be expected, from the coast
inland, with branches leading off in various directions. The Kenya
and Uganda Railway, starting from Mombasa, was opened to
Kisumu in 1901, to Kampala in 1926 and was extended to Kasese on
the western border of Uganda in 1956. There are a number of
branch lines and a northern extension is being surveyed. The
Tanganyika railway system consists of three lines running from
Tanga to Arusha, Dar-es-Salaam to Kigoma and Mtwara to
Nachingwea. The Tanga line is connected with the Kenya Railway
by a branch line from Kahe to Voi. A branch to Mwanza on Lake
Victoria takes off from the Dar-es-Salaam–Kigoma line at
Tabora. There is a short branch line to the lead mines at Mpanda.
The East African Railways and Harbours run regular steamer ser-
vices on the great lakes of the interior.

The principal ports on the East African coast are Kilindini on
the island of Mombasa, Tanga, Dar-es-Salaam and Mtwara. Of
these Kilindini is the greatest. It is the gateway to and from Kenya
and Uganda and is also able to tap the traffic of the northern highlands of Tanganyika by the railway link that passes through Voi.
The port facilities have been greatly improved, and Kilindini is
now able to take large vessels. Half the trade of Tanganyika passes
through Dar-es-Salaam. The harbour is reasonably spacious but
the channel is difficult for large vessels, being tortuous and narrow.
Tanga is overshadowed in importance by its northern and southern
neighbours. These mainland ports have robbed Zanzibar of much
of its former importance.

Most roads in East Africa are of earth and the quality varies. The
best roads are said to be found in Uganda. Earth roads are of course
very much at the mercy of the weather and many become quite
impassable in the rainy season. However, of late years considerable
improvements have been made and long stretches on the more
important routes have been bituminized.

Air transport was very freely used long before the war and in
recent years there has been a considerable expansion in air services.
There are few centres of any importance that have not got some sort
of landing facilities while at the other end of the scale the airport at
Entebbe has been called the Charing Cross of Africa.

Modern Problems

The presence of a community of Europeans and Asians whose importance is out of proportion to its numbers, combined with intense racial consciousness in the African, poses in East Africa a politico-social problem of the greatest difficulty: that of creating a harmonious multi-racial society from among the various elements now living there. The problem is especially difficult in Kenya where there is a *native* European population, born and bred in the country, which looks upon Kenya as its home and which can point with pride to an impressive achievement of colonization. It is indisputable that the economic contribution of these Europeans is very high in proportion to their numbers. It is also difficult to deny that they have, in the past at any rate, been privileged. It would be unjust to say that African interests as a whole have been trampled on. But it is nevertheless true that enterprising and vocal Europeans, and to a lesser degree Asians, have built for themselves a position of considerable wealth and privilege dependent on the not always well rewarded labour of many Africans. One must be careful not to exaggerate in either way. The African has not for instance been harassed to the edge of extinction like the American Indian, or hunted to death like the South African Bushman. But on the other hand he has not been accepted as a fellow-citizen enjoying equal rights, like the Maori, nor has he, as in Nigeria, provided the only object of the administration's benevolence and care. The tendency in Kenya has been to treat the African quite kindly as a perpetual adolescent, useful as a 'boy' on the farm or in the house, picturesque in his 'reserve', but not at all the sort of person to sit in Parliament or in the Club. The result is that his status has always been underrated and his interests played down, and Kenya has presented the aspect of a three-tier society, with the Europeans at the top, the Africans at the bottom and the Asians somewhere in between. The system bore within it the seeds of its own decay and could not in any case have been expected to last indefinitely, even at the leisurely tempo of African advance in the circumstances of two decades ago. It was a predestined casualty of the changes that the last few years have brought to Africa and it has now collapsed in the face of African nationalism. Nothing that is satisfactory to everybody has yet been found to replace it. It should also here be added that the Asians are socially exclusive, conservative, and tenacious of their identity. Much of the wealth of the country is in their hands and they show no disposition to share it. Politically they expect, and for that matter obtain, full representation in the councils of government and their politicians have tended to promote sectarian rather than general interests. They present a more difficult problem of assimilation and adjustment than does the European.

In Uganda the racial problem is an Afro-Asian one, without the European complication. Asians have long held a prominent place in trade and industry which they may find difficult to maintain in a country governed by Africans. The political difficulty is to find a basis for self-government which will not on the one hand isolate the kingdom of Uganda, and on the other place it in an inequitably dominant position among the other units in the Protectorate.

Tanganyika lies somewhere between Kenya and Uganda. The territory was endowed with responsible government in 1960 and this will in due course become self-government. The prospect appears to be quiet and steady progress towards a predominantly African multi-racial state, in which Europeans and Asians will fill their appropriate places. It should at once be said that this will be no revolutionary change. African interests have always been the subject of especial solicitude on the part of the European administrators, and it is yet to be seen whether those interests will be as safe with independence as they have been under British trusteeship.

In Zanzibar Arab dominance is now facing a challenge from the African majority and it seems probable that here as elsewhere the future will see the rise of Africans to positions of power and authority.[1]

In theory the transfer of power to Africans should nowhere be easier than in Ruanda-Urundi. For here, unlike in the Congo proper, there is a ready-made governing class in the Watusi, with a hereditary king and an elaborate constitution. But the indigenous Bantu people have revolted against their Hamitic overlords and although in 1960 Belgian troops prevented the worst excesses, the outlook for the future is unsettled.[2]

In sum, the immediate problem of East Africa is an interracial one, that of the relations between Africans and the immigrant minorities, European and Asian. Since these minorities between them are vital to the economy, much depends on finding a solution.

[1] Early in June 1961 there were fierce inter-racial riots among Arabs and Africans in Zanzibar.

[2] At the end of January 1961 it was reported in the press that the King of Ruanda had been deposed and a republic established. It was also stated that Ruanda would continue to recognize United Nations trusteeship arrangements.

CHAPTER FOUR

THE HORN OF AFRICA

SOMALILAND

JUTTING straight up from the sea at the junction of the Gulf of Aden and the Indian Ocean, towering above a little bay in which huddles a poor fishing village, dangerous to navigators because of winds and currents, stands Cape Guardafui, a notable landmark for travellers, for it is the extreme north-easterly tip of Africa. It is also the apex of Somaliland. *(Plate 38)*

History

The British connection with Somaliland began early in the nineteenth century when the East India Company sought a safe harbour for their ships on the southern shores of the Gulf of Aden. In 1874–5 the Khedive of Egypt claimed jurisdiction over most of the Somali coast and Egyptian forces occupied the main ports; but when the Khedival garrisons were withdrawn in 1884, the British occupied Zaila, Berbera and Bulhar, partly because these places were on the route to the east. From 1899 the British occupation of Somaliland was punctuated by campaigns against Mohamed bin Abdulla, the so-called 'Mad Mullah', who recruited a large number of fanatical followers and dominated the interior for twenty years. During this time British administration was practically confined to the coast, and it was not until 1920, when the Mullah was defeated and driven out, later to die in Ethiopia, that it was possible to begin to govern the country normally. In the years between the world wars some progress was made in introducing modern administration among an independent and very suspicious people. The human population grew in numbers, livestock increased, and trade developed in a limited way. In 1940 British Somaliland was overrun by the Italians but was reconquered in the following year.

In 1889, by treaties with Somali sultans and by agreements with Great Britain, Zanzibar and Ethiopia, the coast east of British Somaliland fell to the Italians. Three years later the Sultan of Zanzibar leased the Benadir ports to Italy and sold them to her in

1905. Italy then obtained the adjacent hinterland from the Emperor Menelik of Ethiopia in 1908 and Jubaland by cession from Great Britain in 1924. In 1941 British Imperial troops operating from East Africa speedily conquered Italian Somaliland, which was occupied by the British until the end of the war.

French Somaliland lies west of the British Protectorate. France had acquired the two towns of Ambabo and Obok in 1856 but did not take formal possession until 1883. In the following years she acquired the whole of the gulf of Tajura by treaty with the local Somali sultans. The seat of government was transferred from Obok to Jibuti in 1896.

At the end of the Second World War the British proposed that most of the country inhabited by the Somali should be brought under a single administration under either British or international trusteeship. For remote and irrelevant political reasons other nations turned this proposal down. Instead, former Italian Somaliland, renamed Somalia, was placed under Italian trusteeship with a promise of independence in 1960. At the same time the British Government encouraged political and economic progress in the Protectorate. Schools were accepted by the Somali for the first time, European medicine began to be appreciated, and later, councils were formed which stimulated among the Somali a wish to play a more responsible part in their own government. As independence for Somalia drew near, the Protectorate people became increasingly anxious to achieve self-government at the same time, so that the two territories might unite in a single nation. The British Government agreed to withdraw its protection and in 1960 Somalia and the former British Protectorate came together to form the independent Somali Republic.

The Haud

The territorial question is complicated by an unfortunate legacy of history. In 1897 Great Britain made a treaty with Ethiopia delineating the boundary between Ethiopia and British Somaliland. It was then realized that the boundary cut across certain grazing grounds called the Haud, which had been used by the Somali since time immemorial, and letters designed to safeguard the use of the area to the Somali were accordingly annexed to the treaty. The Somali remained in ignorance of these arrangements until their frontier with Ethiopia was demarcated by a commission in 1931-35. Even then they were cushioned against the worst effects of the

Treaty by the Italian conquest of Abyssinia, following which the
Haud was administered as part of Italian Somaliland and was thus
still available to the Somali. This situation continued under the
British military administrations set up temporarily to govern the
Italian colonies conquered during the Second World War. But in
1954, at the request of the Ethiopian Government, the Haud was
returned to Ethiopian sovereignty. The Anglo-Ethiopian Agreement of 1954 confirmed the treaty of 1897, reaffirmed the right of
the Protectorate Somali to use the grazing areas, and also provided
a special measure of British protection to the tribes when they were
in Ethiopia. These safeguards soon threatened to break down and
the Somali of the Protectorate became determined to work for the
incorporation of the Haud, by some means, into a fully united
Somaliland, which would include French Somaliland and parts of
northern Kenya where many Somali live. The Ethiopians, on the
other hand, apprehensive of Moslem encirclement, have refused to
contemplate the transfer of any part of the Haud and have actually
claimed that all Somali tribes using it are Ethiopian subjects; the
French Government has opposed the embodiment of French
Somaliland in any Somali Union and it may be assumed that Kenya
would not readily agree to the cession of her northern territories.
The question of the Haud may well continue to cause friction between the Somali and the Ethiopians until some satisfactory solution is reached.

The Country

Somaliland forms a triangle with uneven sides, with its apex at
Cape Guardafui. The northern side of the triangle runs for a
distance of 600 miles along the southern shore of the Gulf of Aden,
and the eastern side is twice as long and extends from Cape
Guardafui southwards to the frontier of Kenya. The depth inland
is 200–250 miles and the total area is something over 270,000 square
miles. The country is on the whole arid and inhospitable, the north
more so than the south, and the coast more so than the middle
plateau and the highlands. Lack of water is the dominant feature of
the region, and characteristically this is more marked in the north,
where the watercourses are usually dry and only flow during, or
immediately after rain. Only in the south are there two rivers with
a perennial flow. These are the Webi Shebeli and the Juba. Of
these only the Juba reaches the sea, as the Webi Shebeli dies away
in sands and swamps inland. For the rest the people depend for

water on scattered well systems, which are closer together in the
south than in the north.

From this description it may well be imagined that the vegetation
is generally sparse, in many places consisting as it does of thin
scrub and short grass when there has been rain. However, trees and
grass grow well towards the Ethiopian highlands and the middle
plateau is covered by fairly thick bush and high grass.

Economy

The economy of the country is dependent on livestock and the
most important form of livestock is the camel. This animal provides
milk when it is alive and meat and a hide when it is dead. It also
furnishes the means of transport at present essential to the people's
way of life. Somali sheep are famous for their skins and their meat
is of good quality. The goats are tough and durable and well
adapted to the harsh conditions under which they live. The skins of
sheep and goats form a valuable export.

The remaining economic resources of Somaliland are slight.
Various gums and resins are collected in the north-eastern part of
the country, fibre is processed from aloe and fishing is an important
local industry. Minerals have so far not been proved in any quantity
but the situation would be entirely altered if the search for oil were
to be successful. The Italians, during their short occupation of
Somalia, promoted the cultivation of cotton, bananas, sugar cane,
durra and maize, but taking it all in all, agriculture is an uphill task
except in some especially favoured areas.

The People

The Somali population in the former five political divisions was
approximately as follows:

Somalia (ex-Italian) 1,300,000
Somaliland Protectorate (British) . . 650,000
Ogaden Province of Ethiopia . . 300,000
Northern Frontier Province of Kenya . 70,000
French Somaliland 25,000

The Somali are Eastern Hamites, tall, handsome, proud and
excitable. They are devout Moslems of the Sunni school of the
Faith. Politically they are divided into tribal groups, tribes, sub-
tribes and clans. At the head of these divisions there are sultans
and chiefs, while the government of the clan, which may consist of

a few families, is patriarchal. The Somali social structure also exhibits well marked class divisions. Holy Men enjoy high esteem; after them come the rich merchants, dhow captains and rich farmers; next, the tribesmen and pastoralists. The lowest social stratum consists of the 'outcast' tribes, smiths, leather workers, hunters, sweepers and refuse collectors, who, though generally despised, have certain ritual and magical properties. The coastal towns house an urban class and it is among these that political ferment on quasi-western lines is most marked. Among the people of the interior, living a predominantly pastoral life and preoccupied with the struggle to live, political excitements are largely tribal.

The Somali's way of life is dictated by the conditions in which he lives. Grazing is sparse and water scanty. Agriculture can only be pursued in a few areas. In the main the Somali is dependent on his camels, goats and sheep. He is therefore essentially a nomad, always moving with his flocks to make the best of the available water and grazing. The nomadic cycle may also be affected by disease, tribal war, natural barriers and several other circumstances, but the factors of grass and water are the dominant ones.

Not all Somali remain for ever in Somaliland. There are many in Aden, where they work as labourers, and in East Africa, where they are cattle traders. There are colonies of them in several ports in the British Isles and Somali sailors are to be found all over the world. They are a tough, enduring race, true sons of the hard, harsh land that breeds them.

Europeans, by controlling disease on the one hand and by repressing tribal war on the other, have destroyed the precarious balance between the human and animal populations and the natural resources. Men and animals have increased in numbers, with no corresponding increase in grazing and water. Thus the country is now overgrazed with the consequent evil of erosion which must get worse. The only remedy seems to be drastic stock reduction and stringent control of grazing. It would be an optimist indeed who would prophesy that either of these two measures may be effectively introduced in the near future.

The Future

The Somali have one asset denied to many African people who have achieved independence, or hope to achieve it in the next few years. In spite of deep domestic and internal divisions, there is among them a certain unity derived from a sense of nationality, a sort of 'Somali-dom', and a common strong religious faith. How far this form of national consciousness will serve to ensure the loyalty of the people of the interior to a government which will certainly at the outset be dominated by the young intelligentsia of the coastal towns remains to be seen. But at least it should cause all Somali to unite against attempts by other nations to step in now that the former European governments have withdrawn.

The greatest handicap of this newly emergent country will be poverty. Unless oil should be found, there are no resources upon which a viable modern state may be built. Having acquired political independence, Somaliland will still be economically dependent on external aid, and most amicable arrangements have been reached with the British, American and Italian Governments. It would be satisfactory if these arrangements were to continue for as long as the economy of the new Republic requires them. Help of a more political kind is readily available from Egypt, who has shown much interest in the area; an equally undisguised interest has been shown by Russia. It is to be hoped that the Somali will choose their benefactors wisely.

ETHIOPIA

Modern Ethiopia is a mountainous massif separating the Nile basin from the Horn of Africa, with lower plateaux falling away to the plains of Somaliland and the Northern Frontier District of Kenya. The mountains are of volcanic origin and the highest is above 15,000 feet, while the tableland is scored by deep valleys and chasms. The Rift Valley divides the plateau of Ethiopia proper from the eastern plateau of the Somali and the Galla and forms a trough which is occupied by a chain of lakes down to Lake Rudolf and then runs on into East Africa. The capital of Ethiopia is Addis Ababa, lying at 8,000 feet above sea-level in the heart of the highlands.

The massif of Ethiopia falls into three zones.[1] The first is the *Quolla*, which extends to an altitude of 5,000 to 6,000 feet and comprises the lower slopes and the valley bottoms. Next is the *Woyna Dega* ('highlands of the vine') an intermediate zone up to about 8,000 feet and the most densely populated of all. The highest zone is the *Dega*, open grass highlands extending from 8,000 to

---

[1] The authorities vary as to the altitudes of the zones. Those quoted here are from Beaver & Stamp, *Africa*, pp. 184–5.

13,000 or 14,000 feet. Temperatures vary according to altitude, but speaking generally the Ethiopian massif is the coolest area in north-east Africa although the deep valleys are very hot. The country south-east of the Rift has a somewhat similar climate but is rather hotter, while the low interior plateau bordering on the Somali littoral is very hot and dry indeed.

Most of the rivers of the massif flow westwards into the great tributaries of the Nile. Of these the most important is the Blue Nile, which has a natural reservoir, Lake Tana, in the heart of the Ethiopian mountains. The most important eastward-flowing river is the Hawash.

History

Some time towards the beginning of the first millennium B.C., Semites from southern Arabia, offshoots of the Sabaean civilization which flourished there before Islam, crossed the Red Sea and proceeded to colonize parts of the Horn of Africa. The people whom they found there were Eastern Hamites who were already in full occupation, having driven their Negro predecessors out to the western confines of modern Ethiopia. The Sabaeans established themselves on the plateau and there perpetuated the superior civilization that they had brought with them from Arabia, thus profoundly influencing the culture and language of the local Hamites with whom they mingled. The fruit of Semitic colonization was the kingdom of Aksum in northern Ethiopia, which reached the zenith of its power and achievement in the fourth century A.D.

In order to remove ambiguities of nomenclature it must here be said that Ethiopia was originally the name bestowed by the Greeks on the vast unknown country south of Egypt, the land of Cush of the Ancient Egyptians and later the Roman Nubia. It was only later that it was applied to Aksum and then to the rest of the plateau, being officially adopted as the name of the whole empire in 1941. The alternative 'Abyssinia' is derived from Habashat, an Arab tribe which lived on the opposite coast of the Red Sea.

Christianity came to Ethiopia in the fourth century and by the seventh the Bible had been translated into Ethiopic or Ge'ez, a Semitic language akin to Hebrew and Arabic but more closely related to Sabaean.[1] Ge'ez ceased to be commonly spoken centuries ago and has only survived as the literary and liturgical language.

[1] The name comes from Agaziyan, like the Habashat an Arab tribe living on the Red Sea coast opposite Ethiopia.

Ethiopian Christianity is monophysite (acknowledging only one nature in the person of Christ) and is closely connected with the Coptic church in Egypt.

From about the eighth century the rising tide of Islam cut Ethiopia off from the outside world, leaving it as a Christian island in a Moslem sea. The glory of Aksum faded and the focus of political power shifted to the south, to Amhara, Lasta and finally Shoa. Semitic language and culture were carried to the central and southern parts of the Ethiopian plateau, and while Islamization of the lowlands proceeded apace, Christianity spread in the highlands. Although Greeks from Egypt had traded down the Red Sea coast in the days of the Ptolemies and Greek influence had spread inland to Aksum, the first western Europeans to reach this remote and mysterious country were the Portuguese, attracted by tales of the fabulous Christian monarch Prester John. They rendered notable service in helping the Ethiopians to repel the Moslems who invaded the country in the sixteenth century, but attempts by Jesuit missionaries to convert Ethiopians to the Roman faith ended in failure. Hardly were the Moslems repelled than a new danger arose, threatening Moslem and Christian alike, and which neither, weakened by war, was in a state to resist. This was the invasion of the country by the Galla, who overran the southern and eastern parts of the plateau, leaving to the Ethiopians only the northern highlands, the area of the old kingdom of Aksum. There followed a period of great confusion. The nominal ruler of the country, while retaining his ancient title of *Negusa nagast*, king of kings, had little real power over largely independent local chieftains. Indeed the period from 1769 to 1855 is called by Ethiopians *mafasent* ('Judges') for it was like the era of the Old Testament when 'there was no king in Israel: every man did that which was right in his own eyes'.[1] European visitors to Ethiopia from the end of the seventeenth century onwards included the French physician Poncet (1699), James Bruce (1769–72), the mission of Lord Valencia and Henry Salt (1805), and later Henry Salt alone (1809), and the French brothers d'Abbadie (1838–48) who collected a great deal of material in various fields of study. In 1854 Richard Burton made his difficult and dangerous journey to Harar.

In 1855 a petty nobleman named Kassa seized power and was crowned king of kings under the name of Theodore. He was very able and in a short time united the country, suppressed the turbulent

[1] Ullendorff, *The Ethiopians*, p. 82.

nobles, revived the spirit of the people and renewed their religious fervour and patriotism. Unhappily his ability and intelligence were allied to a violence of character bordering on madness and this eventually alienated his people and contributed powerfully to his downfall. In 1864, for reasons largely dictated by his own neurotic suspicions, he threw into prison not only a British party including the consul, but also the envoys sent to procure the captives' release. More conciliatory means failing, a British army under Sir Robert Napier was sent to free the prisoners. Theodore's town of Magdala was stormed and taken on 13 April 1868 and the Negus committed suicide, having earlier released the British captives.

After four years of civil war a northern nobleman also named Kassa had himself crowned *Negusa nagast* under the name of John, his accession marking the return of the crown to the home of the kingdom of Aksum. John was a fanatically devout son of the church and a good warrior who crushed two Egyptian attempts to invade the country and then fell in action in 1889 against the Mahdists of the Sudan. He was succeeded by Menelik, king of Shoa, who found himself confronted by a threat far more dangerous than that of the Egyptians or the Mahdists. In 1882 the Italians obtained a foothold in Assab and began to spread inland. They were soon busy consolidating themselves in Eritrea and by 1890 were well established round Asmara in the most northerly part of the Ethiopian plateau. One of Menelik's first actions on becoming emperor was to negotiate the treaty of Uchali with the Italians, but this was regarded by the latter as giving them the right to control Ethiopian foreign policy, an interpretation with which Menelik naturally could not agree. In 1895 the Italians advanced into Ethiopia and occupied Adwa.[1] In the next year Menelik fell upon them with a great army and routed them, inflicting heavy losses. Nevertheless, in the peace treaty that was then concluded, Eritrea remained in Italian hands.

The victory of Adwa caused the powers of Europe to take serious notice of Menelik, and several of them sent diplomatic representatives to Ethiopia. Menelik, free from external threats, now resumed the process which he had begun before his accession, that of absorbing the Galla country into his empire. He died in 1913, to be followed by a regency and then by Lej Yasu, an unsatisfactory young man who was deposed by the great nobles in 1916. Zauditu,

[1] Also spelt Adowa, Aduwa, Adua. The spelling adopted here is that used by Ullendorff in *The Ethiopians*.

daughter of Menelik, was then proclaimed empress, and Ras Tafari, son of Menelik's cousin Makonnen, was made regent and heir to the throne. War followed when Lej Yasu's father raised an army to help his son. The revolt was defeated and Lej Yasu, who was not captured until 1921, died a prisoner in chains in 1935. In 1928 Ras Tafari assumed the title of Negus and in 1930, on the death of Zauditu, he was crowned as the Emperor Hailé Selassié. He had already given evidence of his diplomatic skill when in 1923 he nego-tiated the admission of Ethiopia to the League of Nations. In 1936 an incident at the obscure frontier village of Wal Wal led to war with Italy and the conquest of Ethiopia by the Italians. Hailé Selassié fled into exile first in Palestine, then in England, but was restored to his throne in 1941 on the liberation of Ethiopia by British imperial forces.

The People

Apart from the Negroes who occupy the southern and western borderlands, the population of Ethiopia is basically Hamitic and may be divided into two groups. First the Ethiopians proper, Coptic Christians who live on the central highlands plateau, strongly semiticized by ancient admixtures from Arabia and speaking a Semitic language. Secondly, Hamites comparatively free from Semitic influence, mainly Moslem by religion, the majority speak-ing Hamitic languages, who live in the much larger area below the central plateau. That is a much simplified picture of a highly com-plicated situation. Neither group is pure and each has absorbed so much alien blood from the other, or from the Negroes, as to make clearcut definitions misleading. One interesting community which fits into none of these groups is that of the Falasha, formerly thought to be black Jews, but whom Ullendorff believes are descended from those elements in the kingdom of Aksum who resisted conversion to Christianity.[1] No census has ever been taken in Ethiopia and population estimates range from ten to eighteen million. The true figure may lie between the two extremes.

The official language of Ethiopia is Amharic from the province of Amhara, which has for centuries been the language of the court and of most of the people of the central highlands. It represents the southern development of Ge'ez, so strongly influenced by Hamitic elements as to cause some people to deny that it is Semitic at all.[2]

[1] Ullendorff, The Ethiopians, p. 111.
[2] Werner, Language Families of Africa, p. 133.

The language most nearly akin to Ge'ez is Tigrinya, spoken in the country corresponding to the kingdom of Aksum. Tigré is a form of Tigrinya spoken in the northern lowlands. Almost all Tigré speakers are Moslems.[1]

Christianity is the principal source and inspiration of Ethiopian literature. Apart from devotional works, which are often translations from Arabic or Greek, historiography is the principal branch of the older literature. There are a number of medieval chronicles and also historical romances, of which the best known is the *Kebra Nagast* ('Glory of the kings'). This patriotic compilation includes the legend of the Queen of Sheba, how she visited Solomon and bore him a son Menelik, founder of the royal line of Ethiopia. The use of Amharic instead of Ge'ez as the language of literature received a strong impulse from the Emperor Theodore, and a great number of books in that language have been produced in recent years.

Ethiopian art is expressed in painting and in ornamental writing. As in literature, the inspiration is religious. The style is influenced by several *genres*, of which the Byzantine is the strongest. Architecture is primarily ecclesiastic. The most remarkable examples, though they are by no means typical, are the rock-hewn churches of Lalibala.

Economy

The Ethiopian massif is on the whole a well-favoured land for agriculture and produces a wide variety of crops. The principal cultivated product of the *Quolla* is coffee, and there are also great forests of wild coffee in this zone. The rich valley bottoms grow rice, cotton, and sugar cane and there are also rubber trees, bananas and other kinds of tropical flora. The *Woyna Dega* is the most productive of the three zones. The soil is fertile and there are good pasture lands. Cereals, the vine, the olive and tobacco are among the products of this zone, and horses, cattle, donkeys, mules and sheep are reared in great numbers. The *Dega* tends in places to be rather bleak and barren but it is good country for livestock, and temperate cereals are grown up to 12,000 feet. The lowlands surrounding the massif suffer from poor rainfall and thin soils and remain therefore a pastoral region with hardy fat-tailed sheep as the chief product.

[1] Ullendorff illustrates the relationship of these languages by supposing that Ge'ez corresponds to Latin. In which case Tigrinya would correspond to Italian, Tigré to Spanish and Amharic to French.

Little is known about the minerals of Ethiopia. There is aluminium, some platinum though how much is uncertain, and there is also some gold and copper.

Coffee accounts for over half the exports of the country (1959). It has a high reputation and is akin to the 'Mocha' coffee of Arabia. Other exports are hides and skins, food grains and flour, oil seeds and vegetable oil.

The only railway, that from Addis Ababa to French Somaliland, is French-owned and French-controlled. One effect of the Italian occupation was vastly to improve the roads.

Modern problems

Since his restoration the Emperor Hailé Selassié has bent all his energies to the advancement of his backward country. He has set himself a programme of constitutional reconstruction and social reform which is designed to transform the empire into a properly organized modern state. His rule is intensely personal and for lack of trained Ethiopians he has been compelled to do an enormous amount of work himself. Considerable progress has, it seems, already been made[1] but in spite of a reasonably sound economy and considerable international help the difficulties arising from the nature of the country and its people and the tragic circumstances of the Italian invasion and occupation are such as to daunt the stoutest heart. But the Emperor is single-minded and brave and there is none who will not wish him well in his great undertaking.[2]

ERITREA

Eritrea is a triangle with its hypotenuse a strip of Red Sea coast running north-west for about 670 miles from French Somaliland to the Sudan. The northern part of the territory is simply an extension of the Ethiopian plateau which falls away on the west to the Sudan plain and on the east to the coastal plain of the Red Sea. This plain runs the whole length of the territory and varies in width from ten to fifty miles except at the Gulf of Zula where the hills reach nearly to the sea. South of these hills there is a very dry and torrid

[1] Ullendorff, visiting Ethiopia in 1958, was astonished at the progress that had been achieved since the war (*The Ethiopians*, p. 193).

[2] Very soon after this was written there was a military *coup* in Ethiopia which was designed to remove the Emperor and ostensibly to replace him by the Crown Prince (the latter was in fact innocent of the conspiracy). The Emperor, who was abroad at the time, returned immediately and had no difficulty in suppressing the rising. The great majority of the army and all the people remained steadfastly loyal to him.

zone of lava fields and extinct volcanoes. This is part of the country of the Danakil, of whom many also live in Ethiopia and French Somaliland. The total area of Eritrea is about 45,000 square miles and the population something over one million. About half the population are Coptic Ethiopians and most of the remainder Eastern Hamites predominantly Moslem by religion. In addition to Copts and Moslems there are also some Catholic and Protestant Christians and a number of pagans.

History

Modern Eritrea is an artificial unit formed by the Italians during the Scramble for Africa and retained by them after their defeat by the Emperor Menelik at Adwa. The Christian, Tigrinya-speaking interior highlands are by religion, culture and history Ethiopian and until the arrival of the Italians were part of the empire of Ethiopia. They also constitute the most fertile and populous part of Eritrea. The Ethiopian connection with the plains is much more tenuous and it is doubtful whether the Negus ever exercised any continuous or effective authority over the vast Moslem lowlands. Indeed Ethiopia for many centuries had great difficulty in maintaining her maritime outlets, and was only able to do so by uneasy arrangements with the coastal Moslems.[1] Such unity as there ever was between highlands and lowlands was created by the Italians when they fused the two into one colony, at the same time separating the whole from Ethiopia. The Italian administration was on the whole sympathetic and efficient, but came to an end in 1941 when the colony was captured by the British and governed for some years by a British military administration which managed very well under difficulties. In 1952, by a decision of the United Nations, Eritrea was federated as an autonomous unit under the sovereignty of the Ethiopian Crown.

Economy

The influence of land surface and climatic conditions has largely determined the choice of the inhabitants between an agricultural and a pastoral life. Thus the people of the reasonably well-watered and fertile highlands are settled village-dwellers and agriculturalists. Their principal crops are cereals of various sorts, peas, beans, oil seeds, flax and sisal, onions and pimento. The people of the more arid lowlands are nomadic or semi-nomadic pastoralists, raising

[1] Perham, *The Government of Ethiopia*, p. 436.

sheep, cattle, goats, donkeys and a few camels. Altogether the economic picture is not an impressive one. Neither the agriculturalists nor the pastoralists rise much above subsistence level. The only important exportable asset is the dom-nut, which gives the hard 'vegetable ivory' used for buttons. Minerals in substantial quantities have not yet been discovered. On the other hand the Italians endowed their colony with several splendid modern towns, superb roads, an adequate railway, and a cable-way for the transport of goods between the port of Massawa and the capital Asmara which is the longest in the world.

It is doubtful whether the decision of the United Nations to associate the whole of Eritrea with Ethiopia was just or wise. The affinities of the Moslems who make up half the population are not with the Christian Ethiopians of the highlands but with their own co-religionists in the Nile Valley. Although it is not within the scope of this book to suggest how things might have been better done, one may at least be permitted to express the wish that current inclinations and ancient ties had not been so clearly ignored when the unifying power of the Europeans was withdrawn.

CHAPTER FIVE

THE NILE VALLEY[1]

MEASURED from its most remote source, the Kagera River, a feeder of Lake Victoria which rises in Urundi, the Nile has a length of more than 4,000 miles and is thus the longest river in the world. Leaving Lake Victoria by the Owen Falls near Jinja in Uganda it passes through Lake Kioga, is reinforced by the waters that drain Lake Albert, and then flows northwards into the Sudan across an almost level plain, its course at first much impeded by floating vegetation called 'sudd'. In Lake No it is joined by the Bahr el Ghazal, which is also choked by sudd, and then by the Sobat, a much more tumultuous river which brings down the waters of south-western Ethiopia. During the earliest stage of its journey it is called the Bahr el Jebel. After meeting the Bahr el Ghazal it becomes the White Nile until it reaches Khartoum, where it receives its most important eastern tributary, the Blue Nile. Thereafter it is simply called Nile for the remainder of its course. Two hundred miles below Khartoum the Atbara River flows in, like the Blue Nile from Ethiopia. For the rest of its journey, that is from the Atbara confluence to the sea, a distance of about 1,700 miles, the great river receives no other tributaries and practically no rainfall. Between Khartoum and Aswan there are six so-called cataracts, each a series of rapids representing a descent of the river to a lower level. The Nile enters Egypt a little to the north of the second cataract, which is above Wadi Halfa.

From the air the Nile and the belt of cultivation on either side of it appear like a thin silver-green thread running through an interminable desert on either side. Although the total area of Egypt is nearly 400,000 square miles, the settled and cultivated part is comparatively tiny, being little more than a band seven hundred miles long and only ten to fifteen miles wide along the banks of the Nile. In the Delta the inhabitable area becomes broader, but it is still small. The basic condition for cultivation and settlement is the

---

[1] In this chapter the name 'Sudan' denotes only the Republic of the Sudan, formerly a condominium of Egypt and Great Britain and called the Anglo-Egyptian Sudan.

seasonal flooding of the Nile between July and December. This phenomenon is due largely to the Blue Nile; for whereas the White Nile at Khartoum is a river of almost constant volume, the Blue Nile, rising in the mountains of Ethiopia, is periodically swollen by monsoon rains and melting snow. During the low water season the slower, steadier White Nile contributes 80 per cent of the water available to Egypt, but during the flood season nearly 70 per cent of the water comes from the Blue Nile and 17 per cent from the Atbara. The floods bring down enormous quantities of silt from the mountains of Ethiopia, thus providing the people of the lower Nile Valley with a rich alluvial soil annually renewed. So the Nile waters have created from what would otherwise be a desert a prosperous country and the mother of a very ancient civilization. (*Plate* 37)

Egypt, like North Africa, has her back to continental Africa, and except for her excursions into the Sudan and towards Ethiopia, has been until recently almost exclusively associated with the Mediterranean and with Asia. The population, which numbers between 24 and 25 million, is basically Hamitic, and the peasantry has kept the original strain remarkably pure. The urban middle and upper classes, however, are exceedingly mixed and include many foreign elements. In addition to the settled peasantry and town-dwellers, there are nomadic Arabs in the deserts bordering on the riverine strip.

The greater part of the population is Moslem and Egypt occupies a key position in the Moslem world, forming, as it were, a bridge between eastern and western Islam. The University of Al Azhar in Cairo, home of a great body of Islamic scholarship, enjoys great prestige and influence. The Copts, who number something over one million, are the most important non-Moslem community, being members of one of the oldest Christian churches in the world, descendants of those Egyptians who became Christians in the fourth century. Their head is the Coptic patriarch of Alexandria, and they are especially numerous round Assyut in Middle Egypt, and in the famous oasis of Faiyum.

The Sudan has an area of a million square miles and a population of about 11 million people. It stretches from Uganda and the Congo in the south to Egypt in the north, and is flanked on the east by Ethiopia and the Red Sea and on the west by the countries making up former French Equatorial Africa. It consists of a succession of belts of country running from east to west, starting in the north with the desert that borders on Egypt, progressing southwards to a band of grassy steppe which merges into savannah, and ending in the great marshy basin of the south. The people are exceedingly varied in origin though, as will be seen below, their cultural divisions are simpler. In the north, predominantly Berberine or Nubian peoples live along the river banks and follow a way of life not unlike that of the Egyptians. The desert supports nomadic Arabs in the west and nomadic Hamites, the Beja or 'Fuzzy-wuzzies', in the east. In the steppe and savannah belts there is a diverse population of nomadic Arabs, sedentary people of mixed Arab and Negro blood, and numbers of Nilotes of different tribes. Finally the deep south is the home of the great Nilotic tribes such as the Shilluk, Dinka and Nuer, and some other tribes of non-Nilotic origin.

Broadly speaking the Sudan may be divided into two great zones, the North and the South, one very different from the other but each having certain characteristics that give it some sort of homogeneity. The North, with a population of about eight million, is Moslem, Arabic-speaking, somewhat under Egyptian cultural if not political influence. The people of the few large urban agglomerations and of the Nile bank villages are advanced, vocal and very politically minded. In contrast the South, with about three million people, is primitive, pagan where it has not been christianized, with political organizations at present spreading little further than the tribe, and speaking tribal languages. In order to advance their claim to control the Sudan, Egyptians in the past often used the phrase 'Unity of the Nile Valley'. Like many such slogans, this is somewhat misleading. Although Egypt and the Sudan have a common interest in the waters of the Nile and are bound by old cultural and religious ties, the points of difference are also strong, and must not be overlooked in any appraisal of the relations between the two countries.

History

When we last looked at the history of the Sudan it was as witnesses of Gordon's death at Khartoum and the subjection of the Sudanese to yet another régime of oppression.[1] In 1896 the British Government resolved on reoccupation. There were several motives for this decision: one was to free the Sudanese from the tyranny of the Khalifa Abdulla and to extirpate the Slave Trade; another was to put an end to provocative attacks by the Khalifa's bands on the southern frontiers of Egypt; a third to anticipate other nations,

[1] p. 50.

especially the French, who were casting eyes on the Sudan. National pride also no doubt played some part in the decision. The British public had felt very keenly the disgrace of Gordon's death, and it had always been assumed that the shame of 1885 would one day be avenged.

The invasion of the Sudan fell into two phases. The first was a brisk and inexpensive operation which led to the capture of Dongola. The British commander, Sir Herbert Kitchener, then succeeded in persuading the British Government to authorize a further advance in order that the power of the Khalifa might be destroyed entirely. This proved to be a far more difficult campaign than the first and involved immense problems of supply and transport which were, however, all successfully solved in the end. On 2 September 1898 the Khalifa's army was totally defeated at the battle of Omdurman opposite Khartoum, and the Khalifa himself was killed in a last battle in Kordofan on 24 November. Charging with the Lancers at Omdurman was the young Winston Churchill. By an agreement signed in 1899 the Sudan became a condominium of Great Britain and Egypt. Although the joint sovereignty of Egypt was specifically recognized, in fact she became no more than a sleeping partner. The intention of the agreement was obviously to ensure the predominance of Great Britain in the best interests of everyone concerned. In effect Great Britain assumed a trusteeship of the Sudan, with the result that after many generations of misgovernment and anarchy that country at last received a just and stable administration.[1]

We left Baring in Egypt,[2] where he and a handful of able British administrators between 1890 and 1896 performed the miracle of transforming a backward, oppressed and bankrupt country into a viable modern state. Finance was put on a firm footing, social services were established, the local administration was made reasonably honest and the army was reformed. All these measures were taken ostensibly in the name of the Khedive,[3] for although Egypt was at this time virtually a protectorate of Great Britain, she was still in theory part of the Turkish Empire. When Turkey joined the enemies of Great Britain in the 1914–18 war, the British position became anomalous. Moreover the Khedive, Abbas Hilmi,

[1] At the time of the agreement and for some time after, Egypt had no civil service able to fill the higher posts of government.

[2] p. 49.

[3] Title of the Viceroy of Egypt, accorded to Ismail Pasha by the Turkish Government in 1867.

was openly on the Turkish side. The pretence of Turkish sovereignty was therefore abolished, Egypt was formally declared a British protectorate, and the Khedive was deposed, being replaced by his uncle, Husain Kamil, with the title of Sultan of Egypt. The Egyptian Government threw itself quite wholeheartedly into the war on the British side, and the people bore with patience the disadvantages and hardships that a state of war entailed.

Meanwhile the position of Egypt as a Mediterranean crossroads had tended to make Egyptians very conscious of their position of subordination. Thus it came about that in spite of the undoubted advantages brought by the British, especially to the peasants, Egyptian nationalism, which in the form of impatience of foreign control had existed since the earliest days of the occupation, began to make itself increasingly felt. Stimulated by Turkish intrigues, Moslem religious fervour and an inflammatory press, it had created much anti-European feeling among the masses well before the war. In 1918, under the leadership of Saad Zaghlul Pasha, it became vociferously insistent in its demands for Egyptian independence. Zaghlul was tactlessly treated by the British Government in London, inconclusive negotiations did nothing to allay popular discontent, there were widespread disorders, Zaghlul and a number of his associates were deported, until finally, in 1921, the British Government unilaterally terminated the Protectorate, reserving for itself however security of communications, defence, protection of foreigners and minorities, and the Sudan. At the same time Sultan Fuad, who had succeeded Husain Kamil, was proclaimed King and became a hereditary ruler, parliamentary government was established, and Saad Zaghlul returned from exile, soon to become prime minister. He lost no time in opening a campaign for the complete withdrawal of the British and for the incorporation of the Sudan in Egypt. To these demands the attitude of the British was clear. They were ready to give way on matters affecting domestic and internal affairs, but they insisted on their need to guard the Suez Canal, and they would not compromise on the Sudan. Matters were therefore at a deadlock when Zaghlul died in 1924, to be succeeded as leader of his party, the Wafd, by Mustafa Nahas Pasha. A tragic manifestation of nationalist feeling was the murder in the same year in the streets of Cairo of Sir Lee Stack, Commander in Chief and Governor-General of the Sudan. Attempts in 1927 and again in 1930 to conclude a treaty between Great Britain and Egypt came to nothing, but in 1936 agreement was finally reached and a treaty was signed which provided for co-operation in time of war and the gradual withdrawal of British troops. The treaty was to have a duration of twenty years and it avoided the question of the Sudan. The British High Commissioner was withdrawn from Egypt and the two countries exchanged ambassadors. In 1937, at the instance of Great Britain, Egypt became a member of the League of Nations, and in the same year was helped by Britain to get rid of the 'capitulations', the system of extra-territorial jurisdiction which had survived from the days of dependence.

During the 1939–45 war Egypt faithfully honoured her treaty obligations and was an indispensable base for Allied operations in the Middle East. After the Yalta Conference she herself declared war on the Axis. When the war in Europe came to an end the demand for the evacuation of British troops became violently insistent and to this was added a clamour for the transfer of the Sudan to Egypt. The British Government agreed, perhaps rather tardily, to withdraw troops and evacuation to the Canal Zone began in due course; but on the question of the Sudan they remained adamant, being strengthened in this determination by the preparations that were then being made for the Sudanese to become self-governing and hence eligible to decide the matter for themselves.

On the night of 14–15 May 1948, simultaneously with the termination of the British mandate for Palestine, Egyptian forces entered Palestine, allegedly to restore order and to put an end to 'massacres perpetrated by terrorist Zionist gangs'. Whatever the reasons, the intervention was unsuccessful and the Egyptians had the worst of some rather desultory fighting before an armistice was patched up in the following year.

The internal situation was far from peaceful. The Palace and successive governments were frequently at loggerheads, and there was much popular discontent, which the government usually sought to divert from itself by parading Anglo-Egyptian differences. The ill-success of Egyptian arms in the Palestine campaign and political setbacks in the Sudan supplied material with which the Moslem Brotherhood, a religious, nationalist and terrorist organization under Sheikh Hasan el Banna, used to attack the weakness and corruption of the government. The Prime Minister, Nokrashy Pasha, was assassinated by a member of the Brotherhood at the end of 1948 and two months later Sheikh Hasan el Banna was himself assassinated. Thereafter a series of crises ended in 1952 in a military *coup d'état*, the establishment of a government headed by General

Mohamed Neguib, the enforced abdication of King Farouk who was succeeded by an infant son, and in 1953 in the declaration of Egypt as a republic. The new régime aimed at the eradication of corruption, the abolition of feudalism, land reform, a better distribution of wealth and an improvement in the standard of living of the masses. In 1954 another *coup* removed General Neguib, and his chief lieutenant, Colonel Gamal Abdul Nasser, became president and virtual dictator of Egypt. Whether Nasser will succeed in his ambitious social aims it is too early yet to tell. He has met with considerable opposition on various fronts. The Moslem Brotherhood, now suppressed, tried to assassinate him, and the old landed aristocracy, whose wealth and privileges it is his intention to curtail for the benefit of the poorer classes, can hardly welcome this threat to their position. Moreover the problem of Egyptian poverty is at best an intractable one. But whatever his success in domestic matters there is no doubt of his impact on the international scene. Nasser's role in world affairs is not within the scope of this book but one aspect of his policy is strictly relevant and should be noted: he not only proposes for Egypt a leading place in the world of Islam but he also exhibits a very close interest in the affairs of black Africa. We must therefore expect that under his leadership the cultural, commercial and political contacts of Egypt, which hitherto have been European and Asian rather than African, will tend to become increasingly continental.

The history of the Sudan in the fifty years or so of British administration was an altogether quieter affair than that of Egypt. A few outbreaks among the tribes, occasional disorders in the army and among the townspeople sometimes fomented by Egypt, such were the only interruptions in a steady advance. The Sudanese gave splendid service in the Second World War and when this ended preparations for self-government were pressed forward. The favourable factors here were the high standards of the British administration, improving economic conditions, and the growth of a substantial body of educated Sudanese, many of them the product of the Gordon Memorial College founded by Kitchener in 1902. Obstacles were Egyptian pretensions, some disunity among Sudanese political and religious leaders, and genuine fear bred of ancient memories among the pagan southern Sudanese that they would be maltreated by the Moslem northerners when British protection was withdrawn. After the most careful possible arrangements had been made for parliamentary government on democratic lines, the British withdrew and the new Sudanese government decided to become an independent republic. The elaborate constitution so painstakingly devised did not last long. In 1958 increasing frustration at the lack of a clear policy led a group of army officers to take over the government, and this group has remained in power ever since.

Economy

Egypt is essentially an agricultural country and agriculture in Egypt depends on irrigation from the waters of the Nile. There are three methods of irrigation in use. The first and simplest consists of raising the water directly from the river or canal either by *shaduf*, a lever with a bucket at one end and a weight at the other; or by a wheel with buckets slung round it, worked by a buffalo or a camel; or again by a kind of Archimedes screw worked by manpower. These archaic yet effective methods are still used when the water is too low for flow irrigation, but many people now use modern pumps.

Basin irrigation is also very ancient. In this method cuts are made in the river bank so that at time of flood the rising water flows out on to the neighbouring fields which are arranged in a series of basins separated by embankments. The water remains on the land for several weeks, deposits its silt, and then runs back into the falling river, whereupon seed is planted in the muddy basins.

Basin irrigation, though an improvement on older methods, still only allowed one crop a year. The next step was perennial irrigation. This is effected first by barrages which enable the water at time of flood to flow off into high level canals; secondly by reservoirs for storing water for release during the period when the Nile is low. By these means it is now possible to harvest two, or even three crops a year from the same plot of land. The best known of these reservoirs is the Aswan Dam, completed in 1903 and raised in height between 1907 and 1913. The Sennar Dam on the Blue Nile, a combined barrage and reservoir, irrigates the Gezira plain in the angle of the Blue and White Niles.[1] A third reservoir is that at Gebel Aulia on the White Nile. Several other projects are contemplated.[2] The best known and the most advanced is a high dam at Aswan, on a site $3\frac{1}{2}$ miles below the present dam. The new construction will create a reservoir 400 miles long, of which 150 miles will be in the

---

[1] p. 162.
[2] Suggate (*Africa*, pp. 147–9) gives a list of eight.

Sudan. The estimated cost of the project is immense but the benefits that Egypt may expect from it are commensurately great, including the conversion to perennial irrigation of all land still remaining under the basin system, the greatest possible increase of land under irrigation, and the creation of ample hydro-electric power.

Favoured though he is by a fertile soil and unlimited water, the Egyptian peasant has a hard struggle to live. He uses tools that are traditional and simple. His food crops are corn of different kinds, rice, vegetables, and clover for fodder. The commercial crop is pre-eminently cotton, which is easily the most important agricultural export. The chief reason for the peasant's grinding poverty is that his country is over-populated. The population of Egypt is perhaps 1,600 to the square mile, and it is increasing. In spite of periodic efforts to extend the area under irrigation, pressure on the land is great and individual holdings are therefore small. Colonel Nasser's proposed land reform, involving a re-distribution of the great estates, will no doubt relieve the situation considerably, and, as we have already noted, much is to be expected from various hydrological schemes when these are realized.

There is no serious livestock industry. The peasants raise great numbers of domestic fowls, sheep and goats, and they keep camels and buffaloes for draught purposes. Buffaloes also supply milk for making butter.

Minerals include oil (a developing industry), manganese, phosphates and lead. There are also known to be others which are not, however, exploited on any large scale.

Egypt has a growing industrial economy in which the production of cotton, linen, silk and leather goods, the manufacture of cement and fertilizers, and oil refining play leading parts. The rail and road system is adequate and the Nile navigable throughout its course in Egypt. Of the sea ports, Alexandria is now supreme, and Port Said and Suez have only a small share in the commerce of Egypt. As a great public enterprise the Suez Canal, recently nationalized by Colonel Nasser in the face of considerable international opposition, will no doubt make an important contribution to revenue.

The people of the Sudan have a more spacious if less complicated economy than the Egyptians. Between Wadi Halfa and Khartoum the villagers on the Nile banks practice irrigation and keep small stock. In the deserts on either side of them live camel-owning nomads. The central zone possesses vast grazing grounds and the people's wealth lies in camels and sheep in the northerly parts and cattle in the southerly. Close to the Nile there are mixed farmers who practise irrigation but also receive seasonal rains. The Nilotic tribes of the extreme south are also mixed farmers in the sense that they grow subsistence crops. But with some exceptions their chief interest lies in their cattle, which not only represent their wealth but are also invested with quasi-mystical attributes and play an enormously important part in the social and religious life of the individual and of the tribe.

The Sudan is the world's chief source of gum arabic, which is obtained from two different species of small acacia tree and is collected by the peasants as a supplementary source of revenue. The most important crop grown for export is cotton. A small quantity of American is grown in some places as a rain crop, but the emphasis is strongly on the Egyptian long staple type, grown on irrigated land. The greatest area of production is that of Gezira on the Blue Nile, previously a flat clay plain with a precarious rainfall on which the peasants kept some small stock and grew uncertain crops of millets. After a long period of experiment and on the completion of the Sennar Dam in 1925 this area was put under irrigation and the Gezira Scheme became a highly successful partnership between the government, who built the dam and maintained the canals, two commercial companies who managed the Scheme, and some thirty thousand Sudanese tenants who produced the cotton. Profits were divided between the three parties. In 1950 the companies' concessions expired and they were replaced by a public utility, the Sudan Gezira Board. The total area of the Scheme is now one million acres, of which one quarter is under cotton and one fifth under other crops. It is to be hoped that the republican government will foster the Scheme as assiduously as did the British, for it was of great benefit to the tenants, whose standard of living has been raised from poverty to a level that is high in comparison with that of other peasants in much of Africa and in most of the Middle East. Gezira methods have been applied to several other areas in the Sudan and have influenced a number of projects in other parts of Africa.   (*Plates* 59–60)

Reasonable communications in the northern Sudan make most places of importance fairly accessible. The main railway line runs from Wadi Halfa southwards to Khartoum, then up the Blue Nile to Sennar, with an extension to Roseires. The Red Sea port of Port Sudan is linked to the main line by two branches, one from

Sennar northwards through Kassala, the other crossing the desert eastwards from Atbara. There are two westerly projections: from Sennar the main line strikes westwards to el Obeid, and a 400-mile extension runs from er Rahad (43 miles short of el Obeid) to Nyala in the far west; in the north a line takes off north of Abu Hamed and runs to Karima below the fourth cataract. In the southern Sudan, with difficult terrain and a primitive economy, communications are poor except on the higher ground near the borders of Kenya and Uganda. The only permanent link between north and south apart from air transport is the river. The Nile provides a highway of 2,400 miles from the Egyptian frontier almost to Uganda in the far south. In the northern part navigation is interrupted by the cataracts, but south of Khartoum shallow draft steamers ply freely up and down the White Nile as far as Juba, whence road services operate to Uganda and the Congo.

Air services, internal and international, are well developed, and Khartoum is an important airport lying on the main air routes of Africa.

CHAPTER SIX

MEDITERRANEAN AFRICA

THIS region comprises all the countries along the North African coast, from the western border of Egypt to the Atlantic coast of Morocco, and the Sahara desert behind them. Mauritania and Spanish West Africa are also included, since they have far closer associations with North Africa than with anywhere else.

Morocco, Algeria and Tunisia, the three countries forming the great north-western quadrilateral of Africa, collectively named the Atlas lands for reasons that will shortly be made clear, were formerly known to Europeans as the Barbary States, and to Arab geographers as the Gezira al Maghreb, or Western Isle, because they were isolated by ocean, sea and desert. This isolation is more apparent to a land people like the Arabs than it is to others. To the seafarers of Asia Minor and Europe, North Africa offered no problem of isolation at all, and the Mediterranean has from the earliest times permitted travel from one shore to another of peoples, their cultures, their trade, their armies. From the historical and human stand-points, as well as the physical, north-western Africa is closely asso-ciated with southern Europe and has many claims to be regarded more as the southern shore of the Mediterranean than as part of the north coast of Africa.

Libya, which consists of the two ancient provinces of Tripoli-tania and Cyrenaica, lies east of the Atlas lands between Tunisia and Egypt. In antiquity it served as a road along the North African coast: Phoenician and Greek sailors used Libyan harbours; Greeks and Romans had settlements there. Like the rest of Mediterranean Africa, Libya has been subject to outside influences since very early times.

Mauritania was understood by the ancients to mean the north-western angle of the African continent, but the term was revived by the French in 1904 to describe that part of the Sahara lying between Morocco and the lower Senegal River with a front on the Atlantic between Cape Blanco and St. Louis.

Spanish West Africa consists of two geographically distinct sections. The northern section, Ifni, is a small enclave in the kingdom of Morocco. The southern section is Spanish Sahara which stretches for about 450 miles along the Atlantic coast south of Morocco to Cape Blanco.

The northern part of the region, that is all that part which lies between the Sahara and the Mediterranean sea, falls into two zones. Libya is largely an arid plateau of moderate altitude relieved only by occasional oases and the fertile well watered highlands of western Cyrenaica called by the Arabs Jebel Akhdar (Green Mountain). The overwhelming impression is one of great aridity and emptiness, of rocks and sand and stunted vegetation, of flatness and monotony. The 'Western Isle', on the other hand, is distinguished by a series of lofty mountain ranges known as the Atlas system, running more or less parallel to the coast from Morocco in the south-west to Tunisia in the north-east. These ranges are most extensive in Morocco, where the High (Great or Snowy) Atlas reaches a height of 14,000 feet. South of the High Atlas is the somewhat lower Anti-Atlas, while running eastwards to Tunisia are two other ranges, the Tell Atlas and the Saharan Atlas, the latter of course the more southerly. These rarely reach 6,000 feet and are separated by a high plateau diversified by saline depressions called *shotts*. A branch of the Tell Atlas named the Rif Mountains runs westwards along the coast to the Straits of Gibraltar.

The North African coastal plain is a more or less fertile belt running the whole length of the region from Morocco to Egypt. It varies considerably in breadth and in some places, for instance round the Gulf of Sirte in Libya, where the desert comes down to the sea, vanishes altogether. It is broadest in Morocco where great plains run right up to the mountains from the Atlantic coast. In Tripolitania a sandy steppe called the Jefara lies between the comparatively narrow settled strip of cultivation and the hills that rise to the Libyan plateau.

The Sahara

The Sahara is the world's greatest desert and occupies three million square miles, which is between a quarter and a third of the whole continent of Africa. Not all of this great expanse is desert in the usually accepted sense. There are considerable areas of scrub and steppe where some sort of vegetation just manages to exist, while on the indeterminate margins a poor grassland supports thin nomadic populations.

There are three kinds of surface. First the 'erg', sandy wastes composed largely of drifting dunes. The largest unrelieved area of 'erg' is probably the Libyan desert. The 'hamada' is stony desert with outcrops of bare rocks. The 'reg' or 'areg' is pebbly or gravelly desert. This is the type preferred by caravans since movement there is easier, and vegetation and subterranean water more abundant.

A high ridge widening to a plateau crosses the central Sahara from east-south-east to west-north-west. The most prominent features of this ridge are the mountain masses of Ahaggar and Tibesti, rising in places to 9,000 feet and 10,000 feet respectively. Much of the high ground is volcanic and many of the peaks are extinct volcanoes. The western side of the Sahara, which includes Mauritania, is flat and monotonous and only in one or two places does the altitude exceed 1,500 feet.

Oases occur when underground water is sufficiently near the surface to be reached by vegetation. This underground water can be tapped by wells, and is usually very fresh and pure in contrast to the brackish surface water when that can be found. An oasis is therefore a patch of vegetation in the desert based on a number of wells, usually supporting a settled population. The most important resource of the Saharan oases is the date palm, which flourishes under such conditions, but most inhabited oases have arable land that can be cultivated by the inhabitants. Many of the oases are considerable settlements, or groups of settlements, such as the Fezzan, Tuat and Kufra. Others, such as Jaghbub, are small and poor.

Finally, it goes without saying that the Sahara is in general extremely hot, and during the summer the southern interior districts may be the hottest places in the world. The temperature falls in winter and there is sometimes frost at night.

That man was able, before the days of the internal combustion engine, not only to live in the desert but to master it and to use it, was due to his possession of the camel. This unprepossessing but useful animal is believed to have been introduced into Egypt in the sixth century B.C. and camel transport was used by Alexander the Great on his expedition to Siwa. It was some time before the camel spread westwards into North Africa, but when it did the effect was revolutionary.[1] The adoption of camel transport by their armies enabled the Romans to subdue the hitherto recalcitrant southern tribes;[2] the camel played a large part in the conquest by Berbers and

[1] See Bovill, *The Golden Trade of the Moors*, pp. 41–43 *et passim*.
[2] p. 26.

Arabs of the northern Negro lands and in the founding of the empires of the Sudan;[1] finally it was the camel that made possible the great development of trans-Saharan trade between North and West Africa.[2]

The People

The general substratum of the Mediterranean African population, as we have already noted,[3] is Hamitic and belongs to that group of Northern Hamites called Berbers. Although they have to a surprising extent managed to keep their original stock pure, Berbers have adopted the religion and with it many of the customs of their Arab conquerors. The Berber element is overwhelmingly predominant in the far west and is still strong in the north-west, especially in the hills behind the coastal zone. Eastwards across Libya the Arab strain becomes stronger and civilization notably more Semitic. The people of Cyrenaica, for instance, are of pure Arab stock, descendants of the eleventh century invaders. In general the Berbers tend to be sedentary agriculturalists, whereas Arabs are nomad pastoralists. This contrast is reflected in the political organization of the two races. The Berbers, living in settled village communities, lean towards a democratic form of government based on popular assemblies. The Arabs, exposed to the hazards of desert life and needing strong leadership at times of emergency, tend to be under the despotic control of sheikhs. This pattern is not invariable: under favourable conditions Arabs can become town-dwellers and there are many Berbers who have been forced by their environment to adopt a nomadic way of life.

The dominant people of the Sahara are Moors in the west, Tuareg in the centre, and Tibu in the east. The word Moor comes from the Greek *mauros*, black, which may even be of Punic origin, and in ancient history was used to describe the natives of that comparatively restricted area named after them Mauritania. It later came to be applied generally to the people of north-west Africa of mixed Berber and Arab origin.[4] The Moors of modern Mauritania are properly Shanaqta and the Arabic name for their country is Shinqit.

The Tuareg are a tall, fair-skinned, slender people whose geographic centre is the Ahaggar plateau of the Sahara. Their best

[1] pp. 30–31.
[2] pp. 29–30.
[3] pp. 9, 24.
[4] It is a tricky word and is used in several other senses besides these.

known characteristic is that they wear a veil and hence are known as 'the people of the veil'. They speak a language called Tamahaqq and their alphabet, called Tifinagh, may be derived from the ancient Libyan script. Both the Moors and the Tuareg are Berbers, but many of the latter live in the southerly parts of the Sahara and have become changed in habits and appearance by contact with Negroes.

The Tibu are dark and speak a Sudanic language but are nevertheless not Negroes but probably an old Saharan race. Indeed they are stated to be the direct descendants of the ancient Garamantes who gave so much trouble to the Romans. The greater number now live in the Tibesti massif, from which they take their name, which means 'rock people', but they are also to be found scattered over a vast area of the eastern Sahara. Until ousted by the Senussi they occupied the oasis of Kufra. They were nominally converted to Islam in the eighteenth century but many still observe heathen rites.[1]

The Senussi who supplanted the Tibu at Kufra are members of one of the best known of those Islamic 'orders' which are an important part of North African politico-religious life.[2] The Senussi order was founded in 1843 by Sayyed Mohamed Ali el Senussi and spread very quickly, embracing all the Arab inhabitants of Cyrenaica and many people in the eastern parts of Tripolitania. Cyrenaica was soon dotted with the lodges (*zawiyat*) of the order, half-schools, half-seminaries, unifying the independent tribes of Cyrenaica under the founder and his successors.

Besides the Arabs and the Berbers there are other long-established communities in North Africa. A brief reference has already been made to the Jews. This community has various origins: immigration, traditionally dating as far back as the first diaspora; the conversion of Berber tribes in Roman times; the influx of Jewish refugees from Spain. The oddest Jewish settlement is the troglodytic village at Garian in the hills behind Tripoli. The dwellings consist of sunken shafts in the side of which rooms are excavated. There is an entrance tunnel with its mouth some way from the shaft. The bottom of the shaft is the farmyard and drainage pool. The advantages of this dwelling are that it is cheap,

---

[1] Seligman, *Races of Africa*, pp. 134-5. For Garamantes, see p. 26.

[2] The word 'order' is not strictly appropriate for the Senussi but it is not easy to think of a better one. The founder's aim was to lead people back to the original purity and spirituality of Islam. He did not purport to found a sect or cult but to point a 'way' (*tariq*).

defensible, and protected from heat and cold. The dwellers in these caves speak Arabic and are outwardly indistinguishable from their Arab and Berber neighbours, some of whom also live in caves.

The total population of the region is about 26 million, of whom over 80 per cent are equally divided between Morocco and Algeria.[1]

HISTORY

Mediterranean Africa under Turkish rule

In the flush of the reconquest of Spain the Spaniards and Portuguese carried the war into Africa and by the beginning of the sixteenth century had possessed themselves of a number of towns along the North African coast. The North African states replied by waging war at sea against any Christian nation that did not make special arrangements with them, usually involving payment of money. In Morocco the war was mainly carried on by Moslem refugees from Spain, some of whom at one time actually set up a veritable corsair republic at Rabat and Salé. The central and eastern states called on the Turks for help, and these, having expelled the Spaniards, established a Turkish régime with themselves as rulers in the three 'regencies' of Algiers, Tunisia and Tripolitania. The most powerful of the 'regencies' was Algiers, which became as it were the headquarters of the Barbary corsairs so dreaded by Christian seamen in the Mediterranean.

From the sixteenth to the nineteenth century Libya, Tunisia and Algeria remained part of the great Turkish Empire that stretched from Iraq to the eastern frontier of Morocco. At first governors were appointed who were directly responsible to Constantinople. Gradually all three regencies acquired a considerable degree of autonomy. Although the Sultan's suzerainty continued to be acknowledged, in fact his power became little more than nominal. Early in the eighteenth century the Karamanli family became hereditary and virtually independent rulers of Tripoli, the founder of the dynasty, Ahmed, having murdered all his rivals at a banquet.[2] At about the same time a Cretan Moslem, Husain Bey, founded the Husainid dynasty in Tunis. The first Turkish rulers in Algiers were the brothers Barbarossa, called in by the inhabitants to help them eject the Spaniards. The Barbarossa were

---

[1] Approximate figures are as follows: Morocco 10 million plus, Algeria 10 million plus, Tunisia 4 million, Libya 1 million plus, Mauritania and the Spanish territories ¾ million.

[2] The story was told to the author with much zest and a wealth of detail by a descendant of Ahmed at the very place where the massacre occurred.

followed by a succession of pashas, aghas and deys who took little
interest in the government of the interior and of whom many died
violent deaths. In Cyrenaica the Sultan's authority was not acknowledged until 1640 when Mohamed Sakesli, an able ruler in Tripoli,
appointed one of his men to be Bey of Benghazi.[1] The country
continued in a state of anarchy until the rise of the Senussi order
introduced some sense of unity and cohesiveness among the wild
Arab tribesmen. The Turks, however, frowned upon the Senussi,
and the founder's son, who had succeeded him as leader, withdrew
to the oasis of Kufra to avoid them. By that time all the Arabs of
Cyrenaica were adherents of the order.

The chief interest of the regencies was privateering, and this
pursuit was the main source of their revenue. As time wore on,
however, the scope of the corsairs was greatly curtailed by increased European naval construction and by the eighteenth century
privateering had declined considerably.

In 1801 the United States refused to pay to Yusuf Karamanli of
Tripoli, with whom they had negotiated a treaty, increased
'protection money' for the passage of their ships, whereupon Yusuf
declared war by cutting down the flag pole of the American con-
sulate. This war lasted until 1805 and is commemorated in the
famous marching song of the American Marines. Thereafter Yusuf's
activities became greatly restricted by growing European strength in
the Mediterranean, and he was compelled to abdicate in 1834.
The Turkish Government solved the question of succession by
carrying off the whole Karamanli family and appointing a governor
responsible to Constantinople.

European intervention

The immediate pretext for the French invasion of Algiers in
1830 was a blow from a flywhisk inflicted on the French consul by
the Dey but the major grievance was the Dey's threat to the con-
tinuance of the privileged trading position of the French. Behind
it there was also the need to bolster the uncertain régime of King
Charles X of France with a military success. During the next fifty
years French rule was extended over the whole of Algeria and in
1881 the French declared a protectorate over Tunisia. Turkish rule
survived in Libya until 1911 when war broke out between Turkey
and Italy. The Italians invaded Tripoli and landed troops at several

---

[1] Although *bey* and *dey* differ etymologically, they both mean 'governor' in this
context.

points along the coast. In 1912 the Sultan of Turkey renounced his sovereignty over Libya, granting to the Libyans 'full autonomy'. This did not mean very much, for by the beginning of the 1914–18 war the Italians had occupied the country.

European connections with Rio de Oro, the southern part of Spanish Sahara, go back to the fifteenth century, and it was the scene of some Portuguese activity in the early days. It was not however until 1884 that the Spanish Government formally staked a claim to a protectorate over a large area between Cape Bogador and Cape Blanco. Occupation of the remainder of this area, and of Ifni, was not accomplished until 1934.

In 1903 the emirs of Trarza and of Brakna north of the Senegal River in its lower course were persuaded to put their countries under the direct supervision of French officers. In the following year these areas were constituted as the territory of Mauritania which was later considerably expanded and became part of the Federation of French West Africa.

While the rest of north-west Africa fell first under Turkish and then under French domination, Morocco managed to retain its independence. The cities of Melilla and Ceuta had passed to Spain in the fifteenth and sixteenth centuries but the rest of the country was held together by occasional strong and energetic rulers who also contrived to ward off foreign intervention. When, as often happened, an able ruler was followed by weaker ones, the country fell into anarchy. A particular weakness was the difficulty of succession. The death of a ruler was almost always followed by fighting among his relations, with consequent confusion throughout the country. In the days of independence Morocco was a land of contrasts. There were splendid towns like Fez and Marrakesh, set in beautiful surroundings, with fine houses, mosques and markets, inhabited by dignified, cultured, hospitable people skilled in the art of living. On the other hand the government was despotic and often cruel, politics corrupt, and there were practically no public or social services. Morocco lay in a most important geographical and strategic position and at the beginning of the twentieth century was not surprisingly involved in a number of dangerous diplomatic crises. International rivalries ended in France being given a free hand to pacify and organize the country which she proceeded to do forthwith. In 1912 France and Spain divided Morocco between them, the French establishing a protectorate over the larger part, while a smaller zone in the north fell to Spain.

French and Italian rule—nationalism—present situation

In Algeria the French, and in Libya the Italians purposefully set out to create 'colonies of settlement'. The Italians, newly arrived in Libya, were driven back to the coast by local revolts during the 1914–18 war, and the Senussi of Cyrenaica, as allies of the Turks, attacked the British in Egypt. But with the end of the war, and especially with the rise of the Fascist régime, the Italians took forceful measures to crush opposition and by 1932, at the cost of much suffering on the part of the population, 'pacification' was complete. Numbers of Italian peasants were then imported from the overpopulated districts of Italy and planted both in Tripolitania and Cyrenaica under a scheme that envisaged ultimate large-scale peasant proprietorship. The Second World War broke out before the scheme could have a chance to prove itself.

During the debates that followed the war on the future of the Italian colonies, Libya was governed by two British military administrations, one in each province. Short of money and short of men, they nevertheless gave the country the best government it had had since the Romans. They withdrew in an atmosphere of goodwill at the end of 1951 when the independent United Kingdom of Libya came into being. The first and so far only king of the new state is Sayyed Mohamed Idris, head of the Senussi.

The French, smarting from their defeat by the Germans in 1871, sought to salve their wounded pride by vigorous overseas development, looking to Algeria to provide territorial compensation for the loss of Alsace-Lorraine. Colonization was planned on a massive scale and was assisted by wholesale expropriation of native lands. This process was not accomplished without considerable resistance on the part of the Algerians and there were several insurrections, all suppressed with the utmost rigour. Politically Algeria is a French possession and both northern Algeria and the Algerian Sahara rank as part of France. Algerian Moslems have served with great gallantry in the French Army and have shed their blood freely for France. Nevertheless Algeria is not a country in which there is equality between the races. The effect of colonization has been to create an Algerian people of European origin, about a million strong, who occupy a position of considerable power and privilege. Since General de Gaulle came to power the French Government has become decidedly more liberal towards Algerian Moslems, but events in recent years have sadly demonstrated how far the more reactionary Europeans, the so-called *Ultras*, are prepared to go to resist alteration and reform.

After a period of quiescence at the turn of the century nationalist resistance to the French was renewed about 1920 and has increased in intensity down the years. The last rising began in 1954 and has assumed the character of a long war between a comparatively small nationalist army supported by the mass of the population, and large French forces. The war has actually been carried into France, where Algerian Moslems have committed murder and sabotage. The French Government seems to be incapable of putting an end to this state of affairs, caught as it is between its own apparently liberal inclinations, the intransigence of Algerian Frenchmen, and doubt as to the attitude of the army, which has already brought down one French government suspected of weakness towards the Moslems, and might conceivably bring down another.[1] One can hardly doubt that in the long run the Moslems will achieve their independence; except in the unlikely event of a compromise the process will be a costly one to both sides.

Although Tunisia was nominally a protectorate the country was in fact almost directly governed by a strong French administration, with a resident-general at its head. This administration, acting in the name of the Bey of Tunis, made laws, executed important public works, strictly controlled the native authorities and was all powerful. European settlement was encouraged and in 1956 there were over a quarter of a million Europeans in the country, of whom about three-quarters were French and most of the rest Italians. Resistance to French colonization among Tunisians began in the early days of the present century, and steadily spread in spite of efforts on the part of the French at different times to suppress, divert or canalize it. In 1934 the Neo-Destour party was formed having self-government as its object. After the 1939-45 war agitation by the nationalists became general throughout the country and acts of terrorism began to take place against the police and against Tunisians loyal to the French. The situation improved in 1954 when the French Prime Minister Mendès-France solemnly declared before the Bey at Carthage that France recognized Tunisia's right to autonomy and proposed that negotiations be opened immediately. A Tunisian government was formed largely from Neo-Destour members, and after prolonged discussions agreement was reached with France as to the conditions of Tunisian autonomy. These

[1] There was an unsuccessful military *coup de main* in April 1961.

did not please everybody, and a number of nationalist extremists started a campaign against the more moderate leadership of Habib Bourguiba, head of the Neo-Destour. This campaign was defeated, but the promise to Morocco in 1955 of complete independence made it difficult for the French Government, when pressed by Tunisian leaders, to withhold it from Tunisia. In 1956 Bourguiba became head of the first independent government of Tunisia, and in the following year the monarchy was abolished and a republic proclaimed. The title of President of the new republic was conferred on Bourguiba.

The first French Resident-General in Morocco was Marshal Lyautey, a man of quite exceptional stature. This aristocratic soldier-administrator was very sympathetic to the Moroccan way of life and was endowed with an extraordinary capacity for dealing with people. His policy, similar in some ways to British 'indirect rule', was to preserve Moroccan institutions while at the same time adapting them to the needs of the modern world. When he left in 1926 the old French vice of close direct administration crept in, and the French Government tended increasingly to supplant the authority of the Sultan. Moroccan nationalism began as a reaction against the pervasive tendencies of French administration. Towards the end of the Second World War it developed into a demand for the abrogation of the protectorate treaty and for the independence of Morocco. The Sultan, Sidi Mohamed ibn Yusuf, took a leading part in voicing these aspirations and thus became the head of Moroccan nationalism. The nationalists were opposed by the great provincial nobility who in 1953 procured the deposition and exile of the Sultan and his replacement by an older member of his family. The new Sultan failed entirely to secure popular recognition, disorders broke out, the most influential member of the nobility rallied to Sidi Mohamed, and in 1955 the French had no alternative but to recall the exiled monarch and to meet the public demand for independence. Transfer of power took place in 1956 and Morocco recovered her ancient sovereignty. In 1958 the Sultan announced that the government would be a constitutional monarchy with a national assembly elected by universal suffrage. It is still too early to say how far these intentions will become a reality.

That part of Morocco which became the Spanish zone was a poverty-stricken, mountainous area with an old reputation for restlessness and recalcitrance. The Spanish occupation met with violent opposition, first from a picaresque adventurer named Raisuni and then from the more formidable Mohamed Abdelkrim. Many years were consumed in these struggles and it was not until 1928 that all opposition was overcome. The Spaniards then set about organizing the zone in a businesslike manner but the fall of the monarchy in Spain and the establishment of the Spanish Republic were followed by a period of confusion in Morocco which continued until the Spanish nationalist rising of 1936. The Franco régime was distinctly more liberal towards Moroccan nationalism than its republican predecessor and showed a certain sympathy with the increasing desire of Moroccans for national independence. When in 1956 the French zone regained independence Spain at once agreed to the reintegration of the northern zone with the rest of Morocco and the two zones came together as a united and independent kingdom.

TANGIER

This ancient city, placed at the western entrance of the Straits of Gibraltar, was founded by Phoenician sailors and later formed part of the empire of Carthage. Occupied successively by Romans, Arabs, Portuguese and even British, it passed finally into Moroccan possession in the latter part of the seventeenth century. Large numbers of European merchants established themselves in this busy port which presently became the seat of several legations around which grew a considerable European colony. With the acquiescence of the Moroccan authorities the Europeans set up certain municipal sanitary institutions. These, together with an important diplomatic corps, gave to the city a special character which was generally accepted, and which in 1923 was specifically recognized by an agreement between Britain, France and Spain called the 'Statute of Tangier'. This placed the city under an international government in which the Sultan (which in fact meant the French) was represented by an officer responsible for the administration of the Moroccan population. In 1940 Spain, taking advantage of the fall of France, occupied Tangier but the international régime was re-established after the war by the victorious powers. When Spain and France recognized the independence of Morocco in 1956 the Statute of Tangier was abolished by international agreement and the zone reintegrated with the rest of Morocco.

SPANISH WEST AFRICA AND MAURITANIA

In contrast to her attitude towards Morocco, Spain has so far resisted nationalist pressures in her West African colony. In Ifni these pressures are towards integration with Morocco, of which the country is in every way except the legal a part. In Spanish Sahara there appears some conflict between the irredentist claims of Morocco and a trend among the Shanaqta people of this area towards closer relationships with their fellow-tribesmen who constitute the majority of the population of Mauritania. This territory, the last of France's colonies to come of age, achieved independence smoothly and silently towards the end of 1960. Morocco, with some support from other countries, claims that racially and historically Mauritania is part of Morocco. How far this claim is supported by Mauritanians themselves it is not easy to say. It is, however, fairly clear that the educated few are attached to their newly acquired independence.

Economy

The principal economic resource of North Africa, and until recently the only one, is agriculture, followed by stock breeding. In Morocco, Algeria and Tunisia two forms of agriculture exist side by side. One is advanced, mechanized, uses fertilizers and crop rotation, and is that practised by the European colonists. The other is that practised by the Arabs:[1] archaic, simple though not necessarily primitive, using few mechanical aids, little, if any crop rotation, and practically no fertilizers. Throughout the region Arab agriculture itself falls into two categories. That practised by the people of the fertile coastal strips, static and sometimes assisted by irrigation of a simple kind; and the shifting cultivation of the tribes of the arid hills of the interior, usually associated with stock raising. Europeans grow vines, fruit, tobacco, olives and cereals; static Arab farmers grow cereals, vegetables, fruit, olives and dates; the nomads grow a somewhat precarious supply of barley and not much else. Two crops call for special mention. The vineyards of Algeria cover nearly one million acres and wine production is about one-third of that of the whole of France. Those of Tunisia are not nearly so extensive and wine production is accordingly much smaller, but the olive crop is very much greater. Tunisia is supposed to have sixteen million olive trees, producing eight million gallons

---

[1] I use the word here to describe all the indigenous people.

of oil in the year.[1] The quality of the oil is, or was, very high.

The difficulty facing native agriculture in North Africa is pressure of a growing population on insufficient land. There are huge areas of uncultivable hill and desert, while considerable acreages of the best land in Morocco, Tunisia and especially Algeria are farmed by Europeans. On the whole the peasant has not sufficient land on which to live. Considerable efforts have been made to enable him to make the best of what he has. Water conservation has now made possible the irrigation of large areas; thousands of terraces have been constructed to combat soil erosion; modern methods have been encouraged; there has been some redistribution of land, and also various schemes, rather limited in scope, for resettlement. To be successful all these measures need the co-operation of the peasants which has so far been lacking. Nor have the disturbed political conditions of the last years been propitious for an advance in any field, least of all perhaps the agricultural, where the fruits of success are slow to mature, tradition tenacious, and enthusiasm for reform at the best of times difficult to arouse.

The rearing of stock holds a high place in the economy of North Africa. Sheep and goats predominate, and are to be found almost everywhere. Some of the nomadic tribes devote themselves entirely to the breeding of sheep and there is enormous pressure on the limited pasture, while the management of grazing and water leaves much to be desired.

The other agricultural resources of North Africa are the forests. These have suffered from injudicious cutting and failure to replant but the forest areas are still quite extensive, especially in Tunisia and Algeria, and consist largely of cork trees and oak. Throughout the region there are great stretches of esparto grass which is exported for the manufacture of paper. There are very valuable fishing grounds off the coast of Morocco, and the seas off Tunisia and Libya are also well stocked with fish. Greek sponge-fishers find Libyan waters a rewarding field of operations.

The economy of North Africa, especially that of Algeria and Libya, will probably be revolutionized by the recent discovery of oil in those countries. In Algeria development of wells situated deep in the Sahara has already reached an advanced stage but is complicated by the problem of security. Under present conditions the transport of oil from the Sahara to the coast requires the policing of the whole area through which the pipe line is laid. The Libyan

[1] The figures in this passage are from Beaver and Stamp, *Africa*.

deposits are equally promising and their development is not at present attended by any security risk. These discoveries make it impossible to say anything definitive about the North African economy. The next few years may see the rise for good or ill of an industry equal to that of Arabia and the Persian Gulf. In that case the problem of poverty will no doubt be solved; but new prosperity will no doubt create other problems, as it has elsewhere. Oil is by no means the only mineral found in North Africa. There are very large phosphate deposits in Morocco, Algeria and Tunisia, and these three countries account for a high proportion of the world's total phosphate production.[1] Important reserves of iron ore and copper have been proved in Mauritania, Algeria has high grade iron ore and considerable quantities of zinc, while other minerals in the region include lead, manganese and cobalt. Marine salt is produced by evaporation on the coast of Tunisia.   (*Plates* 78–79)

Much of the mineral wealth of North Africa, especially the oil and a substantial quantity of the iron, lies in the Sahara and is territorially distributed between several political units, including Algeria, Tunisia, Morocco, and the territories of West Africa. The French therefore hit upon the device of a supra-territorial body called the *Organisation Commune des Régions Sahariennes* which came into being in 1957. It is designed to embrace all those countries having an interest in the Sahara (though Mauritania refused to join), and to be an instrument of French-African co-operation for the exploitation of the great desert for the benefit of all.

Apart from mining, the industries of North Africa concern themselves chiefly with the processing of local agricultural and marine products. The most important is the Algerian wine industry but others are oil pressing, fish canning and leather tanning, and the production of local consumer goods.

The French and the Italians have endowed North Africa with a good road system, particularly in the coastal areas, and the most remarkable is the great road through Libya from Tripoli to the frontier of Egypt, well known to those who fought with the 8th Army in the 1939–45 war. A somewhat intricate railway system provides continuous communication from Morocco to Tunisia and south to Beni Abbès in southern Algeria. Between the wars the French showed considerable activity in modernizing the trans-Saharan trade routes, which count among the oldest in the world. Motor roads equipped with rest houses, refuelling stations and a

---

[1] Over 27 per cent in 1956. Morocco is by far the highest producer of the three.

telegraph system link North and West Africa, and the motor lorry has to a great extent replaced the camel caravan.

The interior of North Africa has few great towns except Fez, Marrakesh and Meknes, which are all situated in Morocco. Of these Fez is the oldest, and has long enjoyed great prestige in the Moslem world as the Mecca of the West. Marrakesh is a great market both for the mountain people of the Atlas and for the nomads of the Sahara who come to exchange hides and dates for cereals and European goods. Along the coast of North Africa there is a string of busy ports, beginning in the west with Casablanca, followed by the former international port of Tangier, then by Algiers, Oran, Bone, Tunis, Tripoli, Benghazi, to name but a few.

Comment on the economic situation of North Africa must necessarily be conjectural. It is not possible to say whether Morocco and Tunisia will be able to maintain the same rate of development as they attained when they were French protectorates. Algeria is in the throes of a long civil war of which no one can foresee the end, Mauritania is underpopulated, the future of the Spanish possessions is uncertain, Libya is an artificial combination of two different provinces, held together by the prestige of a delicate old man. It is safe to predict that the oil of Algeria and Libya is a factor that will survive most political vicissitudes. To attempt to look further into the future than that would be unwise.

CHAPTER SEVEN

WEST AFRICA

THIS region consists of the area enclosed on the north and east by an imaginary line drawn due east from the Senegal River mouth to the western frontier of the Republic of the Sudan,[1] thence south-west to the Cameroon Mountain; and on the west and south by the Atlantic Ocean. It therefore includes all the lower part of the great western bulge of Africa between the Atlantic Ocean and the Nile Valley. Politically the region comprises the countries that until recently made up the French West African Federation except Mauritania which we have treated as part of North Africa, the several components of British West Africa, the former British and French trusteeships of Togoland and the British Cameroons, the Republic of Liberia and Portuguese Guinea. To these are added Chad, associated politically with Equatorial Africa, but with so many characteristics in common with the other sub-Saharan countries of West Africa that it must, for our purposes, be treated as part of that region. The French Cameroons, on the other hand, is in every way closer to Equatorial than to West Africa and finds a place in the next chapter. The area of West Africa is about 2½ million square miles and the population about sixty-six million.

The Country

The region reproduces the usual African picture of a coastal plain rising more or less gradually to an inland plateau. This plateau is lower than in most parts of Africa and lies mainly at an elevation of 1,500 feet above the level of the sea. Rising above it, however, there are several lofty massifs, of which the most important are the Futa Jallon in Guinea, where the Niger, Senegal and Gambia Rivers rise, the Bauchi plateau in Nigeria, the Tibesti range in Chad, and the highlands of the Cameroons which terminate seawards in the volcanic peak of the Cameroon Mountain.

The coastline runs from the mouth of the Senegal River in a general south-easterly direction until it reaches the western end of Liberia, whence it turns due east to Lagos at the bottom of the

---

[1] Former Anglo-Egyptian Sudan.

67. Touggourt Oasis.
The reservoir and palms
at this oasis in eastern
Algeria.

68. Desert Reclamation. The dunes at the Judeida Nursery in Tripolitania, Libya.
The technique, which was developed by the Italians before 1914, is to lay down a
network of marram grass squares to stop the sand moving, and then to plant a tree in
each square. Gradually the sand turns to soil and the desert blossoms again

69–70. ROMAN RUINS IN LIBYA. The theatre auditorium at Leptis Magna (*above*), and a general view of Cyrene (*below*)

71–73. ART IN NORTH AND WEST AFRICA. A mosaic showing games in a Roman arena discovered at Gurgi near Tripoli in Libya (*above*); tombs of Touggourt kings in the desert of eastern Algeria (*bottom, left*); and a fine bronze from southern Nigeria of a hunter returning from the chase (*bottom, right*)

74-75. BERBER TOWNS. A casbah surrounded by palms near Ouarzazate south of the Atlas Mountains in Morocco (*above*), and the old town of Jefren in Libya (*below*)

76-77. PEOPLE OF LIBYA. A Berber woman of Ghadames, where Libya, Tunisia and Algeria meet in the desert (*above*), and an Arab family of Derna (*below*)

78–79. THE SEARCH FOR OIL IN ALGERIA. The supply staging-post at the village of El Golea in southern Algeria (*above*); labourers making mud bricks and civil engineers checking levels for the mess-buildings at Azzene (*below*)

80. MOROCCAN
ORANGERY. An
irrigated orangery
at the foot of the
Kansera Dam on
the Oued Beth

81. RICE-DRYING IN SIERRA
LEONE. Rice being raked to
ensure even drying

82. FREETOWN. The capital of Sierra Leone, which was founded in 1788 as a refuge for freed slaves

83. ISLAND OF GOREE. The oldest French settlement in West Africa

84–85. NIGERIAN TOWNS. The walled Hausa city of Kano, which is an old caravanserai (*left*); and the Yoruba city of Ibadan, which is the largest town in Nigeria (*below*)

86. JOS MARKET. Traders in the market at Jos in northern Nigeria; in the background is a stack of yams, one of the staple foods of the area

87. UNIVERSITY OF ACCRA. A student at Accra University (formerly the University College of Ghana) on Legon Hill a few miles outside the Ghanaian capital

88–90. Cocoa in West Africa. Harvesting cocoa pods and cutting them open to extract the beans in Ghana (*above*); sorting cocoa beans in Nigeria (*below*)

91. WAGENIA FISHERMEN. These fishermen in the Congo rapids near Stanleyville use osier traps operated by liana ropes

92. BALOIE POTTERS. Samples of their work in the Congo

93. TIMBER ON THE IVORY COAST. Logs piled on the river-bank to be floated downstream to the coast

94–96. PEOPLE OF GUINEA. A Fulani woman of Guinea with a traditional hair-style; a Bissagos man of Portuguese Guinea about to do a snake-dance; an African boy of Guinea holding pineapples

97. PYGMY OF WAMBA. A pure-blooded pygmy or Negrillo. These people inhabit the dense rain forest of Equatorial Africa and live by hunting and trapping. Their average height is less than five feet

98–99. WATUSI DANCERS. The Watusi are the tall aristocrats of Ruanda-Urundi. Here some girls are doing the "dance of the crowned cranes", which is based on the graceful courtship dance of these birds

100. RUWENZORI MOUNTAINS. The "Mountains of the Moon" between the Congo and Uganda. The tree-groundsels are the first large plants below the glaciers at 15,000 feet

101. THE STANLEY FALLS. The water rushing over the falls on the Congo just above Stanleyville

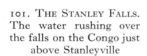

Bight of Benin, thence south-east again to the Cameroons. The coast is generally low lying and masked by sand-bars throughout a long stretch of its length. Cliffs are rare, Cape Verde and the neighbourhood of Abidjan being notable exceptions. The shore is either sandy and in places beaten by a heavy surf, or swampy and intersected by innumerable tidal channels. There are also enormous areas of mangrove forest, especially in the river deltas and creeks. Along a considerable length of the coast a chain of navigable lagoons stretches behind the sand-bars. There are very few good natural harbours. Dakar, focusing a heavy three-way movement of trade between Europe, Africa and the Western Hemisphere, and a vital point in world strategy, is one, Bathurst at the mouth of the Gambia River another, and Freetown, like Dakar protected by a headland, a third. In addition to these a number of river estuaries offer shelter to shipping and access for some distance to the interior, but the ubiquitous sand-bars prevent their use by large ships.

West Africa has five major river systems, the Senegal, the Gambia, the Niger, the Volta, and that of Lake Chad. The Senegal, 950 miles long, rises in the Futa Jallon and runs into the sea at St. Louis. It is navigable for 215 miles from its mouth all the year round, and for short periods to Kayes, about 562 miles. The mouth is blocked by shifting sands. The Gambia has a wide estuary and is navigable for about 250 miles. The navigable stretches correspond to the eponymous British colony, which is a mere narrow strip of land on either side of the river. The Niger also rises in the Futa Jallon and curves in an immense arc first north-east then southwards, entering the sea in the Bight of Biafra. It is navigable from its mouth for 450 miles in the rainy season, and there are long navigable stretches in the upper reaches. The chief tributary of the Niger is the Benue. The Volta is formed by the Black and White Voltas, and flows into the Bight of Benin. Lake Chad is really a large drainage basin with two important feeders, the Shari and the Wobe Rivers. The lake itself has a maximum depth of twenty feet and an area of 10,000 square miles in the dry season and 50,000 square miles in the wet.

Climate

The climate of West Africa formerly had a most vicious reputation, and Europeans frequently succumbed to it. Modern medicine has gone far to protect human beings against its effects, particularly in preventing the insect- and water-borne diseases

13

which are the indirect effect of the heat and humidity. Temperatures
are consistently high, but the variations inland, where there are
occasional night frosts, are considerably higher than on the coast,
where the average temperature is 79° and the annual range only
6°. Rainfall varies both in quantity and incidence throughout the
region. The wettest zones are the south-west, where Freetown, for
instance, has an annual fall of 175 inches, and the south-east,
where the Niger Delta receives more than 100 inches. The coastal
zone of Ghana and Togoland is comparatively dry, with only 30
to 40 inches in the year. Inland, rainfall decreases progressively
almost everywhere northwards from the coast, and there is a long
dry season characterized by the dry and dusty Harmattan wind
which blows off the Sahara.

Vegetation

The vegetational zones reflect the east to west trend of the climatic belts, from luxuriance and profusion on the coast to bareness
and poverty in the remote hinterland. Behind the coastal swamps
there is a zone of equatorial rain forest which stretches from
Sierra Leone to beyond the Cameroons, broken only by the drier
zone of Ghana and Togoland, and extending inland between one
and two hundred miles. The forest gradually thins out into savannah
of various grades and this gives way to grassland which presents
a parched appearance throughout most of the year. These dry
steppes eventually merge into the sandy waste of the Sahara.

Fauna

The fauna of West Africa is not so varied and abundant as that
of East Africa. The dense tropical forest is the home of the great
anthropoid apes. Chimpanzees of different species are to be found
in several parts of West Africa, and the gorilla inhabits the forest
from the Cameroons to the Congo River in Equatoria.[1] One
animal peculiar to the region is the pygmy hippopotamus.

The People

Although true Negroes are the dominant race of the region, and
stretch fairly continuously from Senegal to the Cameroons and
beyond, West Africa presents a scene of great diversity. In spite
of their many common characteristics, true Negroes still exhibit

---

[1] These apes are also to be found in the forested mountains of west and south-
west Uganda in the East African region.

a wide range of differences, whether it be in their domestic life, their religion, or in their social and constitutional practices. Thus we find societies ranging from simple peasants living in hilltop villages to highly organized societies in very large towns; and cultures varying from that of primitive pagans to that of a sophisticated westernized intelligentsia. In several places the old forest kingdoms still survive, and although the introduction of European rule stopped the wars on which their power was based, they preserve much of their splendour, and still play a role of considerable importance.

The largest community of true Negroes in West Africa are the Hausa, who are not of single stock or anything like it. They are a people evolved from a large number of diverse elements who have this in common, that they speak a language fundamentally Hamitic called Hausa. The Hausa are found in colonies and groups all over West Africa and as far away as Tripoli and Bombay.[1] Their largest concentration is in the Northern Region of Nigeria where they number 5½ million and where they appear to have settled in the very remote past. Even then they were organized in states, each named after its capital, a walled town in which the people could take refuge in time of war. The Hausa came under Islamic influence in the fourteenth century, and although religion did not strike very deep it no doubt contributed powerfully towards the development of their policy, which was extremely sound. Each state was governed by a king with an establishment of administrative officials and a trained judiciary. There was also a well-organized fiscal system. In spite of these excellent arrangements, the Hausa states did not play any great part in the West African political scene. They were small, quarrelsome, and frequently exposed to the attacks of stronger neighbours. Their religion, never strong, degenerated still further (in the eighteenth century the rulers were actually pagans) and it was precisely this decay that prompted Othman dan Fodio to launch the *jihad* that made the Fulani masters of most of Hausaland.[2]

In build the Hausas are of medium height, thickset, and possessing great strength and endurance. Their skin is black, but they have rather thinner features than other true Negroes. They are industrious farmers, shrewd traders and fearless travellers. They are splendid fighters, and their services as soldiers in the Nigerian

[1] Newland, *West Africa*, p. 81.
[2] pp. 31, 187.

forces in two wars were oustanding. The Hausa language has become the *lingua franca* over a very wide area.

The other large tribes of true Negroes of Nigeria are the Yoruba and the Ibo. Like the Hausa, these are hardly homogeneous communities but rather linguistic groups deriving from a great variety of ancestral stocks, and the word 'tribe' is therefore not appropriate. It is possible that the Yoruba were not originally pure Negroes and they may have originated from Upper Egypt like the Fulani. However that may be, their civilization was already an ancient one about a thousand years ago, when the people of Ife within the southern bend of the Niger were conquered by migrants of Hamitic stock from the east or the north. The focus of political power in due course shifted to Oyo which became the centre of an empire embracing not only Yorubaland proper but also considerable areas on either side of it. It was an empire based on military aggression, its wealth in great part derived from the sale of slaves. It disintegrated because the subject-peoples resented the manner in which all the wealth of the country always found its way to Oyo and nowhere else. The northern part of the empire fell before the assault of the Fulani while the southern part dissolved in civil wars. Even when the empire had broken up, slaving continued from the original nuclei, Oyo and Ife, and did not end until it was checked and finally abolished by British rule. The Yoruba are the dominant people in the Western Region of Nigeria, and number nearly 5 million. They are a vigorous and intelligent people, highly urbanized and prosperous, who have adapted themselves with ease to modern conditions, while retaining their pride in their own history and institutions.

The Ibo, of whom there are also nearly 5 million, are the Eastern Region counterparts (perhaps one should say the rivals) of the Yoruba. They live in the country which rises gently from the coast and are predominantly subsistence farmers, cultivating yams and cassava. Their main cash crop is palm kernels. They are noted for their very democratic and individualist outlook, and for their resistance to central direction and to complex forms of political organization. They like to live in small village communities separated by an expanse of bush, and large market towns such as Onitsha are exceptional.

As we move westwards the first large homogeneous people we meet are the Akan of Ghana and the Ivory Coast, ethnically a single people, though divided linguistically between Fanti- and Twi-speaking groups. Fanti is spoken along the coast and some distance inland. The Twi group spreads over the central part of the country and includes the Ashanti. Like the rest of the Akan peoples, the Ashanti probably came to their present home from the savannah country in the north and north-west, and having conquered the people then living in the forest land, founded a number of states which during the seventeenth and eighteenth centuries became the Ashanti Federation. It was during the emergence of the Federation that the Golden Stool became in the eyes of the Ashanti the visible symbol of their nationhood. According to tradition the Stool came down from Heaven and rested on the knees of Osei Tutu, chief of Kumasi, whose successors, as keepers of the Stool, are regarded with special veneration as leaders of the nation. When in 1900 a British governor, quite misunderstanding the significance of the Stool, demanded that it be handed over to him, the Ashanti were so outraged that they took to arms. The Ashanti are hardy, proud, strongly attached to their traditions and loyal to their institutions. Their skill and bravery in warfare, together with a great gift of organization, powers of combination and a sense of discipline, made them probably the most formidable people whom any European power encountered in West Africa. In later, more peaceful days they have proved themselves to be go-ahead farmers, and Ashanti now plays an increasing part in the economic life of Ghana.

The Ewe-speaking people of south-eastern Ghana and Togoland deserve mention if only because they have made sporadic appearances on the international scene with a demand that they should be united under one government. Neither the colonial powers, nor the Ghana Government, nor the United Nations have yet provided an answer to this question, but Ewe unification is undoubtedly a matter that will be raised again.

The Kru are really natives of Liberia, but they are to be found distributed in communities round most of the ports of the coast. They are the sailors of West Africa and provide the crews for many of the ships that ply in West African waters.

A group of tribes called Mandingo are the most numerous and important negroid people in the western Sudan.[1] They were the founders of the medieval empire of Mali and are even now spread over an enormous area inland from the coast between the Senegal River and northern Sierra Leone. Their greatest concentration is in the basins of the upper Niger and upper Senegal and in the

[1] p. 30 fn.

northern part of the Futa Jallon plateau. Between 1882 and 1898, under a leader named Samory, they put up a spirited resistance to the French. They are now the great middlemen of that part of West Africa and their language is widely used as a *lingua franca*. In appearance they are tall and lean, and in some cases have high cheekbones and narrow eyes which are taken to indicate some Hamitic blood.

The Songhai are the modern representatives of the empire which destroyed Mali at the end of the fifteenth century. They now stretch from the neighbourhood of Timbuktu southwards across the great bend of the Niger. The Songhai often exhibit strong Hamitic traits, betraying intermixture with the Hamites of the Sahara.

The upper basin of the Volta River is the home of the Mossi, who can claim descent from some of the people who made up the Mossi-Dagomba states from the thirteenth or fourteenth centuries onwards.

The Mende inhabit an area of about 12,000 square miles in the centre and south-west of Sierra Leone and are the largest and most important tribe of the Protectorate. The Temne, their neighbours, originally came from the upper Niger country and settled along the Sierra Leone River and the Port Lokko creek. It was from them that the British obtained the land on which to place the liberated slaves who were the original colonists. The Wollofs or Jollofs are a tall, black, statuesque people of martial traditions, the great majority of whom live in Senegal.

The Hamites are represented in West Africa by the Fulani, often called Peuls, Fula, Fellata or by their own word Fulbe. They are found throughout the region, from Senegal in the west to Darfur in the east. They are thought to have come originally from Upper Egypt and to have migrated westwards to the Atlantic Coast. They are distinctive in appearance, having fine features, a slim and tall physique, and light coloured skin. In character they are reserved and withdrawn, and they have a reputation for 'slimness'.[1] They number about six million and are for the most part disseminated among the Negro population, though the main concentrations are in Futa Jallon in Guinea, Massina in the former French Sudan,[2] and Adamawa in Nigeria.[3] Some are nomadic pastoralists, others sedentary farmers, and others both agricul-

---

[1] An untranslatable South African expression implying smoothness, speciousness, elastic standards of honesty.
[2] Now Mali (p. 194).
[3] Seligman, *Races of Africa*, p. 137.

turalists and pastoralists. The nomadic pastoralists are those who have best preserved the physical characteristics of the race. The sedentary Fulani are more negroid in appearance than either the nomads or the semi-sedentary farmers, sometimes because they are in fact Fulani-speaking Negroes, or else because they have intermarried with Negroes.

In some parts of West Africa the Fulani have attained a dominant social and political position. During the European Middle Ages they penetrated peacefully into the country that later became Northern Nigeria and here their influence steadily grew until about 1802 when a Fulani sheikh named Othman dan Fodio launched a religious war which won him an empire over a large part of West Africa and the remote hinterland. Although this empire later decayed, the Fulani remain the ruling class in much of Northern Nigeria, and constitute the aristocracy of Guinea.

The Bantu play but a small part on the West African scene. They live in the Cameroons, on the north-western edge of the Bantu world, and generally speaking occupy the forest areas, while their Sudanic-speaking neighbours prefer the mountains and the grasslands. There are also in this racial borderland certain tribes who have mixed characteristics and are called semi-Bantu.

Finally it must be mentioned that there are throughout the region between the forest and the desert large groups of strongly hamiticized negroid pastoralists, descendants, it must be supposed, of the people of the ancient sub-Saharan empires. Such, for instance, are the people of the Chad territory.

A number of foreign races have made their home in West Africa. Liberia, as we have seen, was settled by emancipated Negroes from the United States in the first half of the nineteenth century. These people, though of African descent, were entirely alien to African conditions and formed an exclusive society in the coastal towns, while professing to exercise sovereignty over the indigenous tribes of the interior, who resented their presence. During the last twenty years or so there have been genuine efforts on the part of the Afro-American rulers to replace this 'colonial' situation by co-operation with the local tribes, while the financial position has improved under the stimulus of American enterprise, and there has been some expansion of social and economic services. Sierra Leone, like Liberia, was originally settled by immigrant Negroes but the presence of the British Government prevented a reproduction of the Liberian situation here. Nevertheless the so-called 'creoles' in the Colony claim social superiority over the indigenous peoples in the neighbouring Protectorate though of course unable to exercise political sovereignty over them. The Akus are to the Gambia what the creoles are to Sierra Leone, descendants of liberated slaves.

Another important group of foreigners are the so-called Syrians (they are in fact mostly Lebanese) who play the same part as the Asians in East Africa. But they are far less numerous than the East African Asians, nor are their roots in the country so deep.

Finally the Europeans, mostly officials, soldiers, traders, miners, missionaries and teachers, who are in a different category from the others. The great majority are transients, that is to say they do not expect to end their lives here. After working in West Africa, either for themselves, or like the officials and the missionaries, for others, they will in due course retire to their homes in Europe. Unlike Kenya or Algeria, West Africa has no *native* European population.

Aspects of Culture

The strong, highly organized, settled, predominantly agricultural true Negro societies of West Africa have, as was briefly indicated in Part I,[1] evolved a culture that has several most remarkable characteristics. The most noteworthy of these are the system of secret societies and a strong artistic tradition that finds its chief expression in sculpture. Most secret societies are associations in some ways corresponding to the English conception of a friendly society, a group of people who have come together for mutual benefit, and who derive a certain social distinction from membership. Some of these societies are exceedingly powerful and have important religious, judicial and social functions. Such, for instance, is the Poro Society of Sierra Leone, which has a very wide membership and which may, according to one author, have been at one time an association for protection against slave traders.[2] Another is the Egbo Society among the Ibibio of Nigeria, so influential and widespread as to have assumed the character of a government. While most societies are harmless and indeed beneficial, others, such as the Leopard, Crocodile and Baboon Societies, may be directed to sinister and anti-social purposes.

African sculpture is confined to a well-defined geographical area which corresponds to the basins of the Niger and the Congo, and

[1] p. 20.
[2] Newland, *West Africa*, pp. 193-4.

hence to the regions of West Africa and Equatoria in this book.
Why this should be so is not easy to explain but it is worth observing
that the people of the sculptural zone are mainly sedentary agriculturalists who have been settled in their present homes for a
long time, while the people of East and South Africa follow a
pastoral or semi-pastoral economy and arrived where they are now
comparatively recently. The climates and vegetation of the several
regions are also dissimilar, a great part of the area where sculpture
is practised corresponding to that of heavy rainfall and thick
forest.[1]

At one time sculpture flourished throughout West Africa, but
the art has now declined and is only perpetuated in a few places.
The change is due to the decay of those institutions with which
sculpture was most closely associated, the tribal customs and the
tribal religion. Modern changes in the conception of chiefship and
in the role of the chief have also deprived artists of the patronage
which was formerly in many cases their stimulus and inspiration.

There are two different styles in West African sculpture, that of
the western Sudan and that of the Guinea Coast. This classification
is a very broad one, and certainly does not imply that the two styles
fall rigidly into separate categories. Like the frontiers of race,
climate and vegetation, the artistic frontiers are ill-defined and not
easily perceptible.

The western Sudan is a predominantly Moslem area, and icono-
clasm is an essential tenet of Islam. It is perhaps for this reason
that pagan art in this area shows a tendency towards asceticism and
restraint and is highly formalized. It consists largely of human
and animal figures and of masks carved in wood, many of the forms
being of a geometric design characteristic of the Moslem art of
decoration.

The Guinea Coast, which in this context runs from Senegal to
the Cameroons, has a more varied artistic tradition. It is also an
ancient one, as is proved by the discovery over a large area in the
neighbourhood of Nok in Nigeria of terra-cotta figures from a
culture dating from the latter part of the first millennium B.C.
There is also some evidence that the Nok culture survived long
enough to influence the art of Ife, which flourished after the first
millennium A.D. Since the latter is believed in turn to have affected
the development of the art of Benin, there is therefore perhaps a

[1] Exceptionally, there are fine sculptors among the tribes in the north of Portuguese East Africa.

continuous thread in the artistic tradition of this part of Africa that goes back for over two thousand years. It is indeed from Ife and Benin that are derived the best known examples of West African art. Ife produced admirable bronzes of outstanding naturalism and elegance, terra-cottas, elaborate shrine furniture from quartz and granite, and megalithic monuments. The bronzes and ivories of Benin are the product of an art which was essentially associated with the ruler and his court and which seems to have reached its *apogée* in the fifteenth and sixteenth centuries. The earliest examples known to us are thin and naturalistic and in style not far removed from that of Ife. Later, representation became static and stylized and the early simplicity became overlaid by a profusion of decorative detail. By the nineteenth century the art of Benin had fallen into decadence. (*Plate* 73)

The art of metal casting was by no means confined to Ife and Benin. Small bronze gold-weights are the most representative examples of Ashanti art, although Ashanti metal work reaches its highest level in the small bronze urns and vessels made for ceremonial use. In Dahomey a restricted family guild worked as retainers of royalty and nobility and cast human figures and animals representing the fauna of the country and scenes from daily life.

Throughout the region there is a distinguished tradition of wood carving, a special feature being the carving of masks connected with religion and with the rites of the secret societies, decorative sculpture, clay modelling, and appliqué work on cloth.

Though it is to trespass on the next chapter a word may be said here of the art of Equatoria. This region is peopled with few exceptions by Bantu, but there do not seem to be any fundamental differences in aesthetic between their art and that of the true Negroes of the Guinea Coast. Wood carving predominates and reaches perhaps its peak in the rich and varied production of the Ubangi-Congo river system. In particular the art of the tribes commonly grouped under the name Bushongo,[1] between the Kasai and Sankuru Rivers, is distinguished by boldness of design, descriptiveness, and superb craftsmanship.

History

The end of the Scramble for Africa saw West Africa practically

---

[1] J. Vansina prefers to call them Bakuba, as 'Bushongo' is properly applicable only to the Bambala tribe (Ethnographic Survey of Africa, Central Africa, Belgian Congo, Part I, *Les tribus Ba-Kuba et les peuplades apparentées*).

divided between Britain, France and Germany. Portugal retained
a small footing in Portuguese Guinea and there was also the Afro-
American colony of Liberia, administered by the descendants of
former slaves. The largest share fell to France, with Britain well
behind in the second place, and Germany third. The Federation
of French West Africa, as it ultimately emerged, consisted of
seven colonies: Mauritania, Senegal, French Guinea, the Ivory
Coast, Dahomey, Upper Volta,[1] French Sudan and the Niger
Colony. British West Africa consisted of the Gambia, Sierra
Leone, the Gold Coast, and Nigeria.[2] France, with her three
colonies of Mauritania, the Sudan and the Niger, occupied the whole
of the vast hinterland and reached the sea in four great wedges
represented by the coastal zone of Mauritania and the other five
colonies. From the Senegal these wedges were separated from each
other by the British, German and Portuguese dependencies and
Liberia.

Although the maps of the period of the Scramble show vast
areas of West Africa coloured in this shade or that, so reflecting
the claims of the Powers, the realities of the situation on the spot
were very different. European influence was by no means as extensive as the maps suggest. Many of the people of the great
hinterland marked out as colonies and protectorates were still
quite unaware of their new status and not at all disposed to submit
to European government. Yet the Slave Trade could not be stopped,
nor peace and good order secured, nor economic development
begun, unless effective administration were first established. So
the main preoccupation of the colonial Powers in the years following the Scramble was to induce the African people to recognize the
new authority. The subjugation of the Gold Coast by the British
was completed in 1901 by the annexation of Ashanti as a Crown
Colony. In Nigeria the British first revived the idea of the chartered company with powers of government and entrusted the
extension of British authority to Sir George Goldie's Royal Niger
Company. Goldie brought the slave-trading states of Nupe and
Ilorin under control and succeeded in keeping Germans and
French out of Northern Nigeria, but in 1900 the government
took over the administrative responsibilities of the Company,

[1] Upper Volta was suppressed as a separate unit in 1932 but reinstated in 1947.
[2] In 1906 the governments of Lagos and the Protectorate of Southern Nigeria (the
former Niger Coast Protectorate) were amalgamated to form the Colony and Protectorate of Southern Nigeria. In 1914 Northern and Southern Nigeria were
amalgamated to become the Colony and Protectorate of Nigeria.

which continued, however, to function as a commercial concern. In the same year Sir Frederick Lugard was given the task of forming an administration in Northern Nigeria and was fully occupied till 1906 in consolidating his position in the great Fulani emirates.

The establishment of European government in the French colonies took even longer. There were military operations in Guinea and on the Ivory Coast as late as 1915, while the Niger Colony was not transferred from military to civil administration until 1920. There was a reallocation of territory after the First World War when the German colonies of Togoland and the Cameroons were divided between Great Britain and France to be administered under a mandate from the League of Nations. They continued to be held by the same Powers after the Second World War as trusteeships under the United Nations. The British administered their sections of Togoland and the Cameroons as part of the Gold Coast and Nigeria respectively. French Togoland was at one time brought into fairly close association with French West Africa but its autonomy was restored in 1946 and it became an 'associated territory' under the constitution of that year.[1] The French Cameroons was originally attached to French Equatorial Africa for purposes of administration, but was organized as a separate unit when France was entrusted with the mandate. It also became an 'associated territory' under the 1946 constitution.

When France collapsed in 1940 official French West Africa rallied to Vichy. In September 1940 British and Free French forces tried to take Dakar, capital of the Federation, but the attempt failed, and in the event the fear that Dakar might be used by the Germans was never realized. Many Africans did not share the early pro-Vichy leanings of their government and refused to accept the 1940 armistice. Large numbers of men went over to French Equatorial Africa, which had joined the Free French, and thus made no small contribution to the Allied war effort. When the British and Americans landed in North Africa in 1942, Governor-General Boisson threw in his lot with Admiral Darlan and thus brought French West Africa in on the side of the Allies. The British colonies were uniformly loyal and made a notable contribution in materials, money and men.

Both in British and French West Africa the Second World War very much accelerated the movement towards self-government. At a conference held at Brazzaville in Equatorial Africa in 1944 the

[1] See below.

Provisional Government of France gave a new turn to French colonial policy. True to the theory of assimilation the conference repudiated any suggestion of self-government. The aim was to be one of still closer integration, the participation of the dependencies in the reconstruction of the French political system and thereafter in the political life of France. These political advances were to be accompanied by social reforms and economic development. At the same time concessions were made to the local situation in the recognition by the conference of the value of African institutions. The constitution that emerged from these discussions in 1946 was that of a 'union founded on equality of rights and duties', in which the French West African colonies, with others, were described as 'overseas' territories, their people the equal of French nationals, entitled to representation in the institutions of the French Republic and endowed with their own representative assemblies called *Assemblées territoriales*. An 'Investment Fund for Economic and Social Development' was set up in order to promote capital investment. Although this constitution went some way to meet the demands of the élite, it fell far short of establishing the full political equality of Africans and Frenchmen that the theory of assimilation implied. As the years passed, the new African leaders began to demand a much larger measure of self-government and even the substantial changes introduced in 1956 (which virtually substituted a federal relationship for the old idea of assimilation) were soon seen to be insufficient to stem the rising tide of nationalism. The new constitution presented by General de Gaulle after his assumption of power in 1958 radically altered the French system of overseas administration. It enabled overseas territories to become members of a community of autonomous states sharing only foreign policy, defence, currency and some common economic questions. Rejection of the constitution would mean immediate independence and the right of secession was recognized even if the constitution had once been accepted. All the West African territories approved the new constitution by a large majority except French Guinea. The latter was then held to have seceded from France, all French aid was withdrawn and Guinea is now an independent republic. It is described as a 'centralized democracy' which in effect means that the country is governed by Sekou Touré, the President, through a single political party of which he is head. The former trust territories, the French Cameroons and French Togoland, are also independent republics outside the

French Community. After trying to unite in a federation called Mali
after the medieval empire of that name, Senegal and the French
Sudan are now independent states within the French Community,
the latter taking the name of Mali. The former Niger Colony, the
Ivory Coast, Dahomey and Upper Volta (now the Voltaic Republic) are independent states associated for purposes of economic
co-operation in the so-called Benin-Sahel Union. Their position in
regard to the French Community is not clear. Chad is also an
independent state apparently in some not very well defined
association with the Central African and Congo Republics of
Equatorial Africa.

The political evolution of the British colonies was considerably
simpler, largely because self-determination, including the right to
secession, had long been implicit in British colonial policies. In
Nigeria particularly, Lugard's policy of 'Indirect Rule', that is
administration through the traditional authorities, was an education in local government designed to enable the people ultimately to stand on their own feet. At the centre, the first Legislative Council in British Africa with a majority of unofficial members was set up in the Gold Coast in 1946. After riots in 1948 a
commission of inquiry recommended radical changes. In the
following year an all-African committee made recommendations
which were accepted as a basis for fuller constitutional development. A new constitution was published in 1950, elections were
held in 1951, and in the following year a cabinet was appointed
with an African Prime Minister and African ministers in charge of
departments. Further elections and the victory of the Convention
People's Party in 1956 led to the grant in 1957 of complete independence within the British Commonwealth. The new nation,
which includes the former British trust territory of Togoland, took
the name of Ghana on the strength of a supposed connection with
the medieval empire of that name. Ghana has now become a republic within the British Commonwealth.

Although Ghana was the first of the British West African colonies
to become independent, she will not in the long run be the most
powerful nor perhaps the most influential. In 1960 Nigeria's
three regions became an independent federation within the
Commonwealth. The federal constitution was adopted of necessity,
since the territory has no natural unity and was only kept together
by the presence of the British Government. The problems now
facing an independent Nigeria are the relationship between the

three regions and the federal government, and the relations
between the regions themselves. Southern Nigeria, which comprises the Eastern and Western Regions, is predominantly Christian
and pagan and has a large and influential middle class, active,
vocal, western-educated, politically minded, from which most of
the leaders come. The north is predominantly Moslem and aristocratic. Relations between north and south have not always been
easy. There has also been some lack of cordiality between the
Eastern and Western Regions, the homes respectively of the Ibo
and Yoruba peoples. Provided these various fissures and rifts
can be healed or bridged, Nigeria, with a population greater than
that of the whole of the rest of West Africa, will no doubt make a
profound impression on the future of the African continent.

Sierra Leone has become a self-governing country in 1961.
The chief problem here seems to be the division between the
Colony, populated by the descendants of liberated slaves, and the
Protectorate, home of the indigenous people. The Gambia, part
colony, part protectorate, seems too small ever to attain complete
independence. Under the present constitution elected members are
in the majority both in the Legislative Council and in the Executive
Council. If the people of the Gambia seek a more adventurous
future then it would seem to lie in some sort of federation with
neighbouring states. An unbiased observer might suggest that
they would be wise to remain as they are.

There has been some doubt about the future of the British
Cameroons. In 1960 the southern part of this territory, or Southern Cameroons, which had already in 1954 set up as a region
on its own, finally parted altogether with Nigeria when the latter
attained independence. There will shortly be a plebiscite to decide
between unification with the former French Cameroons, now an
independent republic, or integration with the Federation of
Nigeria. The northern part, or Northern Cameroons, voted in
1959 for the continuation of British trusteeship but another vote
will be taken in 1961.[1]

ECONOMY

Agriculture
   West Africa is climatically unsuitable for European settlement

---

[1] In the event, the Northern Cameroons joined Nigeria, and the Southern
Cameroons voted to join the former French Cameroons.

and apart from the activities of the Firestone Company in Liberia, of which more will be said later, and a number of somewhat specialized plantations in the French and Portuguese territories, all agriculture is in the hands of the natives of the country. In West Africa as elsewhere most Africans are primarily concerned with ensuring their food supply and with certain important exceptions export crops are often just the surplus from their small gardens. Staple food crops include yams, cassava and other roots, pulses, plantains, rice, groundnuts, cereals and large varieties of subsidiary crops such as pumpkins, tomatoes and peppers.

The most spectacular and valuable export crop is cocoa, which originated in South America and was introduced by the Portuguese to the island of St. Thomas. After an unsuccessful attempt to grow it on the Gold Coast early in the nineteenth century, a man named Tetteh Kwashi[1] (to whom, if they have not already done so, the people of Ghana should certainly build a memorial) brought six beans from Fernando Po to his native village. From these small beginnings there has grown an industry which accounts for about two-thirds of the value of the exports of Ghana. Cocoa is also an important element in the exports of the Ivory Coast, Togoland and Nigeria. Unlike most other edible crops, cocoa is cultivated exclusively for export, and some observers have expressed the fear that the economy may become dangerously weighted in favour of this one crop. These fears are underlined by the prevalence of a deadly virus disease called 'swollen shoot' for which no cure has yet been found. African farmers were slow to accept the harsh truth that the only really effective way to save the industry was to cut out affected trees but they now appear to have become more co-operative in this respect. They receive compensation from the Cocoa Marketing Board[2] for any trees so destroyed. (*Plates* 88–90)

The groundnut is not only a useful African food but an important export crop. Groundnuts and their derivatives represent no less than 90 per cent of Senegal exports, while in the Gambia groundnuts are practically the only cash crop and make up about 98 per cent of exports.

The oil palm likes a fairly high rainfall and though reasonably tolerant of poorish soils prefers rich moist ones. It flourishes in the forest areas near the coast. Some countries, especially Nigeria,

---

[1] The name has various spellings.
[2] In 1947 Cocoa Marketing Boards were set up in the Gold Coast and Nigeria with power to devote their profits to the maintenance of price stabilization and to the furtherance of any purpose that will assist the industry.

express the oil prior to export; others export the kernels and leave the processing to the purchasing countries.

Shea nuts are collected in the dry savannah country and provide oil and 'butter' for food, and oil for fuel. The shea tree plays a similar part in the life of the African in these areas to that of the oil palm in the forest zone.

Cotton is grown in French West Africa but is practically confined to the irrigated lands of the Niger basin. In Nigeria it is grown in the Niger Delta. Bananas are exported from Guinea and the Ivory Coast. Among other smaller exports are coffee, piassava fibre, sesame, and ginger.

In 1926 the Liberian Government allowed the Firestone Corporation of America to take up a 90-year lease of a large area of land for the establishment of a rubber plantation. The Firestone Plantations cover an area of about 100,000 acres, and produce 80 million pounds of rubber a year. This and other recently established American enterprises have made an improvement in the economic condition of Liberia.

Livestock

Large areas of West Africa are infested by the tsetse fly. Varieties of small humpless cattle, believed to be immune to trypanosomiasis, are kept in the forest country towards the coast, but the great cattle zones are in the north, from which there is a considerable trade to the south. The greatest commercial cattle centre in West Africa is Kano in Northern Nigeria. Great numbers of cattle are sent from here to Lagos by train and even on the hoof. Sheep and goats are ubiquitous and enormous numbers are kept by the tribes of the western Sudan. There is a thriving export of hides and skins from Nigeria, and in the northern part of that country tanning is an ancient industry. Kano is thought to be the original home of 'morocco' leather.

Fishing

Sea fishing is practised all along the coast and is a particularly flourishing industry off Senegal and Ghana. Fresh water fishing is an important occupation with several of the inland riverain people, especially among those living on the Senegal River and on the great bend of the Niger.

Forests

Since the end of the Second World War there has been a great expansion of the timber industry in Nigeria and Ghana. West African forests consist largely of hardwood trees yielding beautiful timbers which can be used for the highest quality work. Unhappily there is a conflict between the conservation of forest and the needs of farmers for land, and the tendency is for agriculture to encroach on forest, whatever governments may do to try to conserve the latter.

Mining

The history of gold mining on the west coast of Africa is an old one. Europeans were trading for gold as early as the fifteenth century and the indigenous people mined gold and traded it with the great inland empires long before that. Ghana is still the leading producer of gold, but there is also some gold mining in Guinea and Sierra Leone. Ghana is also the largest West African producer of diamonds. These are small and mainly of industrial quality. Large diamonds are found in Sierra Leone and there is a growing production in Guinea and the Ivory Coast. There are very large bauxite deposits in Guinea and in Ghana. Full exploitation of the Ghana deposits will depend on the progress of the Volta River project, which envisages the construction of a barrage and hydro-electric power station for smelting the ore. Ghana is among the largest producers of manganese in the world. Iron ore is being worked in Sierra Leone, Liberia and Guinea. The Guinea deposits constitute one of the three greatest so far discovered. There are lesser ones in Nigeria. Nigeria has long been a leading producer of tin but the present deposits show signs of exhaustion and deeper mining will be necessary in order to get at further reserves. Nigeria is the largest world producer of columbite, which is a by-product of tin mining. Nigeria also possesses at Enugu the only coal mine in West Africa. Most of the production is consumed locally though there is a small export. Senegal is an important producer of ilmenite and deposits of this metal will soon be developed in the Gambia. There are phosphates at various places throughout the region, the most important workings at present being in Senegal. Other minerals known to exist in West Africa are silver, lead, zinc, tungsten, platinum, copper and uranium. Production of oil from fields in the Niger Delta began in 1958.

Railways

As in most parts of the continent, the railways of West Africa run inland at right angles to the coast in order to give the most direct access to the interior. Because the British colonies were isolated enclaves in French West Africa, the British West African railways are not interlinked, since none could reach the others without passing through French territory. Each colony has its own railway system, serving none but itself. The French had more room for manœuvre in their vast hinterland and planned their railway system to supplement navigable stretches of the Niger and Senegal Rivers and to link their inland territories to the coastal ports. They succeeded in doing so in Senegal and Guinea, but the two southern railways both stop well short of the Niger. The Ivory Coast railway ends at Wagadugu in the Voltaic Republic and the Dahomey line goes no further than Parakou, 230 miles from the coast.

The Gambia, having its river, needed no railway, and the only railway in Liberia is that constructed by the Liberia Mining Company to bring haematite from the Bomi Hills to the coast.

Roads

Road making is more difficult and more expensive in West Africa than in East Africa. The cost of unskilled labour is high and the material for road metal rather scarce. Nevertheless both the British and French territories possess networks of roads of reasonably good quality by African standards, and the French have displayed considerable energy in creating a road system which links the whole of the interior of French West Africa with the railways.

Intense competition between roads and railways is a feature of the West African transport system, and lorry transport is a most important private enterprise. For short hauls at least it seems likely that this competition will continue, as it is far more likely that roads will be improved than railways extended.

Waterways

Several rivers of West Africa besides those already mentioned[1] are navigable for part of their length and carry a considerable volume of traffic. Light craft can navigate the lower reaches of the Great and Little Scarcies in Sierra Leone. The Benue can take sizeable vessels according to the time of the year and farther to the

[1] p. 181.

east the Cross, Calabar, Imo and Bonny Rivers are used extensively for transport. Several rivers in the Southern Cameroons afford access some distance inland, as also does the Casamance in Senegal south of the Gambia. The Bani, affluent of the Niger in its upper reaches, carries traffic for a long distance, and all along the coast of West Africa there are a great number of navigable lagoons and channels.

Air Transport

The loss of the Mediterranean–Suez route to the Middle and Far East during the Second World War made West Africa a nodal point on west-east communications. There was a rapid development of airfields in British territory on this new and important supply line, and other airfields were built round Freetown for the defence of the naval base and Atlantic convoys. With the development since the war of international air travel, West Africa is now served by several European airlines, and is within a day's flight of Europe. There is also a good network of internal air services and most big towns are now connected by air.

Conclusion

The new states of West Africa vary widely in their ability to support the weight of their recently acquired independence. Some, like Ghana, the Ivory Coast, Senegal and parts of Nigeria, are comparatively well-to-do, having achieved a fairly high standard of development under the former colonial Powers. Others, like Niger and Chad, are thinly populated and poor. Yet others lie between the two extremes. By and large they are all faced with the problem that they have not at present the resources to finance their requirements, and help from overseas will be needed, in some cases on a massive scale. This, however, is a general problem and will be touched upon again in the concluding chapter.

CHAPTER EIGHT

EQUATORIA

THIS is the region of the Congo basin, together with that block of country which lies between the mouth of the Congo River and the Cameroon Mountain and drains directly to the Atlantic Ocean. The Equator runs through the heart of the region but Equatoria does not stretch across the continent, since the highlands of East Africa lie to the east and are of a quite different character. The region therefore comprises the whole of the former Belgian Congo, former French Equatorial Africa excluding Chad,[1] Spanish Guinea, the Cameroons formerly under French trusteeship, and the Spanish and Portuguese islands. The former Belgian Congo is now in name an independent republic and the countries that made up French Equatorial Africa are also independent, one of them having assumed the style of Congo Republic. We shall therefore refer to the former Belgian Congo simply as Congo, reserving the term Congo Republic for the ex-French colony across the river. As for the northern part of the region, that great land mass stretching north from the Congo to the Cameroons and Chad, there seems to be no better collective name for it than Equatorial Africa.

THE CONGO RIVER AND ITS BASIN

The Congo River, known as Zaïre to the Portuguese who discovered it, forms the largest of African river systems and in this respect is only exceeded in the world by the Amazon. The drainage area is nearly $1\frac{1}{2}$ million square miles and the length of the main stream is estimated at 3,000 miles which places it among the five longest rivers of the world.[2] It rises in Katanga at an altitude of 4,659 feet and is called the Lualaba until it reaches Stanleyville. It was in the headwaters of the Lualaba that Livingstone thought that he might find the source of the Nile. The Congo River receives innumerable tributaries throughout its length, many of

[1] Chad has already been dealt with in the chapter on West Africa.
[2] The other four are the Nile, the Mississipi-Missouri, the Yangtze and the Amazon.

them considerable rivers in their own right and perennial in their
flow owing to a well-distributed and fairly high rainfall. Although
there are long navigable stretches the flow is broken by many
cataracts and falls.   (*Plate* 101)

The Congo basin is a vast shallow depression in the African
plateau crossed by the Congo River and its tributaries and enclosed by uplands. The lowest part of the depression is in the south-
west, where the altitude is about 1,000 feet above sea-level. From
here the ground rises more or less gradually towards the north,
south and east. The height of the surrounding uplands is by no
means uniform. In the north the divide between the Congo and
Chad basins is hardly perceptible whereas the eastern side of the
rim is marked by the mountainous wall of the Ruwenzori range,
with several lofty peaks, the highest reaching almost 16,800 feet.
Between these extremes the highlands separating the Congo basin
from the Benue, Nile and Zambezi systems and from the Atlantic
coastal plain have a range of about 1,500 feet to 6,000 feet. The
centre of the depression has a cover of dense rain forest with trees
so tall and a canopy of leaves so thick that they exclude the light of
day. The floor of the forest is a mat of almost impenetrable under-
growth which gives way to considerable areas of swamp. The
higher ground which surrounds the central plain and gradually
rises to the mountainous edges is the same more or less wooded
savannah that we have observed elsewhere in Africa.

THE CONGO

The Country

Except for comparatively small areas in the west and north-east
the whole of the Congo is situated within the Congo basin. It is
an immense land mass over 900,000 square miles in area, occupying
the centre of western Africa between latitudes 5° 20' N and
13° 40' S. One peculiarity of the huge territory is that the outlet
to the sea is exceedingly small, being only a narrow strip some
twenty-five miles across at the Congo River mouth.

About 43 per cent of the Congo is in the rain forest zone with a
rainfall of over 63 inches. This is fairly well distributed throughout
the year, with two very short dry seasons and also two periods at the
equinoxes when the rainfall is rather heavier than at other times.
Constant humidity is accompanied by high temperatures which
show little variation throughout the year. In the eastern highlands

the climate is cooler owing to the altitude, and the savannah country on either side of the Equator has well-defined wet and dry, hot and cool seasons. North of the Equator the dry cool season corresponds roughly to the European winter. South of the line this season falls in our late summer.

The People

The people of the Congo are predominantly Bantu and belong to the western branch of that great family. The habitat of this branch coincides fairly accurately with our region of Equatoria, with the addition of Angola, whose African peoples are also Western Bantu.[1] The Congo has seen the rise and fall of several important and extensive kingdoms, of which one was the eponymous Congo, befriended by Portugal in the fifteenth century.[2] Now the Bantu of the Congo can be regarded as falling into three groups, a western, a southern and a central, each containing a great number of different tribes.[3] They include the Bushongo, in several ways the most developed of the Western Bantu, whose artistic skill has already been mentioned.[4]

In the extreme north-west of the country, occupying most of the Ubangi-Uele basin, is a group of Sudanic-speaking tribes with characteristics which distinguish them both from the Bantu and from the Nilotes of the Sudan. The most important are the Mangbetu and the Azande. The other non-Bantu minority are the Negrillos or pygmies, hunters, trappers and collectors, whose home is the thick tropical forest on either side of the Equator. They are generally on good terms with the neighbouring Bantu tribes, whose languages they speak and with whom they barter game meat for their simple necessities. The total population of the Congo is believed to be between 13 and 14 million.   (*Plate* 97)

History

On his second expedition to Africa in 1874–7 H. M. Stanley solved the problem of the Lualaba and other rivers west of Lake Tanganyika and followed the Congo River down to the sea. On his return to Europe he pressed the British Government to take the Congo basin, and when his proposals were rejected, turned to King Leopold II of the Belgians, who readily fell in with Stanley's

[1] Angola was described in Chapter Two.
[2] pp. 109–110.
[3] Seligman, *Races of Africa*, p. 186.
[4] p. 190.

plans. The King had already shown his interest in Africa when in 1876 he convened a meeting of geographers and others from which emerged the 'International Association for the exploration and civilization of Africa'. When Stanley came home a committee of the Association was set up called the 'Comité d'études du Haut Congo', which later became the 'International Association of the Congo'. The Association was international only in name for it soon passed entirely into the hands of the King of the Belgians. Stanley went back to the Congo as agent of the Association and spent four years building stations and making treaties with the chiefs. All the powers that took part in the Conference of Berlin in 1884–5 gave formal recognition to the Association, and the General Act of the Conference provided, *inter alia*, for freedom of trade in the Congo basin and free navigation of the river. Soon after the conference King Leopold was proclaimed sovereign of the 'Independent State of the Congo' or Congo Free State, which he proceeded to rule as a personal domain and in no way as a dependency of Belgium.

Serious opposition to the new state came from the Arab slave and ivory traders who had settled in the country west of Lake Tanganyika. This culminated in 1892 in a war which lasted several months and which ended in the total defeat of the Arabs by the State forces.

In order to develop his vast tropical estate King Leopold gave out great concessions based on a monopoly of trade and industry, and it was not long before well-founded charges of gross abuses and oppression began to be levelled against the administration. These had to do with atrocities committed during the collection of wild rubber from the Natives. Following vigorous international agitation the King appointed a commission of inquiry whose recommendations led to some changes in the administration. These were not however of a character to satisfy the critics and in 1908 Leopold finally yielded to the pressure of international opinion and ceded the State to the Belgian Government. At the end of the 1914–18 war the districts of Ruanda and Urundi, formerly part of German East Africa, were entrusted to Belgium to be administered as a mandated territory under the League of Nations. They became a U.N.O. trust territory at the end of the Second World War.[1] During that war and after the fall of Belgium to the Germans, the Congo continued to fight beside the Allies. Congolese troops took

[1] Chapter Three.

part in the Abyssinian campaign and the Congo was also a valuable source of much needed materials.

On assuming responsibility for the administration of the Congo in 1908 the Belgian Government lost no time in correcting the abuses which had brought the Free State Government into disrepute. A sound administration was set up and the resources of the country were vigorously developed. The political aim seems to have lain somewhere between that of the British and the French. There was little tendency towards decentralization, certainly no suggestion of future colonial self-government. Only very limited opportunities were given to Africans to acquire the social or official status of Europeans, and the number of educated Africans is even today very small. Neither Africans nor Europeans had franchise rights. On the other hand the Belgians laid great emphasis on African advance in the field of technology. Every form of skilled employment of a technical nature was open to Africans and the Native became increasingly absorbed into the industrial life of the country with a consequent progressive improvement in his standard of living.

The labour policy of the Belgians was profoundly different from that of the other European powers in Africa. The latter have usually encouraged, or at least tolerated, the migration of labour. Working for wages is regarded as a somewhat abnormal occupation, to pursue which a man travels some distance to a place of employment and stays there for a period of months or years, ultimately, however, returning to his home. Indeed this procedure fits in very well with the African's own attitude towards paid labour.[1] The Belgians on the other hand aimed at the stabilization of labour, that is to say at the creation in due course of a settled population of whole-time industrial workers. This meant the provision of facilities far more attractive and permanent than the compounds and labour lines of other African industrial areas. The Copper Belt in particular has well laid out native villages, good houses, adequate water supplies and sanitation, hospitals, schools and training centres, everything in fact that from the material standpoint may contribute to a full and comfortable urban life.

The winds of change blew over the Belgian Congo as they did over the rest of Africa. This vast area, where comparatively high industrial achievement stands out in contrast with conditions which are among the most primitive in Africa, which had until recently

[1] But see Southern Rhodesian policy, p. 99.

shown no sign of political consciousness, suddenly developed an overpowering thirst for independence. The Belgian Government quickly acceded to the demands of the leaders, elections were held and independence followed in the middle of 1960. Hardly were the independence festivities over when the country began to fall apart, and, as everyone knows, is now one of the trouble spots of the world. Some reference to the present situation will be made later.

Economy—Minerals

This section must, alas, be written in the past tense. The economy of the Congo is grinding to a standstill and no one can predict how and when it will recover. It is therefore only possible to describe things as they were under Belgian rule.

Minerals are the most important factor in the economic life of the country and formerly represented about two-thirds of the exports. Mineral development played a decisive part in determining the direction taken by rail and river transport; it influenced Belgian policy in regard to the lines planned for African advance; and it was long the principal object of investment for Belgian capital. Moreover it is to minerals that are due the rapid rise in the prosperity of the Congo during the last twenty years, an impressive industrial advance in certain areas, the improvement in communications and the development of social services.

The focus of the mineral industry is the province of Katanga, an undulating plateau of an average altitude exceeding 3,500 feet, situated in the south-west of the territory. Katanga is especially noted for its copper, mined by Natives long before the appearance of the Europeans, and worked by the Belgians since 1911. The Katanga copper field is one of the richest in the world and makes this province, after the Witwatersrand, the most important commercial and industrial area in Africa.

The Congo was the world's largest producer of cobalt, which is found in association with copper, and it also produced 90 per cent of the world's requirements of industrial diamonds. Most of these came from the province of Kasai. Other important minerals are tin, manganese, zinc, cadmium, uranium, radium and coal. Most mining operations were in the hands of large companies, almost all Belgian-owned, but the state held the rights in the land, and mining could only be done under concession from the state. The government was in the practice of retaining a substantial share in the stock of the mining companies, and the state therefore had an important interest in the development of the country's minerals.

Agriculture

Native food crops include cassava, maize, bananas, rice, corn and groundnuts. The principal cash crops were rubber, cotton, coffee and vegetable oils, which together accounted for nine-tenths of the agricultural exports.

At one time the collection of wild rubber represented 80 per cent of the exports of the Congo Free State, and it was indeed with this industry that were associated most of the abuses with which the Free State was charged and which led to the transfer of the administration to the Belgian Government. But wild rubber could not withstand the competition of plantation rubber, and although the wild product came in for renewed demand during the last war, it is now uneconomic and off the market. Most of the rubber from the Congo was grown on European plantations. Cotton was an entirely native-grown crop but was sold and processed through several large companies established in the Congo. Coffee was grown both by Europeans and Africans, but the African contribution was a small one. About one-third of the production was *Arabica* and the remainder *Robusta*.

It was to the oil palm that the Belgians first turned when plantation rubber from the Far East first began to supplant wild rubber, hitherto the mainstay of Congolese economy. But in this field too the wild product proved to be comparatively of inferior quality and in 1911–12 the Belgian Government accepted an offer by the Leverhulme interests to establish plantations and generally to assist in the organization of the industry. The Leverhulme interests were represented by the *Huileries du Congo Belge*, and other concessions were later granted to plantation or oil processing companies.

Transport

The Congo system of river transport is easily the most important and extensive network of inland waterways in tropical Africa. There are 9,000 miles of navigable river and although the main stream and its tributaries are interrupted at critical points by falls and rapids, there are very long stretches of unobstructed waterway, notably between Leopoldville and Stanleyville, a distance of nearly 1,100 miles, and from Leopoldville to Port Francqui, about 378 miles up the Kasai River from its junction with the Congo. In days of prosperity each of these stretches carried 400,000 tons of traffic yearly. In several cases the unnavigable spots have been by-passed by rail links, and although this involves repeated unloading and reloading of goods in transit, it does provide a fairly comprehensive surface transport system from one end of the country to the other.

The railways of the Congo were originally designed to supplement the river system, but in recent years the relative importance of these two means of transport changed. With the opening up of new sources of production in areas distant from the rivers, the railways came to be regarded as ends in themselves, indeed as the major arterial lines of communication. Even more recently, with the discovery that within certain limits the cost in the Congo of carriage by road is less than by rail, plans for road construction were given precedence over new railway projects. As it is the Congo has six railway systems. Comparatively the busiest was the Leopold-ville–Matadi line, 227 miles in length, and carrying more freight to the mile of track than any of the others. In the east there is a great combined rail-water system connecting Stanleyville with Albertville on Lake Tanganyika with a total length of 1,470 miles. The *Chemin de fer du Bas-Congo au Katanga* (B.C.K.) serves the great mineral area of Katanga and is connected to the Rhodesian and Benguela railways. The remaining systems are the Vicicongo in the north (425 miles), the 'Cefaki' or Kivu line in the east (57 miles) and the 2′ gauge Mayumbe line running 87 miles northwards from Boma near the mouth of the Congo River.

The Congo after Independence

The present situation in the Congo, of which no coherent account can be given in a book designed to be factual, is proof that although a country can rub along quite well without politicians, it can hardly exist for a moment without a reasonable civil service, whether that service be on modern or on traditional lines. When the Belgians left there was not a single African officer for the security forces, not a single African doctor, lawyer or engineer, nor any individual who had ever filled a post of even moderate seniority in the public service. Nor apparently were there any chiefs or representatives of the old order to whom the people in their extremity might turn for reassurance and leadership. Apart from Katanga, which remained reasonably stable, the country was without an administration of any kind. As a result law and order broke down, the economy disintegrated, and although a rural community with a low standard of living can resist the worst effects of such a situation for some time, famine conditions already exist in several areas and must inevitably spread. One supposes that somewhere, somehow, a sort of authority is maintained at village level, but the civil population is bullied and plundered by a drunken and disorderly rabble which was once the Congolese army, now split into a number of undisciplined factions. The country itself is divided into several mutually antagonistic parts under phantasmagoric 'leaders' who in some cases are the tools of foreign powers African and European. The United Nations, whose early intervention aroused high hopes, are divided in counsel and ineffective in action. In the present climate of world opinion there is no possibility of applying the obvious remedy, nothing less than a massive dose of neo-colonialism, administered if need be under international mandate. Even if it were possible to disarm and disband the army, this alone would be an important step towards normality. As things are, we can only support the agencies providing relief in the distressed areas, encourage the United Nations to play a more positive part in restoring order, and avoid any gesture that could serve as an excuse to the Russians or to their fellow-travellers again mischievously to intervene. Beyond that we can only pray for a miracle.

EQUATORIAL AFRICA

History

French interest in Equatorial Africa began in the days when France was engaged with Britain in suppressing the Slave Trade. In 1839 a naval officer named Bouët-Guillaumetz obtained the right of residence at two small places on the left bank of the Gaboon estuary and in 1843 similar rights on the other bank. During the next few years arrangements of the same kind were made up and down the coast and in 1849 the French followed the British example in Sierra Leone and deposited a number of ex-slaves[1] at a settlement which they called Libreville. It was not for some years that the French did anything to spread from the coast of the Gaboon into the hinterland; not, in fact, until 1875 when the explorer Savorgnan de Brazza travelled up the Ogowe River and crossed over to the Congo basin. In the course of a second

[1] They had been rescued from a slaving vessel.

expedition in 1880–82 he founded Brazzaville, and using this as a base made treaties with the local peoples which placed large areas north of the Congo River under French protection. Between 1885 and 1891 the French secured most of the Gaboon and Middle Congo and then proceeded to expand eastwards towards the Nile and northwards towards the French possessions in North Africa. The spearhead of the eastward advance was Major Marchand's fruitless expedition to Fashoda[1] but the northward movement succeeded, after many years of effort, in securing the whole of the Chad territory and hence through the Niger Colony a continuous empire from Equatorial Africa to the Mediterranean.

After several experiments in government the area was divided into four colonies which were the Gaboon, the Middle Congo, the Ubangi-Shari and the Chad territory, joined in a federation with a governor-general whose headquarters were at Brazzaville. In Chad the French met with prolonged resistance from the tribes and the territory was not transferred from military to civil administration until 1920.

When France fell in 1940 the Governor of Chad, a Negro named Eboué born in French Guiana, proclaimed that his colony would join General de Gaulle. The other French Equatorial territories and the French mandated territory of the Cameroons followed this example with the result that Brazzaville became the capital of Free France in Africa and Equatorial Africa became an important base for the Allies. In particular Chad played a most valuable part in the North African campaigns. Eboué himself was appointed to be Governor-General and continued in that office until 1944 when his death robbed France and Africa of a most remarkable man.

The four French colonies availed themselves of their opportunity under the new constitution of 1958[2] to become autonomous republics within the French community. Of the three with which we are here concerned,[3] the Middle Congo has been re-christened the Congo Republic, Ubangi-Shari is the Central African Republic, but the Gaboon has retained its former name.

The Country

The coastline is about 800 miles long and is low and swampy,

---

[1] p. 53.
[2] p. 193.
[3] The reader is reminded that Chad has been included in West Africa.

and fringed with sandspits and lagoons, in this way resembling parts of the coast of West Africa. The southern and longer section is very straight and has few if any good natural harbours. The northern section has several bays and inlets, of which the largest is the Gaboon estuary.[1] The ground rises quickly to the plateau, which averages 2,000 to 3,000 feet. Several massifs of greater height tower above the general level. The western slopes are drained by the Ogowe and Kwilu river systems, flowing directly to the Atlantic. The rest of the territory is drained by tributaries of the Congo such as the Mbomu, Ubangi and Sanga. There is dense forest in the Gaboon and in the Congo Republic. In the north the vegetation is savannah degenerating to thorny bush towards the dividing line between the Chad and Congo basins. The total area is rather less than half a million square miles.

There are two principal climatic belts, the Equatorial and the Sudanic. The former is that of the lower part of the territory and is characterized by temperatures which are fairly constant round 77° and by heavy rainfall, high humidity and a very short dry season. The Sudanic climate is hotter, with a longer dry season, but it has fairly wide daily and seasonal variations. This is the climate of the more northerly part of the region.

The People

The estimated African population is under $2\frac{1}{2}$ million, and there are about 22,000 Europeans. Most of the African people of the great forest zones of the Ogowe and the Congo, including the Ubangi in its lower course, are Bantu of whom the best known are perhaps the Pangwe, the most important people of the Gaboon. Across the upper half of the Central African Republic there are communities of Negroes with a mixture of Hamitic blood, having much in common with their neighbours in the Sudan and Northern Nigeria but distinguished from Negroes with stronger Hamitic strains not only by physical traits but also by the fact that they are primarily agriculturalists and not pastoralists.

Economy

Like the King of the Belgians in the Congo, the French first sought to develop Equatorial Africa by means of concessions. These concessions gave to the grantees monopolistic control over

[1] So called by the Portuguese navigators who discovered it because of a fancied likeness to a gabão or cabin.

forest produce, with a guarantee of an ultimate freehold over selected areas of land. The first rush of concessions involved about two-thirds of the whole of Equatorial Africa, seriously affecting the use by Natives of their own land. Public feeling in France against the abuses of monopolies led to a drastic revision of the system. Long negotiations ended in the abandonment of their concessions by a number of the companies concerned in return for compensation in various forms, including the grant of freehold over considerable areas. The country was thus relieved, at considerable cost to the Africans, of the commitments so precipitately incurred in the early days of European rule, and new legislation in 1947 placed further limitations on the disposal of land. The total area covered by concessions in 1951 was stated still to be 330,000 acres, but it is impossible to foresee what the attitude of the new independent republics will be towards land alienation by the former colonial Power. The emphasis placed in the past on development through European agencies has not resulted in any startling advance in the country's prosperity. On the contrary, economic standards are rather low, and this is due, not to the absence of possibilities, but to a weakness in the foundations on which the country's economy is built.

Basic native foodstuffs are cassava, yams, bananas, maize, sorghum, sweet potatoes and rice. In the southern forest area, especially in the Gaboon, timber is of the greatest economic importance. The forest also yields palm oil and palm kernels and rubber, and there are European-owned oil palm plantations. Cotton dominates the economy in the Ubangi area. The forest zones are infested with tsetse fly, and there are consequently very few cattle in the Gaboon and Congo Republic. The Central African Republic also has tsetse but is not so densely infested, and is consequently able to maintain a small cattle population.

The mining industry is of growing importance but is hampered by inadequacy of transport and the nature of the country. There is gold in all three territories and there are diamonds in the Ubangi area. Other minerals are lead, zinc and copper. The most important mineral find of recent years is a very large manganese deposit in the Gaboon.

Industrial equipment is not rich, especially in comparison with the Congo next door as it was under Belgian rule. Industry has suffered from a lack of cheap power, scarcity of labour, low domestic consumption and a small population. Hydro-electric power is potentially great and several schemes have lately been brought into operation. The other deficiencies are less easily remedied. The largest manufacturing activity is the lumber industry, followed by the processing of crops such as the fruit of the oil palm, groundnuts, sesame and cotton seed. Cotton ginning is a rapidly growing industry.

The only railway is the so-called Congo–Ocean line, 306 miles long, completed in 1934 and recently modernized and provided with diesel locomotives. It runs from Pointe Noire on the Atlantic coastline of the Congo Republic to Brazzaville at Stanley Pool, which is the beginning of the navigable part of the Congo. Considering the peculiar difficulties presented by the terrain, the road system is remarkably good, and air transport facilities both internal and external are quite well developed.

Inland waterways are about 3,000 miles long but the course is interrupted in places by rapids and by seasonal variations in water levels. The most important is a stretch of 720 miles along the Congo and Ubangi rivers from Brazzaville to Bangui, the capital of the Central African Republic. This is navigable for six months in the year throughout its length, and on the Congo section during the whole year. The Gaboon has a number of navigable rivers used mainly to float logs from the forest to the Atlantic ports.

THE CAMEROONS

The Cameroons is largely a plateau which rises towards the west and falls away in the south-east towards the Congo basin. The coastal plain is narrow, with mangrove swamps, sand-bars and lagoons. The Cameroon Mountain rises majestically above it to a height of 13,430 feet. From the central highlands of the territory rivers flow in all directions, some direct to the Atlantic Ocean, some to the Benue, some to the Congo system and some towards Lake Chad. The vegetational pattern is similar to that found in other parts of this region of Africa. There is dense forest in the south, giving way in the north first to wooded savannah and then gradually to dry scrubland where the territory touches Lake Chad. The highlands have a variety of fine mountain scenery. On the coast the rainfall is heavy and well distributed throughout the year. Duala receives an annual fall of 155 inches. This decreases towards the north and the annual rainfall round Lake Chad is no more than 12–15 inches. (The western side of the Cameroon Mountain receives 400–430 inches a year but the conditions are special.)

15

The temperature is fairly high, being between 72° and 89° in the south and rising considerably higher in the Chad basin.

Formerly a Germany colony the Cameroons was divided after the 1914–18 war between the British and the French to be administered under mandate from the League of Nations. The British mandated territory has already been described as part of West Africa,[1] but the French territory, the more easterly and by far the larger, 166,500 square miles in area and with a population of over three million, gives the impression of being essentially equatorial in character and hence is more fittingly dealt with here.

The French mandate became a trusteeship under the United Nations Organization like its British counterpart, and in due course an 'associated territory' of the French Union. It became independent on 1 January 1960 with the name Cameroun Republic. Political difficulties assailed the independent government immediately. While the country was still administered by France a man named Ruben um Nyobe founded a militant party called the 'Union des populations Camerounaises' (usually shortened to U.P.C.), with a programme of independence and union with the British-administered Cameroons. The U.P.C. was declared illegal in 1955 and Ruben was killed by the French in 1958. Shortly after his death the French announced that the country would be granted full independence in 1960, whereupon one section of the U.P.C. agreed to work in a constitutional manner and was disbanded under an amnesty that was offered at the time. The other section, directed from outside the Cameroons by a Dr. Felix Moumié, a man with strong communist affiliations, continued the campaign even though the French Cameroons is independent and the U.P.C. has been legalized. This section is particularly powerful among the Bamileke tribe on the frontier between the former British and French Cameroons, whose country the mandate arrangements of 1919 arbitrarily divided. The campaign has now lost all association with a political programme and is simply an affair of gang warfare, brigandage and resistance to authority. It is estimated that some fifty thousand people are in revolt against their government and that there is an average of 200 killings a month, often of a most gruesome character. Moumié died under mysterious circumstances in Switzerland in 1960.[2] The Government can do nothing and the

---

[1] p. 180 et al.

[2] According to press reports, Moumié said before he died that a French organization called the Red Hand had poisoned him.

only stable factor in an anarchic situation are some French troops who are doing their best under difficulties to stop the disorders. Meanwhile, to their great alarm, the people on the British side have found themselves forced to give shelter to rebels using British territory as cover and as a springboard for new raids. Nigerian troops were sent to patrol the frontier and deport terrorists, but they were withdrawn and replaced by a British regiment when Nigeria became independent.

Racially the people are extremely mixed but may be divided into two main groups according to whether they speak Bantu or Sudanic languages. The Bantu live in the southern and central areas and the Sudanic speakers in the north. The northern areas have in the past been frequently invaded by fair-skinned Semites and Hamites, for example the Fulani who founded the empire of Adamawa which straddled the north of the future German Cameroons and the eastern side of Northern Nigeria. This empire collapsed with the coming of the Europeans and the partition of the country between the British and the Germans. There are pygmies in the forests of the Sanga River.

The economy of the Cameroun Republic is based on agriculture and the exploitation of forest produce, both largely in African hands. Apart from food crops, Africans produce cocoa, coffee, groundnuts, palm oil and palm kernels. European settlers grow coffee and bananas. Mining is still comparatively undeveloped. Cattle and horses are reared in the northern and central parts of the country. The southern part is infested with tsetse fly and pastoral pursuits play little part in the economy.

THE SPANISH AND PORTUGUESE COLONIES

Spanish Guinea includes a small enclave on the mainland between the Rio Muni and the Cameroons and a number of islands, the largest of which is Fernando Po. The seat of government is at Santa Isabel on Fernando Po, which has an area of 800 square miles, a population (with the other smaller islands) of under 30,000, including 3,000–4,000 Europeans, and is a collection of extinct volcanoes, being part of the southerly extension of the Cameroons volcanic chain. It is from here that the cocoa bean is said to have been carried to the Gold Coast in 1870. In more recent years Fernando Po came into prominence less auspiciously when international investigation in the 'thirties of the present century proved that high Liberian officials had been selling slave labour from their country to the Spanish colony. There are extensive European plantations and the principal export crops are cocoa and coffee. The indigenous Africans belong to a tribe called Bubi but they are considerably outnumbered by immigrant labourers, mainly Ibo from Nigeria.

The mainland territory, which is equatorial in climate and aspect, has an area of something over 10,000 square miles and a population under 200,000. There are large timber concessions and plantations of oil palm and coffee. The Africans grow coffee and cocoa for export.

The Portuguese islands of St. Thomas and Principe lie south of Fernando Po and form part of the same volcanic chain. They have an area of 372 square miles and a population of something over 60,000. St. Thomas in particular has well-developed European-owned plantations of cocoa, coconuts, oil palm and cinchona. Immigrant labourers from Angola form the majority of the population.

It would be unfitting to close this description of Equatorial Africa without reference to one of the great men of the age who lives and works there. This is Dr. Albert Schweitzer, priest, theologian, philosopher, musician and doctor. Schweitzer came to Africa in 1913 and built a hospital at a place called Lambarene, 175 miles up the Ogowe River in the heart of the Gaboon. Schweitzer was then thirty-eight years of age but had only recently qualified as a doctor of medicine, having already attained some eminence in philosophy, theology and music. He paid for the expedition to Africa out of gifts from the parish where he was curate, and from his earnings as lecturer and organist. His work at Lambarene is too well known to need further description here. Now, at the age of eighty-six, assisted by a small staff of doctors and nurses, Schweitzer still presides despotically and lovingly over his creation, an embodiment of practical idealism in the service of the African.

CHAPTER NINE

SMALL ISLANDS

ATLANTIC OCEAN

MADEIRA is the largest of a group of islands belonging to Portugal and lying about 400 miles from the coast of Morocco. The islands have an aggregate area of 314 square miles and a population of about 270,000. They are volcanic and rise abruptly from the ocean. Pico Ruivo, the highest point on Madeira, reaches a height of 6,056 feet and some of the other peaks are not much lower. The steep slopes are carefully terraced to prevent soil erosion. Many kinds of fruit grow in abundance, early vegetables are raised for the European market, and the wines, especially the dessert varieties, are famous. Local industries, which include lace making, wickerwork and woodwork, centre largely on providing for tourists whom the agreeable climate attracts to Madeira in large numbers. Funchal on the south of this island is an important port of call for vessels bound for West and South Africa. The population is basically Portuguese but contains Moorish, Italian and Negro elements.

The Canaries are a group of islands belonging to Spain, of which the best known are Tenerife and Grand Canary. They were originally inhabited by a Berber people called Guanche, now extinct, but they fell to Spain in the course of the fifteenth century. The present inhabitants are a little darker than Spaniards but in other respects are indistinguishable from them. The total area of the group is 2,800 square miles and the population about 800,000. Like Madeira, the Canaries are volcanic and rise steeply from the sea. The snow-capped peak of Tenerife reaches a height of 12,000 feet. Lying as they do close to the African coast these islands are more arid than Madeira, especially on the eastern side. However, the soil is fertile, and when irrigated produces an abundance of fruit, vegetables and other crops. Fishing is an important industry and lace making and embroidery are local handicrafts. The islanders lean heavily on the tourist trade. Puerto de la Luiz on Grand Canary and Santa Cruz on Tenerife are considerable ports of call for shipping.

The Cape Verde Islands, 300 miles off Cape Verde on the African mainland, are an old Portuguese colony with a total area of 1,500 square miles and a population of 180,000. There are fourteen islands in all, of which ten are inhabited. They are of volcanic origin, and the highest peak, Fogo, has only recently become extinct. The average annual temperature is high and the rainfall low, but in spite of their aridity the islands produce a large variety of crops, including coffee of high quality, castor seed, tobacco, corn and beans. The majority of the inhabitants are of Negro origin.

INDIAN OCEAN

Socotra is an island about 150 miles east-north-east of Cape Guardafui, seventy-five miles long and twenty-two miles wide, with an area of 1,400 square miles. Politically it represents the insular part of the Mahri sultanate of Kishin and Socotra in the Eastern Aden Protectorate. The Sultan himself lives on the island in the village of Hadibu on the northern coast.

The island is mostly mountainous along its axis with granite peaks that rise to a height of nearly 5,000 feet above a limestone plateau of 1,000 to 1,500 feet. The mountains are cool and usually cloud- or mist-covered, but the lowlands are hot and malarious. The island is seamed with gorges which are normally dry but sometimes become raging torrents during the rainy season from November to April. The flora has affinities not only with that of Asia, Africa and the Mascarenes, but also with that of Polynesia and South America.

The population is about 8,000 and consists of two main elements. The coastal people are mostly Arabs and Africans, the latter being largely descendants of slaves from East Africa, though some are the offspring of West African soldiers stationed on Socotra during the last war. The nomadic pastoral inhabitants of the mountainous interior are Socotri proper, some tall and fair-skinned, others shorter and darker. The Socotri speak a language which with Mahri, to which it is related, and the pre-Islamic dialects of Arabia, forms an independent branch of the south Semitic family. Although they were Christians for centuries, the Socotri are now nominally Moslem.

The economy is a poor one. The principal occupations are fishing and raising the small Socotran cattle. The main exports are ghee (clarified butter), said to be the best in the whole of the northern Indian ocean, and mother of pearl. Other exports, of which the volume is small, are the red-coloured resin called dragon's blood, aloes' juice, lichen, ambergris, civet musk, dried shark, pottery, pearls, rugs, skins, and tobacco. Agriculture is precarious, and the islanders are compelled to import foodstuffs such as maize and rice. Dates are an important article of diet.

Socotra was known to the Greeks and Romans and appears in the *Periplus of the Erythraean Sea* as a busy trading station. During the European middle ages it was a notable haunt of Indian pirates. It was seized by the Portuguese in 1507 but abandoned in 1511. With the opening of the Suez Canal Socotra lay right astride the sea route to India and thus became of some importance to Great Britain. From 1876 onwards the Sultan received a subsidy from the government in Aden and in 1886 he formally placed himself under British protection. In effect this means that the Sultan's government has complete control of all internal matters, British supervision being limited to foreign affairs.

Abd-el-Kuri is a small island lying between Socotra and Cape Guardafui inhabited by pearl divers and fishermen. Other islands in the group are Kal Farun and The Brothers.

PART III

CONCLUSION

CONCLUSION

IF a survey of Africa in this time of change may seem a bold undertaking, an attempt to prophesy the future is positively foolhardy. Yet this is just what the author now intends to do. And since the views about to be expressed are his own and certainly will not commend themselves to everybody, he will abandon the impersonal style which he has till now been at pains to maintain and air his opinions freely in the first person singular.

Reservations must first be made. Perhaps the most important is that in discussing Africa we must never underestimate our ignorance. It is of course true that in the last hundred years much light has been shed on a continent that until modern times was little known to the outside world. But this light has, as it were, only illuminated the surface. Here and there a few scholars, a handful of scientists, some missionaries and administrators have dug deeper; but they themselves would be the first to admit that their researches are in a restricted field and that the results only reach a very limited public. Most people take their knowledge of Africa from other Europeans, publicists, journalists, travellers, who are usually ignorant of African languages and get their own information from western-educated Africans who are often almost as remote from the common people as are the Europeans themselves. We simply do not know what the African thinks and feels, what he is told and what he believes, and our approach to all we read and hear about Africa must therefore be exceedingly cautious, in the recognition that the material on which it is based is flimsy and at best second-hand.

Next, we must bear in mind that the effects of the Cold War are incalculable and that there are many who believe that Africa, or large parts of it, may ultimately fall under communist domination. Just as it is impossible, so runs the argument, to regard the destiny of south-east Asia except as that of a sphere for Chinese colonization, so must we be prepared to see the newly emergent states of Africa fall one by one to the Russian drive to capture the continent.[1] On this question I have an open mind. I can only say here that two and possibly three African states lend some support to these pessimistic speculations and have approached perilously near to

[1] This drive is circumstantially described in *The Times*, 12 January 1961.

the communist camp, which is a country 'from whose bourn no traveller returns'. But since a collection of Russian satellites offers us no basis for discussion here, we must assume for the purpose of this book that emergent Africa will retain as long as we can foresee freedom to shape her own future, influenced perhaps, but not dominated, by external forces.

The basic fact of Africa today is the change from a colonial form of administration to full independence, a process enormously hastened since the Second World War and largely accomplished during 1960. The dynamic factor in this change is African nationalism, a complex phenomenon for which nationalism is perhaps the wrong name, since there are in Africa very few nations in the European sense. African nationalism is rather a racial consciousness which on its negative side is a rejection of control by people regarded as outsiders, and on the positive a yearning for equality, the search for an African 'personality' which will fill a respected place in the world alongside other nations and races. This emotion has found a base and a springboard in the various territorial divisions created by Europeans at the time of the partition of Africa and has already acquired an extensive martyrology and *mystique*. Its exponents are a highly articulate if somewhat restricted group with wide popular appeal, and if the propagation of nationalism has been accompanied by a good deal of hocus pocus and intimidation, and if on its positive side it appears at present to lack direction and content, it must be recognized that it is irresistible and is the force that is fashioning Africa now. The measure of its success is the fact that with the exception of one or two territories the whole of Africa down to the Congo and Tanganyika inclusive is independent or nearly so.

How long nationalism in its present form will survive its own success appears to me doubtful. It is, as we have seen, based on territorial divisions created by Europeans and it would be surprising if these unnatural boundaries were henceforward long to resist the facts of ethnology, religion, geography and economics. The map of Africa at the end of this century will be surprisingly different from what it is now. Nor do I see much probability of unions, amalgamations and federations of territories. It is more likely that as independence becomes consolidated and the boundaries rearranged, emphasis will be on differences rather than on similarities. I suggest that Africa for many years to come will be fissiparous rather than coalescent.

As it matures nationalism will also lose something of its idealism. It was after all the product of the European impact, and as that impact lessens, so must the movement change. If, on the one hand, the African nationalist rejects European control, he has on the other wholeheartedly embraced the western values of equality and in one area at least he has adopted the catchword 'one man, one vote' as a popular slogan. It is doubtful whether these liberal concepts will survive the reality of power. Present indications are that the governments of independent Africa will be highly centralized and will tend to perpetuate the dominance of a single party managed by a small group of top people, between whom and the masses there is a deep gulf. The one man may get his one vote, but he probably will not use it more than once. Authoritarianism of this type is not characteristically nor traditionally African but it will not be challenged until the spread of education develops an informed and effective public opinion.

Colonial rule in Africa set in motion a process of social change that is now irreversible. Many Europeans regarded the process with misgiving, as being too brutal, too sudden, too demoralizing. Indeed the British in particular often sought to slow it down by the caution with which measures of reform were introduced, always deferring, whenever possible, to conservatism and custom. Such gradualism makes no appeal to the African nationalist, in whom we may here note a curious dualism. On the one hand he looks back with nostalgia to his quasi-mythical past, which he sees as a golden age of culture and prosperity and which he seeks to evoke by bestowing on new countries such ancient names as Ghana and Mali. On the other he has by no means rejected European methods and techniques but on the contrary has adopted th em wholeheartedly as the key to the modern world. We shall not see in Africa, as in India in the time of Gandhi, a deliberate return to the spinning wheel as a protest against Europeanization and the 'dark satanic mills'. The modern African wants his mills and he does not think that they are dark or satanic. We must therefore expect that independent African governments will ruthlessly brush away those customary and social institutions which they believe stand in the way of progress, and that the rate of change will be accordingly accelerated.

African nationalism has been much more concerned with politics than with economics. It is natural that this should be so. Economics, let us face it, are rather dull stuff to most people,

AFRICA

Former Political Divisions

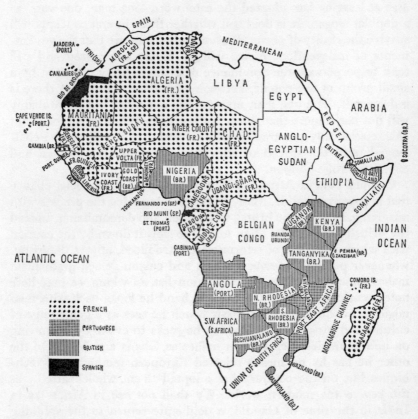

This map represents the position as it was in the early 1950s. The powers administering dependencies are shown by the various hatchings. The distinction between colonies, protectorates and trusteeships is not shown on the map, but may be found in the text.

AFRICA

Regions and Territories

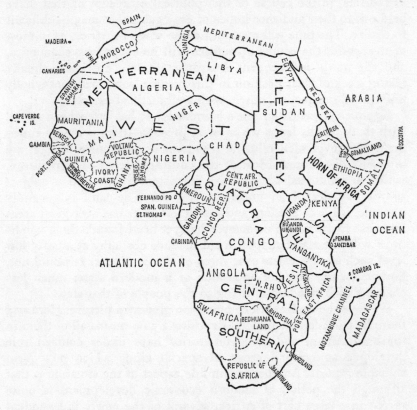

- - - - - - - - - - - -   Territorial boundary

—————————   Regional boundary

whereas politics, besides being exciting in themselves, offer to those educated Africans with magnetism and a gift for oratory immediate rewards in terms of power and popularity. This is not to say that African nationalism is altogether without economic content of a kind. Some leaders, and certainly a number of their supporters, in the course of this political campaign or that, have held out to their audience hopes of easy gains that may be difficult to realize. The time will no doubt come when in Africa, as in most of the world, the course of politics will be shaped by economics, and the newly independent African states are no doubt already taking stock of their position in this respect, some with not wholly unfounded satisfaction, others with well justified anxiety.

So much depends on one's standards! It has often been stated with truth that as far as we know at present Africa is a poor continent. Moreover such valuable resources as are known to exist are unevenly distributed. Most of the continent relies on agriculture, which is conducted largely on a subsistence basis and is subject to the vagaries of an uncertain climate. The land is generally infertile, liable to erosion, and restricted in its use over great areas by tsetse fly, to which no answer has yet been found. Such conditions will just about support a subsistence economy at a fairly low level such as now exists over most of the continent. It would not, however, carry the full apparatus of a modern state, much less ensure a high standard of living to the people of that state.

We must be careful not to paint too gloomy a picture. Here and there lie considerable mineral deposits, by no means all of them in southern Africa, and some territories have under colonial rule developed agricultural crops of special kinds which now form valuable exports. Another favourable aspect of the situation is that although the period of modern economic development is quite recent in a large part of Africa, several of the newly independent states have inherited from the colonial powers quite buoyant economies and useful capital equipment.

Finally, we must remember that Africa still has many assets that remain unexploited. The mineral resources are still by no means known, the rivers represent an immense reserve of unused power and could also be still further developed for transport, tourism is potentially an important industry especially if timely steps are taken to preserve game, the land, now so sadly abused, could be made to produce more and yet be protected against exhaustion and erosion, fisheries could be developed. In all these aspects of development and in many more the colonial powers have shown the way. The successor governments will find ample scope for their energies in pursuing and widening them.

It is however to foreign skill and capital—European and Asian—that are largely due such economic advances as have already been achieved in Africa. It follows that at the present early stage of development this skill and capital must be encouraged and conserved. Alongside a programme of education designed to produce the classes from which professional men, craftsmen and artisans are drawn, African governments will, if they are wise, aim at creating a situation of economic and political security which will attract men and money from abroad and persuade them to stay.

There is no ex-colony in Africa with an adequate indigenous civil service. In each case the heavy responsibility of self-government has come before an educated middle class had emerged of the type from which officials are normally drawn. In some countries, for instance the Congo, this deficiency was so glaring as to result in anarchy. In others it has been supplied, and disaster thus averted, by the good sense of the educated minority, the existence of respected agencies of traditional rule such as chiefs and headmen, and good relations between the old colonial government and the new independent one. One of the virtues of colonial rule was that in most cases it provided Africa with a devoted and efficient administration. If the aspirations of modern Africa are to be realized these standards must be maintained, and until a fully efficient and reliable African bureaucracy can be trained (and this includes doctors, veterinary officers, police officers, teachers and so on) the new states would be wise to offer every inducement to Europeans, who may well be members of the old colonial service, to remain in the country. Some metropolitan powers were more imaginative than others in preparing the public service for the transition from colonial rule to independence. The Belgians were the worst of all, but the British were by no means free from reproach. Nevertheless there are still plenty of devoted men and women who would be happy to serve in the new states if they were assured of a satisfying career—I am not now thinking of material rewards but of opportunities for service—and this fund of goodwill should not be wasted.

When all is said and done the most perplexing problem of modern Africa is that of the relationship between Africans and the other races, European and Asian, that have taken root in various

16

places of the continent. It may generally be said that the larger
the non-African community the more difficult it is to strike a
balance of interests that will satisfy all parties. It must however be
recognized that time and the climate of world opinion are on the
side of the African and that it is impossible in the long run to
foresee any outcome other than an Africa for the most part governed and controlled by the indigenous peoples. This is already
the situation in much of West, North and North-East Africa and
we may expect in due course to see it repeated in East and at least
in parts of Central Africa. One would suggest that even in South
Africa European hegemony will one day come to an end, though
not without blood and tears.

Under the most favourable circumstances regions like East
Africa, with comparatively small but economically indispensable
European and Asian minorities, may evolve into reasonably
homogeneous multi-racial states, each immigrant group recognizing the power of the majority, but contributing, in security and
without fear of victimization, its own special aptitude to the welfare
of the community. The difficulties in the way of such an ideal
situation are enormous, as experience has shown, but there are
nevertheless distinct signs here and there that racial feelings are
by no means always bitter and uncompromising. Personal relations
between black, brown and white are often very warm and friendly
and there are everywhere many generous and imaginative people
who are seeking to bring into politics the same forbearance and
charity as infuses the lives of many individuals.

With independence a great part of the continent of Africa also
acquired a new significance on the world stage. A few years ago
the only African members of the United Nations, apart from the
Union of South Africa, were Egypt, Ethiopia and Liberia. Now,
with the recent emergence of new independent African states,
the number has increased to well over twenty and may soon be
thirty, thus forming a substantial part, nearly a third, of the voting
power of the General Assembly.

It is of course unlikely that all these states would always vote
together. On certain matters they seem to have marked diver-
gencies of outlook, and in particular there is a line dividing the
attitude of some of the old French colonies from that of Ghana and
Guinea, the former tending to be more conservative. But on
matters on which all may be expected to vote the same way, such for
instance as the issues of peace and security and in condemnation

of racial discrimination, their attitude in principle will undoubtedly
be one that the West could not fail to approve. It may here be
added that at the 1960 session of the General Assembly, when the
great influx of new African states took place, the delegates made
a splendid impression by their dignity and statesmanship. Their
deportment was certainly more fitting to the place and the occasion
than that of delegates from certain states of longer standing. It
was also more effective.

Historians will probably regard 1960 as the *annus mirabilis* for
Africa, the year in which the colonial Powers withdrew their
tutelage from a large part of the continent, devolving their duties
and responsibilities on to wholly indigenous governments. In that
sense the year marks the close of an era. But self-government is
not an end in itself. It is merely the opening phase of an entirely
new relationship between Africa and the rest of the world, and one
in which the former colonial powers are particularly involved and
bear a special responsibility. Independence has not solved the
economic and social problems of Africa. It has only thrown on
Africans themselves the onus of finding a solution; and Africans,
courageous and adaptable as they are, will need help to do so. To
provide that help, while at the same time enabling the new states
to preserve their independence and self-respect, is now a chal-
lenging task for the Free World.

READING LIST

Books on Africa are legion and it is impossible to compile a short bibliography which will satisfy everybody. The books in the following list are in English, most are reasonably accessible, and some contain bibliographies which will suggest further reading.

GENERAL

Beaver, S. H. and Stamp, D. L., *Africa, a regional geography* (Longmans 1960).

Davidson, B., *Old Africa re-discovered* (Gollancz, 1959).

Fitzgerald, W., *Africa, a social, economic and political geography of its major regions* (Methuen, 1957).

Hailey, Lord, *An African Survey* (Oxford University Press, 1957).

Hance, W. A., *African Economic Development* (Oxford University Press, 1958).

Perham, M. F. and Simmons, J., *African Discovery, an anthology of exploration* (Faber & Faber, 1949).

Seligman, C. J., *Races of Africa* (Oxford University Press, 1957)

Suggate, L. S., *Africa* (Harrap, 1960).

Werner, A., *The Language Families of Africa* (Kegan Paul, Trench, Trubner & Co., 1925).

Wingert, P. S., *The Sculpture of Negro Africa* (Columbia University Press, 1951).

REGIONAL

Southern Africa

Ashton, H., *The Basuto* (Oxford University Press, 1952).

Cole, Monica, *South Africa* (Methuen, 1961).

Marquard, L., *The peoples and policies of South Africa* (Oxford University Press, 1952).

Marwick, B. A., *The Swazi* (Cambridge University Press, 1940).

Pienaar, S. and Sampson, A., *South Africa: two views of separate development* (Oxford University Press, 1960).

Schapera, I., ed., *The Bantu-speaking tribes of South Africa* (Routledge & Kegan Paul, 1953).

Sillery, A., *The Bechuanaland Protectorate* (Oxford University Press, 1952).

The Year Book (*State of the Union, economic, financial and statistical year-book for the Union of South Africa*) is full of facts and figures.

The year book and guide published by the Union Castle Company is also useful.

CENTRAL AFRICA

Debenham, F., *Nyasaland, Land of the Lake* (H.M.S.O., 1955).

Duffy, J., *Portuguese Africa* (Harvard University Press, 1959).

Hanna, A. J., *The Story of the Rhodesias and Nyasaland* (Faber & Faber, 1960).

Handbook to the Federation of Rhodesia and Nyasaland (Cassell, 1960).

Mason, P., *The Birth of a Dilemma* (Oxford University Press, 1958).

Mason, P., *Year of Decision* (Oxford University Press, 1960).

Maugham, R. C. F., *Zambezia* (John Murray, London 1910).
Most of the best material on Madagascar and the Comoro Islands is in French. The following book is simple, informative and reasonably up-to-date: Decary, R. and others: *La France de l'Océan Indien* (Series 'Les Terres Lointaines' published by the Société d'Editions Géographiques, Maritimes et Coloniales, 1952).

EAST AFRICA

Coupland, R., *East Africa and its invaders* (Clarendon Press, 1939).

East Africa Royal Commission 1953–1955 Report (H.M.S.O., Cmd. 9475).

Hollingsworth, L. W., *The Asians of East Africa* (Macmillan, 1960).

Huxley, Elspeth, *White Man's Country* (Macmillan, 1953).

Huntingford, W. B. and Bell, C. V. R., *East African Background* (Longmans, 1950).

Ingham, K., *The making of modern Uganda* (George Allen & Unwin, 1958).

Ingrams, W. H., *Zanzibar* (H. F. & G. Witherby, 1931).

Mitchell, Sir P. E., *African Afterthoughts* (Hutchinson, 1954).

Moffet, J. P., ed., *Handbook of Tanganyika* (Tanganyika Government, 1958).

Wraith, R. E., *East African Citizen* (Oxford University Press, 1959).

THE HORN OF AFRICA

Longrigg, S. H., *A short history of Eritrea* (Oxford University Press, 1945).

Ullendorff, E., *The Ethiopians* (Oxford University Press, 1960).

Collins, D., *A Tear for Somalia* (Jarrolds, 1960). This is a story by an officer of the Administration during the post-war British occupation of Somalia. It gives a good picture of the country and people.

THE NILE VALLEY

Duncan, J. S. R., *The Sudan* (William Blackwood, 1952).

Fisher, W. B. *The Middle East* (Methuen, 1957).

Issawi, C., *Egypt at mid-century* (Oxford University Press, 1954).

MacMichael, Sir H., *The Anglo-Egyptian Sudan* (Faber & Faber, 1934).

MEDITERRANEAN AFRICA AND SAHARA

Bovill, E. W., *The Golden Trade of the Moors* (Oxford University Press, 1958).

Barbour, N., ed., *A Survey of North West Africa* (Oxford University Press, 1959).

Gautier, E. F. (trans. D. F. Mayhew), *Sahara, the great desert* (Columbia University Press, 1935).

WEST AFRICA

Church, R. J. Harrison, *West Africa* (Longmans, 1960).

Fage, J. D., *An introduction to the history of West Africa* (Cambridge University Press, 1957).

Pedler, F. J., *Economic Geography of West Africa* (Longmans, 1955).

Pedler, F. J., *West Africa* (Methuen, 1959).

Thompson, V. and Adloff, R., *French West Africa* (George All en & Unwin 1958).

J. D. Fage (pp. 199–210) gives good advice on books about West Africa generally and on works particularly devoted to the British territories. To the latter should now be added the following which have been published since Fage wrote his note:

Lewis, R., *Sierra Leone* (H.M.S.O., 1954).

Ward, W. E. F., *A History of Ghana* (Allen & Unwin, 1958).

Material in English on French Africa is thin but Thompson and Adloff have an extensive bibliography of publications mainly in French.

EQUATORIA

Kuczynski, R. R., *The Cameroons and Togoland* (Oxford University Press, 1939).

Legum, C., *Congo Disaster* (Penguin Books, 1961).

Slade, Ruth, *The Belgian Congo* (Oxford University Press, 1960).

Schebesta, P., *Among Congo Pygmies* (Hutchinson, 1933).

Schweitzer, Albert, *On the Edge of the Primeval Forest* (Fontana Books, 1961).

Thompson, V. and Adloff, R., *The Emerging States of French Equatorial Africa* (Stanford University Press, 1960).

Torday, E., *On the trail of the Bushongo* (Seeley, Service & Co., 1925).
A compact and informative book in French on Equatorial Africa is:
Trezenem, E. and Lembezat, B., *La France Equatoriale* (Series 'Les
Terres Lointaines' published by the Société d'Editions Géographiques,
Maritimes et Coloniales, 1950).

SOCOTRA

Botting, D., *Island of the Dragon's Blood* (Hodder & Stoughton, 1958).

Publications cited in footnotes, but not included in the above list, should
not for that reason be ignored. They are as follows:

Africa. Journal of the International African Institute.

Bantu Studies (now *African Studies*). A journal published by the University of the Witwatersrand.

Baumann, H. and Westermann, D., *Peuples et Civilisations de l'Afrique*
(Payot, Paris, 1948).

Coupland, R., *Kirk on the Zambezi* (Clarendon Press, 1928).

Ethnographic Survey of Africa. A series published by the International
African Institute.

Hailey, Lord, *Native administration in the British African territories*
(H.M.S.O., 1950–54).

Gray, R., *The two nations* (Oxford University Press, 1960).

Joelson, F. S., *ed.*, *Rhodesia and East Africa* (East Africa and Rhodesia,
1958).

Newland, H. O., *West Africa* (Daniel O'Connor, 1922).

Perham, M. F., *The Government of Ethiopia* (Faber & Faber, 1948).

Posselt, F. W. T., *A survey of the native tribes of Southern Rhodesia*
(Government of Southern Rhodesia, 1927).

GENERAL INDEX